D1616968

Country Cakes

Published by

BLAIR OF COLUMBUS, INC.

Columbus, Georgia

1984

Additional copies of
COUNTRY CAKES
may be obtained by addressing
BLAIR OF COLUMBUS, INC.
P. O. Box 7852
Columbus, Georgia 31908

First Printing, 1984, 10,000
Second Printing 1984, 10,000

Printed by Columbus, Productions, Inc.
Columbus, Georgia

Library of Congress Catalog Number: 84-72948
ISBN: 0-9613709-0-4

Little girls have an inborn urge to bake a cake and we big girls remember the warm and light-hearted experience of watching Mama or Grandma baking. By following these "Country Cakes" recipes you will rediscover that little girl feeling because "Country Cakes" is a treasured collection of tested cake recipes that I have developed over the years...each of them very special; many treasured recipes never before published. Others are favorites of friends and acquaintances. All of them have been kitchen tested and enjoyed in many homes through the years.

How happy I am that you have selected "Country Cakes" to be your very own. It's my hope it will become a nostalgic keepsake that you will want to pass on to your children. If you've never baked a homemade cake...do it now!! Good Luck!

Bevelyn Blair

Bevelyn Blair, Author/Editor

Blair of Columbus, Inc.

3

TABLE OF CONTENTS

Cakes and Frostings

ALMOND CAKE

1/2 pound butter, softened
2-1/4 cups sugar
3 cups flour
2-1/2 teaspoons baking powder
1 cup milk

1 cup chopped, blanched
  almonds
1-1/2 teaspoons vanilla
1/2 teaspoon salt
6 egg whites, stiffly beaten

Cream butter and sugar until light and fluffy. Add sifted flour, baking powder and salt alternately with the milk and vanilla. Fold in the chopped almonds and then the stiffly beaten egg whites. Bake at 350° F. for around 30 minutes or until done in 3 or 4 9-inch pans that have been greased and lightly floured. Spread Candied Fruit Icing between layers and on the top and sides.

CANDIED FRUIT ICING

2 cups sugar
1 cup water
4 egg whites, stiffly beaten

1/2 cup chopped, candied cherries
1/2 cup chopped, candied pineapple
1 teaspoon vanilla extract

Boil the sugar and water over a low flame until syrup spins a thread. Pour slowly into the egg whites. Beat mixture until smooth and stiff enough to spread. Add the vanilla, cherries and pineapple. Spread between layers of Almond Cake and on top and sides.

You will have a delightful experience when you bake and serve this beautiful cake! One of President Abraham Lincoln's favorite cakes.

ALMOND CRUNCH CAKE

Crust: 3 cups sifted cake flour
       1-1/2 cups butter
       2 eggs

1-1/2 cups sugar
1/2 teaspoon salt

Cream butter and sugar thoroughly. Add eggs, one at a time, blending well after each addition. Add sifted flour and salt and mix until dough forms. Divide in half and spread half in bottom of greased springform pan.

Filling: 1 cup grated or very finely chopped almonds
         1/2 cup sugar
         1 teaspoon grated lemon peel
         1 egg, slightly beaten
         whole almonds for garnish

Blend together all ingredients except whole almonds; spread over crust. Press remaining dough over top of filling and press lightly together. You may want to make a circle the size of springform pan and press the dough the size of the circle before placing dough over the filling. Garnish with whole almonds.

Bake at 325°F. for 45 to 50 minutes, or until golden brown. Cool and then remove from pan. Cut in wedges or diamonds.

ALMOND LEGEND CAKE

1/2 cup slivered almonds, chopped
2 cups sugar
2 Tablespoons lemon juice
2 teaspoons vanilla extract
3 cups cake flour
1/4 teaspoon baking soda
1/2 teaspoon salt
1/4 teaspoon cream of tartar

1 WHOLE almond
1 cup butter
4 eggs, separated
1 teaspoon grated lemon
  rind
2 teaspoons baking
  powder
1 cup milk
1/2 cup sugar

Sprinkle chopped almonds into a well greased Bundt pan and set aside.

Cream butter and sugar together until light and fluffy. Add egg yolks, one at a time, beating well after each addition. Add lemon juice, rind and flavoring and continue to beat well. Add sifted dry ingredients alternately with the milk.

Beat egg whites and cream of tartar and gradually add 1/2 cup sugar, beating until stiff peaks form. Fold mixture into batter. Pour into pan and press the whole almond just below surface of the batter. Bake at 300°F. for 1 hour and 20 minutes or until cake tests done. Cool completely and pour glaze over cake.

LEMON GLAZE

1 cup sifted confectioners sugar   3 Tablespoons lemon juice

Mix ingredients together until well blended to make a glaze.

A delicious cake...and fun to see if you will be the lucky one to find the whole almond in your slice...

ALMOND CREAM CAKE

1-1/2 cups cake flour	2 teaspoons baking powder
1/2 teaspoon salt	1 cup whipping cream
2 eggs	1 cup sugar
1 teaspoon vanilla	1 (3-ounce) package cream
1 cup sifted confectioners sugar	cheese
1 cup slivered almonds	1/2 teaspoon almond
toasted	extract

Sift together flour, baking powder and salt and set aside. Beat the whipping cream until soft peaks form; add eggs, one at a time, beating well after each addition. Add one cup sugar and beat until smooth and dissolved. Stir in vanilla and fold in dry ingredients. Pour into a greased and floured 8-inch square pan. Bake at 350° F. for 25 to 30 minutes. Cool.

Beat cream cheese until light and fluffy. Add confectioners sugar and beat until smooth. Add almond extract and blend well. Stir in almonds; spread on cooled cake.

A treat is in store for those who receive a portion of this marvelous cake!

ALMOND TEA CAKES

2-1/2 cups sifted flour	1 egg
3/4 cup sugar	1 teaspoon almond extract
1/4 teaspoon salt	36 whole almonds, blanched
1 teaspoon baking powder	1 egg yolk
3/4 cup butter	

Sift flour with sugar, salt and baking powder. Using pastry blender or 2 knives, cut in butter until mixture resembles coarse cornmeal. Beat egg with 2 tablespoons water and the almond extract. Add to flour mixture, mixing with fork until dough leaves side of bowl. On lightly floured surface, knead dough until smooth. Wrap in waxed paper; refrigerate 1 hour. Preheat oven to 350° F. Form dough into balls 1 inch in diameter. Place 3 inches apart on ungreased cookie sheets. With palm of hand, flatten each cookie to a circle 1/2 inch thick; press almond into center of each. Combine egg yolk with 1 tablespoon water. Brush on cookies. Bake 20 to 25 minutes or until golden brown. Remove to wire rack and let cool.

These little cakes are easy to make and are delicious served with tea or coffee!

ALMOND LOGS

3/4 cup butter, softened
1/3 cup sugar
1 teaspoon almond extract
2 cups sifted flour
1 teaspoon sugar

1/4 teaspoon salt
1 egg, slightly beaten
1/4 cup finely chopped,
   unblanched almonds

Cream together butter, 1/3 cup sugar and almond extract until light and fluffy. Add sifted flour and salt and mix well. Place dough on lightly floured surface. With hands, shape dough into a roll 6 inches long. With sharp knife, cut roll crosswise into 6 parts. With hands, shape each part into a roll 12 inches long and 3/4 inch in diameter. Cut each roll into 6 (2-inch) pieces. Place 1 inch apart on lightly greased cookie sheets. Brush tops lightly with egg; then sprinkle with 1 teaspoon sugar and chopped almonds. Bake at 350° F. for 15 to 20 minutes or until delicately browned. Remove to wire rack to cool.

You will be envied when you bake and serve these luscious little cakes!

APPLE CAKE

1-1/2 cups liquid vegetable shortening
3 eggs, well beaten
1 cup chopped pecans
3 cups cake flour
1 teaspoon soda
1 teaspoon vanilla

2 cups sugar
3 cups finely chopped
   apples
1 teaspoon salt
1/2 teaspoon cinnamon

Combine shortening and sugar, blending well. Add eggs, apples and nuts. Sift together and add to above mixture the flour, salt, soda and cinnamon. Add vanilla. Pour batter into a greased and floured tube or bundt pan. May be baked in 2 loaf pans. Bake in preheated 350° F. oven for 1 hour and 15 minutes.

GLAZE FOR APPLE CAKE

1/2 cup butter
1/4 cup milk

1 cup light brown sugar

In saucepan melt butter and sugar; bring to a boil and cook for 2-1/2 minutes. Add milk and mix well. Pour mixture over hot cake. Let stand in pan for 2 hours before removing cake.

CINNAMON APPLE CAKE

2 cups sifted cake flour
2 teaspoons ground cinnamon
2 eggs
1 teaspoon vanilla
1/2 cup chopped pecans

2 cups sugar
1 teaspoon baking soda
1/4 teaspoon salt
1 cup cooking oil
4 cups chopped apples

Sift together flour, sugar, cinnamon, baking soda and salt. Beat eggs and oil until light and foamy. Add vanilla. Gradually blend in dry ingredients. Stir in apples, pecans. Pour into greased 13x9x2" cake pan. Bake 350°F. for 1 hour. Dust with confectioners sugar.

Be sure to bake one of these cakes soon!

APPLE-PINEAPPLE CAKE

1 can (8-ounces) crushed pineapple
1-1/2 cups sugar
1-1/2 cups wesson oil
3 eggs
2 cups cake flour
2 teaspoons baking soda
2 teaspoons ground cinnamon

2 teaspoons vanilla
1 teaspoon salt
2 cups peeled
   shredded apples
3/4 cup chopped
   pecans or walnuts

Drain pineapple thoroughly; reserve 2 tablespoons syrup for frosting. Combine all ingredients well and pour into 2 greased and floured 9-inch cake pans. Bake in preheated 350°F. oven for 35 minutes or until cake tests done. Cool in pan for 5 minutes.

Turn out on rack and cool completely. Frost between layers and top with Maple Flavored Frosting.

MAPLE-FLAVORED FROSTING

1 package (3-ounces) cream cheese, softened
2 Tablespoons softened butter
1-1/2 cups confectioners sugar
2 Tablespoons reserved pineapple syrup
1/4 cup chopped pecans or walnuts
1/4 teaspoon maple flavoring
Dash of salt

Blend cream cheese, butter and the confectioners sugar until soft and fluffy. Add pineapple syrup, nuts, maple flavoring and salt, mixing well. Add more sugar if necessary to make frosting easy to spread.

A very special cake...

DUTCH APPLE CAKE

1/3 cup butter
1/2 cup brown sugar, packed
1 egg
1 cup cake flour
1 teaspoon baking powder
1 teaspoon cinnamon
1/4 cup milk

4 ounces sharp natural
    cheddar cheese, shredded
1/2 cup sugar
1/2 cup pecans, chopped
3-1/2 cups peeled, sliced apples
1 carton whipping cream
    sweetened to taste

Beat butter and sugar together until light and fluffy. Sift together the flour, baking powder and 1/2 teaspoon cinnamon. Add to first mixture alternately with milk, mixing well after each addition. Stir in 1/2 cup of the cheese.

Pour into a greased 10x6-inch baking dish. Combine remaining cinnamon, apples and sugar; spoon over the batter and then sprinkle over the nuts. Bake at 350°F. for 35 minutes. Sprinkle over remaining cheese and return to oven until cheese slightly melts. Serve warm topped with whipped cream.

Allow yourself enough time to bake a cake...

APPLE-COCONUT CAKE

3 cups cake flour
1 teaspoon soda
3 eggs
2 teaspoons vanilla
3 cups peeled, chopped apples

1 teaspoon salt
1 cup vegetable oil
2-1/4 cups sugar
2 cups chopped pecans
1/2 cup coconut

Combine flour, soda and salt; mix well and set aside. Combine oil, eggs, sugar and vanilla; beat at medium speed of electric mixer for 2 minutes. Add flour mixture; mix at low speed just until blended. Fold in pecans, apples and coconut. (Batter will be stiff.)

Spoon into a greased and floured 10 inch tube pan. Bake at 350°F. for 1 hour and 20 minutes. Cool in pan 10 minutes. Remove from pan; immediately drizzle glaze over cake.

GLAZE

1/2 cup firmly packed light brown sugar
1/4 cup milk
1/2 cup butter

Combine all ingredients in a heavy saucepan; bring to a full boil and cook stirring constantly, for 2 minutes. Let cool to lukewarm.

DRIED APPLE CAKE

2 (6-ounce) packages dried apples
4 to 5 Tablespoons sugar
1 cup melted butter
2 eggs
1 Tablespoon soda
1 Tablespoon cloves
1 cup milk
1 cup chopped pecans

1-3/4 cups water
2 cups firmly packed
brown sugar
4 cups cake flour
1 Tablespoon nutmeg
1 Tablespoon cinnamon
1 box (15-ounce) raisins

Combine apples and 1-3/4 cups water. Cover and cook until water is absorbed. Cool slightly; mash. Add 4 to 5 Tablespoons sugar and set aside. Combine brown sugar, butter and eggs; beat well. Stir in apples. Combine dry ingredients and add to apple mixture alternately with 1 cup milk, beating well after each addition. Stir in raisins and pecans. Pour batter into a greased 13x9x2 inch pan. Bake at 350°F. for 1 hour.

APPLESAUCE-NUT CAKE

2 cups sifted flour
1 teaspoon baking soda
1 teaspoon baking
powder
1 teaspoon cinnamon
1 teaspoon nutmeg
1 teaspoon cloves
1/2 teaspoon salt

1/2 cup butter
1 cup sugar
1 egg
1 cup applesauce, sweetened
1 teaspoon vanilla
3/4 cup raisins
1 cup chopped walnuts
or pecans

Sift together flour, baking soda, baking powder, cinnamon, nutmeg, cloves and salt. Cream together butter and sugar until light and fluffy. Add egg, applesauce and vanilla. Blend well. Gradually blend in dry ingredients. Stir in raisins and nuts. Pour batter into greased 9x5x3-inch loaf pan. Bake in 350°F. oven for 55 minutes or until cake tests done. Cool for 10 minutes.

You will find nothing better than these outstanding cakes and a good cup of coffee...

APPLE CHEESE SQUARES

1/2 cup butter
1 cup cake flour
2/3 cup apple butter
1 (7-ounce) jar
marshmallow cream

1/3 cup brown sugar, packed
1/2 cup finely chopped pecans
1 (8-ounce) package cream cheese
1 egg

Cream butter and sugar until light and fluffy. Add flour and pecans, mixing well. Reserve 1 cup of this mixture. Press remaining mixture onto bottom of a 9 inch square pan. Bake in 350° F. oven for 15 minutes.

Spread 1/3 of the apple butter over the baked crust. (If you can't find the apple butter, substitute 2/3 cup of applesauce plus 1/4 teaspoon cinnamon for the apple butter.) Combine cream cheese, marshmallow cream and egg, mixing with electric mixer until well blended. Pour over the apple butter.

Top with remaining apple butter and the remaining crumb mixture. Bake in 350° F. oven for 45 minutes.

Be creative -- Bake a cake and surprise yourself or someone...

APPLE-PECAN CAKE

1-1/2 cups salad oil
3 cups cake flour
2 cups sugar
3 eggs
2 teaspoons vanilla

1 teaspoon soda
1 teaspoon salt
3 cups tart apples, diced
1 cup chopped pecans

Beat together the salad oil and sugar until light and fluffy. Add the eggs one at a time, beating well after each addition. Sift together the flour, salt and soda and add to mixture. Blend well. Stir in the apples and pecans. Pour into a greased tube pan and bake 1-1/4 hours at 300° F. While hot pour the glaze over the cake.

GLAZE

1 stick butter
1/3 cup milk

1 cup light brown sugar, packed

Combine and boil for 3 to 4 minutes and pour over hot cake.

ICING FOR APPLE CAKES

This icing may be used instead of the cooked icings, if preferred.

1-1/2 cups powdered sugar
3 Tablespoons butter
1 teaspoon vanilla

1 (6-ounce) package cream cheese
Dash salt

Soften cream cheese and butter. Mix in mixer until smooth. Add remaining ingredients. Spread over cooled cake. Very rich and good.

Bake and share this cake...

DELICIOUS APPLESAUCE CAKE

1/2 cup butter
1 cup sugar
1 egg, well beaten
1-1/2 cups sweetened applesauce
2 cups flour
2 teaspoons cocoa
1 teaspoon cinnamon
1 teaspoon vanilla

1/2 teaspoon cloves
1/8 teaspoon salt
3/4 cup raisins
3/4 cup chopped
   pecans
1/4 cup hot water
2 teaspoons soda

Cream butter and add sugar gradually, creaming until light and fluffy. Add egg and the applesauce. Mix well. Sift flour. Measure and sift again with the cocoa, cinnamon, cloves and salt. Mix with raisins and nuts. Add gradually to apple mixture and beat well. Combine soda and hot water; add to mixture and mix well. Add vanilla. Bake in 2 greased and floured layer cake pans for 35 minutes at 350° F. Spread Caramel-Nut Frosting on cake when cool.

CARAMEL-NUT FROSTING

1-1/2 cups light brown sugar,
   firmly packed
1/2 cup granulated sugar
1/4 teaspoon salt

3/4 cup whipping cream
2 Tablespoons butter
1 Tablespoon Cream
1/2 cup chopped nuts

Combine sugars, salt, cream and butter and bring to a boil, stirring constantly until sugar is dissolved. Cook slowly, keeping crystals washed from sides of pan. When small amount forms a soft ball in cold water, remove spoon and set pan aside to cool. Do not move pan until mixture is lukewarm. Beat until thickens. Add cream. Beat until spreadable. Add nuts.

I hope you will enjoy baking this cake...

COVERED APPLE CAKE

2-1/2 sticks butter
5 eggs
2 cups cake flour
3 pounds tart apples, peeled and sliced

1 cup sugar
1 teaspoon vanilla
2 teaspoons baking
   powder

Cream butter and sugar. Add eggs one at a time, mixing well after each addition. Add vanilla. Add sifted flour and baking soda a tablespoon at a time. Cream well. Grease and flour a 10 inch springform pan. Put one-half of batter in pan and add apples, spreading evenly. Place remaining batter on top and bake 1-1/2 hours in 350°F. oven.

While cake is warm mix: 1/2 cup apricot jam with 2 table-spoons water, heat to boiling point and spread over cake. Let cool and then mix: 1/2 cup powdered sugar with enough lemon juice to make mixture just thin enough to drizzle over cake.

APPLE SNACK CAKE

3/4 cup vegetable oil
2-1/2 cups cake flour
1 teaspoon soda
1 teaspoon salt
3 cups peeled, chopped
apples
1 6 ounce package
butterscotch morsels

2 eggs
2 cups sugar
1 teaspoon baking
powder
1 teaspoon ground
cinnamon
1 cup chopped
pecans

Combine oil, eggs and sugar in large mixing bowl; beat at medium speed until well mixed. Combine flour, soda, baking powder, salt and cinnamon; stir. Add dry ingredients alternately with apples to egg mixture, mixing well. Stir in pecans and half of butterscotch morsels. Spread batter into a greased 13x9x2 inch baking pan. Sprinkle batter with remaining morsels. Bake at 350°F. for 55 to 60 minutes or until done.

Lots of Luck! - Bake and share these great cakes...

APPLE PRESERVE CAKE

If you are lucky enough to have some good homemade apple preserves, try this cake and you will love it!

2 cups sifted cake flour
1/4 teaspoon salt
3/4 cup butter
1 cup sugar
1/2 cup sour cream
1/2 cup apple preserves
1/2 cup chopped pecans

1 teaspoon baking soda
1 teaspoon baking powder
1 teaspoon cinnamon
1 teaspoon nutmeg
1 teaspoon allspice
3 eggs

Sift flour, soda, baking powder, salt and spices together 3 times. Cream butter with sugar until fluffy. Add sour cream and apple preserves, mixing well. Add eggs, one at a time, beating well after each is added. Add sifted dry ingredients gradually, beating well. Fold in nuts and pour into a greased loaf pan. Bake at 350°F. for 50 minutes or bake in layers 25 to 30 minutes.

APPLE UPSIDE-DOWN CAKE

This cake will be a conversation-piece and delicious.

1/4 cup butter	1 cup brown sugar, light
2 large baking apples	1-1/2 cups sifted cake flour
1/2 teaspoon salt	3 teaspoons baking powder
1/3 cup butter	1/2 cup granulated sugar
2 eggs, well beaten	1/2 teaspoon vanilla
2/3 cup water	

Melt 1/4 cup butter in skillet or baking pan. Add brown sugar and stir until melted. Cool. Peel, core and slice apples; place on sugar. Sift flour, salt and baking powder together. Cream butter with sugar until fluffy. Add eggs and vanilla and beat thoroughly. Add sifted dry ingredients and water alternately in small amounts, beating well after each addition. Pour over apples and bake in 350° F. oven 40 to 50 minutes. Turn on plate immediately and serve with whipped cream.

APRICOT NECTAR CAKE

This cake is made with a cake mix but it is delicious!

1 box Lemon Supreme Duncan Hines Cake Mix	1/2 cup sugar
	3/4 cup Wesson oil
4 whole eggs	1 cup Apricot Nectar

Beat eggs at high speed on mixer; mix with rest of ingredients. Cook in tube pan approximately one hour at 350° F. Cool in pan on rack and while cooling, punch holes in cake and pour over warm cake: juice of two lemons mixed with 1-1/2 cups powdered sugar.

APRICOT TEA CAKE

1 cup dried apricots	1 cup sugar
1 large orange	1 egg
1/2 cup chopped nuts	2 Tablespoons butter, melted
2 cups flour	
1 teaspoon baking soda	1 teaspoon vanilla
2 teaspoons baking powder	

Simmer apricots in boiling water for 30 minutes. Drain and mash. Squeeze juice from orange. Add enough boiling water to juice to make 1 cup. Sift together: flour, soda, baking powder and sugar. Add nuts, fruits, juice, egg, melted butter and vanilla, mixing well. Bake in a greased loaf pan at 350° F. for 50 minutes. Serve hot and buttered or cold.

Baking a cake for a friend is a special way of saying you care...

ARABIAN RIBBON CAKE

3 cups sifted cake flour
3 teaspoons baking powder
1/4 teaspoon salt
2/3 cup butter
1-1/2 cups sugar
3 egg yolks, well beaten
3 Tablespoons dark molasses

1 cup milk
3 egg whites, stiffly
 beaten
1-1/2 teaspoons cinnamon
1/4 teaspoon cloves
1/2 teaspoon nutmeg
1/4 teaspoon mace

Sift flour and measure. Add baking powder and salt and sift together three times. Cream butter thoroughly. Add sugar gradually and cream with the butter until light and fluffy. Add egg yolks and beat well. Add flour, alternately with milk, a small amount at a time, beating well after each addition until smooth. Fold in stiffly beaten egg whites.

Fill one greased 9-inch layer pan with 1/3 of batter. To remaining batter add spices and molasses and blend. Pour into two greased 9-inch layer pans. Bake layers in 350° F. oven 20 to 25 minutes. Place white layer between spice layers. Spread Fruit Filling between layers and Lemon Frosting on top and sides of cake. Sprinkle grated lemon rind over the top.

FRUIT FILLING

Combine in saucepan: 1 cup water, 2 tablespoons butter and
 dash of salt
 1 cup finely cut raisins
 1 cup finely cut figs
 1/2 cup finely cut dates

Boil slowly 6 to 8 minutes or until thick enough to spread. Cool. Then add 1 tablespoon lemon juice and 1/2 teaspoon grated lemon rind.

LEMON FROSTING

Cream together 1 teaspoon grated lemon rind and 4 Tablespoons butter. Add gradually 3 cups confectioners sugar alternately with 3 tablespoons lemon juice, beating thoroughly after each addition. Add dash of salt. If too stiff to spread, add little more lemon juice.

You won't be able to forget the fine flavor of this delicious cake. If you bake it once, you will bake it again!

APRICOT CAKE

1 cup dried apricots
6 Tablespoons sugar
1/2 teaspoon salt
1/2 teaspoon baking soda
1/2 cup butter
1 teaspoon vanilla

2 cups water
1-3/4 cups sifted cake flour
1/2 teaspoon baking powder
1 cup sugar, 2 egg yolks
1/4 cup milk

Simmer first 3 ingredients together 30 minutes. Mash and measure 1/2 cup pulp. Sift flour, soda, salt and baking powder together 3 times. Cream butter and sugar until fluffy. Add yolks and vanilla; beat thoroughly. Add dry ingredients alternately with milk and pulp in small amounts. Bake in greased 8 x 8-inch cake pan at 350°F. for 45 minutes or until tests done.

APRICOT CHOCOLATE CAKE

The apricot variation has just the right touch to set off the chocolate flavor.

Sift together . . . . *1-3/4 cups sifted cake flour*
1/2 teaspoon baking powder
1 teaspoon soda
1 teaspoon salt
1-1/4 cups sugar

Add . . . . *1/2 cup butter*
2/3 cup milk

Beat . . . . for 2 minutes until batter is well blended.

Add . . . . *1/3 cup milk, 3 squares (3 oz.) chocolate, melted and cooled; 2 eggs, unbeaten; 1 teaspoon vanilla*

Beat . . . . for 2 minutes

Fold in . . . . *3/4 cup chopped, drained cooked apricots*

Pour . . . . into two well-greased and lightly floured pans

Bake . . . . at 350°F. for 30 to 35 minutes. Cool and frost with Browned Butter Frosting. Decorate with pecans.

BROWNED BUTTER FROSTING

Brown 1/4 cup butter in saucepan; add 1/4 teaspoon salt. Blend in 4 cups (1 Lb.) Confectioners sugar alternately with 1/3 to 1/2 cup hot CREAM. Add 1 teaspoon vanilla. Beat until creamy.

BANANA NUT CAKE

1/2 cup butter
3 egg yolks
1 cup mashed bananas
1 teaspoon soda dissolved
  in 1/4 cup buttermilk
1/2 cup chopped pecans
1 teaspoon baking powder

1-1/2 cups sugar
3 egg whites
1/4 cup boiling water
2 cups flour
1/4 teaspoon salt
1 teaspoon lemon juice

Cream butter and sugar; add egg yolks and mashed bananas. (Pour water over pecans.) Add lemon juice; sift baking powder with flour and add alternately with buttermilk and soda mixture. Add pecans. Fold in beaten egg whites. Bake in layers at 300° F. for 30 to 35 minutes. Spread with Banana Filling.

BANANA FILLING

1 package powdered sugar
1/2 cup mashed bananas
1 Tablespoon orange or lemon juice

1/2 cup softened butter
1/2 cup chopped pecans

Mix softened butter and sugar until creamy. Add bananas and nuts and juice. Spread between layers and on sides and top.

BANANA CHIFFON CAKE

This cake is moist and delicious. Frost it with your favorite Butter Cream Icing.

2 cups sifted cake flour
1 cup sugar
1 teaspoon baking powder
1 teaspoon baking soda
1 teaspoon salt
1/3 cup cooking oil
1 cup mashed bananas

1/3 cup buttermilk
1 teaspoon vanilla
2 eggs separated
1/3 cup buttermilk
1/3 cup sugar
1/2 cup chopped pecans

Sift flour, 1 cup sugar, baking powder, baking soda and salt. Make a well in center. Pour in oil, bananas, 1/3 cup buttermilk and vanilla. Beat 1 minute, mixing well. Add egg yolks and 1/3 cup buttermilk. Beat 1 minute. Beat egg whites until frothy, gradually beat in 1/3 cup sugar. Beat until stiff peaks form. Fold into batter. Fold in pecans. Pour into ungreased 9-inch tube pan. Bake at 325° F. for 55 minutes.

BANANA SPLIT CAKE

1 cup butter, divided
1-1/2 cups graham cracker crumbs
2 cups powdered sugar
2 eggs
1 teaspoon vanilla
1/2 cup chopped pecans

3 or 4 bananas, sliced
1 (20 oz.) can crushed
  pineapple, drained
1 pint whipping cream
  (whipped and sweetened
  to taste)

Melt 1/2 cup butter and add to crumbs. Mix well and pat into a 13x9-1/2x2-inch pan. Combine sugar, eggs, 1/2 cup softened butter and vanilla. Beat until smooth and creamy. Spread over graham cracker crust. Add a layer of banana slices and pineapple; spread whipping cream mixture evenly over fruit. Sprinkle with chopped pecans. Refrigerate until set.

A delicious party cake of good flavor...

BERRY TEACAKES

Serve these teacakes while warm and you will find they are a dainty addition to the tea table; try them with butter!

1 cup sugar
2 eggs
1-1/2 cups milk

1 heaping teaspoon
  baking powder
1/2 stick butter

Flour, sufficient to make a STIFF batter. In this batter stir a pint bowl of fruit -- any fresh or canned berries with juice poured off -- lightly dredged with flour. Bake in greased muffin tins at 350° F. until tests done.

BLUEBERRY MOUNTAIN CAKE

1/2 cup shortening
1 cup sugar
1/4 teaspoon salt
1 cup milk
1 cup coconut

2 cups flour
3 teaspoons baking powder
2 eggs, beaten
1-1/2 cups blueberries

Sift flour, baking powder, salt and sugar together; cut in shortening until mixture appears like cornmeal. Combine eggs and milk and mix until all is just moistened. Fold in blueberries and pour into two 9-inch round greased cake pans. Sprinkle coconut on top. Bake at 350° F. for about 25 minutes.

A great favorite... make it often!

BROWNIES

1 cup sugar
4 tablespoons cocoa
Dash salt
1 teaspoon vanilla

1 cup chopped nuts
1 cup self-rising flour
2 eggs
1/2 cup wesson oil

Mix sugar, cocoa, salt and flour; add other ingredients mixing well. Bake for 20 minutes at 350°F. Ice with chocolate icing, if desired or serve plain. Cut into squares.

BURNT SUGAR CAKE

This is a different and delicious cake that you will want to bake again and again.

1/2 cup sugar
1/2 cup water
1 cup butter
3-1/2 cups plus 1 tablespoon
   cake flour
1 teaspoon vanilla

3 teaspoons baking powder
1 teaspoon salt
1 cup milk
2 cups sugar
3 eggs

Put 1/2 cup sugar into hot skillet. Stir constantly until sugar turns to a light brown syrup. Remove from heat. Add water. Replace over heat and simmer until just dissolved. Pour into measuring cup. Should be 1/2 cup syrup. Cool, then add milk to make 1-1/2 cups. Proceed and mix cake: Cream butter and sugar until light and fluffy. Add eggs one at a time beating well after each addition. Add sifted dry ingredients alternately with the milk. Pour into greased and floured cake pans and bake at 350°F. from 24 to 26 minutes. Spread with Penuche Frosting.

PENUCHE FROSTING

2 cups brown sugar, packed (light)
2 cups granulated sugar
1/2 cup butter, room temperature

2 tablespoons white
   Karo syrup
2 cups whipping cream

Measure sugars, cream and syrup into 3 quart saucepan; place over medium heat to boiling, stirring frequently until sugar dissolves. When reaches steady brisk boil, add butter and cook 20 to 25 minutes or until forms soft but not sticky ball when dropped in cold water. Cool without stirring. Beat until spreading consistency. Add cream, if necessary to thin.

Nothing can take the place of the wonderful aroma of a cake baking . . .

BLACK FOREST CAKE

The most elegant chocolate cake of all.

2 *(15 or 16-ounce) cans pitted tart cherries,*
  drained and each cut in half
1/2 *cup kirsch (cherry-flavor brandy)*
1 *package chocolate cake mix for 2 layer (or bake a*
  chocolate cake from scratch in 3 layers)
3 *squares semi-sweet chocolate*
2 *cups heavy or whipping cream*
1/2 *cup confectioners sugar*
14 *maraschino cherries, well drained*

In medium bowl combine tart cherries and 1/3 cup kirsch; set aside, stirring occasionally. Prepare cake mix as label directs but pour into three 9-inch round cake pans; or bake your own from scratch. Cool on racks for 10 minutes; remove from pans; cool completely.

Meanwhile, with vegetable peeler, shave a few curls from chocolate for garnish; grate remaining chocolate. With fork, prick top of each cake layer. Drain cherries well and slowly spoon the drained liquid from cherries over cake layers.

Beat cream, sugar and remaining kirsch until stiff. Place one cake layer on cake platter; spread with 1/4 whipped cream and top with half of cherries; repeat. Top with third layer.

Frost side of cake with half of remaining whipped cream. With hand, gently press grated chocolate into cream. Garnish top of cake with dollops of remaining cream; top each dollop with a maraschino cherry. Pile chocolate curls on center of cake. Keep refrigerated until ready to serve. Delicious!

BROWN SUGAR NUT CAKE

1 *cup butter*
1/2 *cup margarine*
1 *pound light brown sugar*
1 *cup sugar*
3 *cups flour*

2 *teaspoons baking powder*
5 *eggs*
1 *cup milk*
1 *teaspoon vanilla*
1-1/2 *cups chopped pecans*

Cream butter, margarine and sugars until light and fluffy. Add eggs one at a time beating well after each addition. Add sifted four and baking powder alternately with the milk and vanilla. Fold in the chopped pecans. Bake in a greased tube pan for 1-1/2 hours at 325°F. Ice with a white icing or serve plain, as desired.

BROWNIE BAKED ALASKA

A rich and sophisticated dessert!

1 quart vanilla ice cream,
  softened
2 cups sugar, divided
1 cup flour
2 tablespoons cocoa
1 teaspoon vanilla

1/2 cup butter
2 eggs
1/2 teaspoon baking powder
1/4 teaspoon salt
5 egg whites

Line a 1-quart mixing bowl with waxed paper, leaving an overhang around the edges. Pack ice cream into bowl and freeze until very firm.

Combine butter and 1 cup sugar, creaming until light and fluffy. Add eggs one at a time, beating well after each addition. Sift flour, baking powder, cocoa and salt; add to creamed mixture, mixing well. Stir in vanilla.

Spoon batter into a greased and floured 9-inch round cake pan. Bake at 350°F. for 25 to 30 minutes. Let cool completely.

Place cake on an ovenproof serving dish. Invert bowl of ice cream onto cake leaving waxed paper intact; remove bowl. Place cake in freezer.

Beat egg whites and gradually beat in 1 cup sugar until stiff peaks form. Remove cake from freezer and peel off waxed paper. Spread meringue over entire surface, making sure edges are sealed.

Bake at 500°F. for 2 to 3 minutes or until meringue peaks are browned. Serve immediately.

BUTTERNUT LOAVES

3-1/2 cups flour
1 cup chopped pecans
2 cups sugar
1-1/2 cups cooked, mashed
  butternut squash
1-1/2 teaspoons nutmeg
1 teaspoon mace

2 teaspoons soda
1 cup vegetable oil
4 eggs
1/2 cup honey
1 cup milk
1-1/2 teaspoons cinnamon
1-1/2 teaspoons salt

Combine flour, soda and pecans; stir well and set aside. Combine oil, sugar, and eggs; beat well. Stir in squash, honey, milk, spices, and salt. Add flour mixture; stir just until all ingredients are moistened.

Pour batter into 3 greased 9x5x3-inch loaf pans, or 3 greased 1-pound coffee cans. Bake for 1 hour at 350°F. until done. Cool.

BROWN VELVET CAKE

2 cups cake flour, sifted
1 teaspoon soda
3/4 teaspoon salt
1-1/2 cups brown sugar,
    firmly packed
1/2 cup shortening

2 eggs
3 squares (3 ounces) unsweetened
    chocolate, melted
1 cup, plus 2 tablespoons milk
1 teaspoon vanilla

Sift together flour, soda and salt. Cream together the shortening and sugar in electric mixer. Beat in eggs, one at a time, beating until mixture is fluffy. Stir in chocolate and vanilla. Add milk alternately with the dry ingredients, beginning and ending with the flour. Pour into 2 greased and floured 9-inch cake pans and bake in 350° F. oven for 25 minutes or until the cake tests done. Cool in pan for 10 minutes; remove to cake rack and finish cooling. Spread the cake with your favorite white icing.

Make the Brown Velvet Cake for plain or "most elaborate" meals!

BLUEBERRY BUCKLE

1/4 cup butter
3/4 cup sugar
1 egg
2 cups flour
2 teaspoons baking powder

1/2 teaspoon salt
1/2 cup milk
2 cups blueberries
Crumb topping

Cream butter and sugar until light and fluffy. Add egg and beat well. Add sifted dry ingredients alternately with milk, beating until smooth. Fold in berries. Pour into greased 9x12-inch pan. Sprinkle with topping. Bake 35 minutes at 375° F.

CRUMB TOPPING

1/4 cup butter
1/2 cup sugar

1/3 cup flour
1/2 tablespoon cinnamon

Cream butter and sugar, then add flour and cinnamon. Sprinkle on Blueberry Buckle before baking.

LUSCIOUS BLUEBERRY CAKE

3 cups sifted cake flour
2 teaspoons baking powder
1/2 teaspoon salt
1 cup butter
1/2 sugar
4 eggs, separated
2 teaspoons vanilla

2/3 cup milk
1-1/2 cups sugar
3 cups blueberries,
    fresh, frozen or
    canned, drained
1 tablespoon flour
confectioners sugar

Sift flour, baking powder and salt. Cream butter and 1-1/2 cups sugar until light and fluffy. Add egg yolks and vanilla. Blend well. Add dry ingredients alternately with the milk. Beat egg whites until stiff. Gradually beat in 1/2 cup sugar. Fold into batter. Combine blueberries and 1 tablespoon flour. Fold into batter. Pour into greased 13x9x2-inch cake pan. Bake at 350° F. for 50 minutes or until tests done. Sprinkle with confectioners sugar.

The taste of these Blueberry Cakes will haunt you...

BETSY ROSS CAKE

1 cup butter, softened
5 eggs, separated
1/2 teaspoon baking soda
4 cups sifted cake flour
3 cups sugar
Grated rind and juice
of 1 lemon
1 cup milk
(If you plan to decorate the cake to resemble our first American Flag, you will also need: 1 cup hulled blueberries and 4 cups hulled strawberries)

Cream butter, adding sugar gradually until light and fluffy. Add egg yolks, grated rind and juice of lemon, baking soda, flour and milk. Mix until well blended. Beat egg whites stiff but not dry. Fold into batter. Pour into greased and floured 13x9x4-inch baking pan. Bake at 325° F. for about 45 minutes or until done. Cool cake and spread the White Chocolate Cream Cheese Frosting over it. Reserve 1/4 of the frosting if decorating.

WHITE CHOCOLATE CREAM CHEESE FROSTING

4 cups confectioners sugar (1 pkg.)
6 ounces white chocolate
2 tablespoons butter
1 8-ounce package
cream cheese
1 teaspoon vanilla

Gradually beat sugar into cream cheese until evenly blended. Melt chocolate. Off heat, stir in butter and cool. Blend with cream cheese mixture. Add vanilla.

Serve with icing only or for FLAG:

Arrange drained blueberries in a 4x6-inch rectangle in upper left hand corner. With the point of a knife, trace wavy 2-inch stripes from left to right lengthwise. Set strawberries, pointed end up, in alternate stripes. Pipe remaining frosting in remaining stripes and pipe a few stars on the blueberry field to resemble our First American Flag. Beautiful as well as delicious!

My personal wish to you that you will enjoy baking and serving this cake as much as I have!

BUTTER CAKE

1 cup chopped pecans
4 eggs
2 cups sugar
1 teaspoon vanilla
1/2 cup butter

2 cups flour
1 teaspoon baking powder
1/4 teaspoon salt
1 cup milk

Preheat oven to 350°F. Grease a 9-inch tube pan generously. Line the bottom of the pan with waxed paper and grease the paper. Sprinkle the nuts over the bottom of the pan. Beat eggs until lemon colored and very thick. Gradually beat in the sugar and continue beating until mixture is very thick. Beat in the vanilla. Mix the flour with the baking powder and salt and blend in with the mixer on the lowest speed. Heat the milk and butter together in a pan until the butter is melted and the mixture is boiling. Pour all at once into the batter and mix just sufficiently to blend all ingredients together. Immediately pour into the prepared pan and bake about 50 minutes. Cool in the pan 10 minutes before turning upside down onto a serving plate. The cake will shrink during the cooling.

Believe you can and you will bake this beautiful, delicious cake to perfection...

BUTTERMILK CAKE

4-1/2 cups cake flour
1-3/4 cups butter = 3-1/4 sticks
3-1/3 cups sugar
8 eggs

1/4 teaspoon baking soda
1 tablespoon vanilla
1/2 cup buttermilk

Cream butter and sugar together until very light and fluffy. Add eggs, one at a time, beating well after each addition. Add sifted dry ingredients alternately with the vanilla and buttermilk. Bake in a buttered loaf pan 10x5x3-inches and lightly flour the pan. Bake at 325°F. for around 1 hour and 15 to 20 minutes. Remove to cake rack and immediately turn out onto cake rack carefully to cool, right side up.

This cake can't be beat for flavor...the authentic, old-time kind...

BLACKBERRY CAKE

1 cup milk
1 egg
1 cup sugar
1/2 teaspoon nutmeg
Dash of salt
Confectioners sugar

1/4 cup butter, melted
2 cups cake flour
1 teaspoon baking powder
1/2 teaspoon baking soda
2 jars (10 ounces each)
    blackberry jam

Cream butter and sugar until light and fluffy. Add egg, beating well. Beat in the dry ingredients that have been sifted together alternately with the milk. Pour into 3 greased and floured 9-inch round cake pans and bake in 350° F. oven for 25 to 30 minutes or until done. After cakes have been removed from pans and cooled completely, sift confectioners sugar over top layer after you have stacked and spread the blackberry jam between each layer.

BLACK WALNUT CAKE

2 cups flour, sifted
2-3/4 teaspoons
    baking powder
1/4 teaspoon salt
2/3 cup butter
1-1/2 cups sugar

1 teaspoon vanilla
3 eggs, separated
3/4 cup milk
1-1/2 cups black walnuts,
    chopped in small
    pieces

Sift flour, baking powder and salt together. Cream butter with sugar and vanilla until fluffy. Add beaten egg yolks. Beat thoroughly. Add sifted dry ingredients and milk alternately in small amounts, beating well after each addition. Add nuts then the stiffly beaten egg whites. Pour into greased pans and bake in moderate oven, 350° F. for 30 minutes. When cool, frost with caramel frosting.

CARAMEL FROSTING

1 cup sugar
1 cup butter

2 cups sugar
1 cup milk

Put one cup sugar and one cup butter in heavy saucepan or skillet and brown...stirring CONSTANTLY. Bring 2 cups sugar and 1 cup milk to a boil and mix slowly with sugar-butter mixture. Boil for 2 minutes, stirring constantly. Let cool until lukewarm and add 1 teaspoon vanilla. Beat until creamy and spreading consistency. Spread on cake.

An unusual and distinctive cake!

BUTTER AND NUT CAKE

1 cup butter
2 cups sugar
3 cups cake flour
   (sift before measuring)
1 cup buttermilk
1 teaspoon soda

1/4 teaspoon salt
3 eggs, separate and
   beat whites until stiff
3 teaspoons SUPERIOR
   Vanilla, Butter and
   Nut Flavoring

Cream butter and sugar thoroughly; mix soda and salt in buttermilk and add alternately with the flour, mixing well. Add egg yolks one at a time, mixing well after each addition. Blend in the flavoring. Fold in the stiffly beaten egg whites. Pour into greased and floured 10-inch tube pan and bake at 350°F. for 1 hour or until it tests done.

This cake is delicious and fine textured. You may serve as it is or with an icing.

BUTTER NUT CAKE

Another variation that I like baked in layers and frosted.

4 eggs
1 cup crisco
2 cups sugar
2 teaspoons SUPERIOR "The Original"
Vanilla, Butter and Nut Flavoring

2-1/2 cups cake flour
1 cup milk
1/2 cup self-rising flour

Cream shortening and sugar with mixer at high speed for 10 minutes. Add 1 egg at a time, beating well. Add one cup flour and mix on low speed for one minute. Add remaining flour and milk alternately, mixing well. Add flavoring, mixing well and bake at 325°F. for 45 minutes.

BUTTER NUT ICING

8 oz. package cream cheese
1 box confectioners sugar
1 cup chopped pecans
1/2 cup softened butter

1 tablespoon Superior
   "The Original" Vanilla,
   Butter and Nut Flavoring

Cream butter and cream cheese well; add confectioners sugar and flavoring, blending well. Stir in pecans and then spread on layers.

Bake this beautiful and delicious cake...

BUTTER PECAN CAKE

3 tablespoons butter
2/3 cup butter, softened
2 eggs
1-1/2 teaspoons baking
  powder
2/3 cup milk

1-1/3 cups chopped pecans, toasted
1-1/3 cups sugar
2 cups flour
1/4 teaspoon salt
1-1/2 teaspoons vanilla

Melt 3 tablespoons butter in a 13x9x2-inch baking pan. Stir in pecans and bake at 350° F. for 10 minutes. Cool.

Cream butter and sugar until soft and fluffy. Add eggs one at a time, beating well after each addition. Combine flour, baking powder and salt; add to creamed mixture alternately with the milk. Stir in vanilla and 1 cup pecans, reserving remaining pecans for the Butter Pecan Frosting. Pour batter into 2 greased and floured 9-inch cake pans. Bake at 350° F. for 30 minutes or until cake tests done. Cool completely and then spread top and sides of cake with frosting.

BUTTER PECAN FROSTING

3 tablespoons butter
3 tablespoons plus 1 teaspoon milk
Reserved toasted pecans

3 cups confectioners sugar
3/4 teaspoon vanilla

Cream butter; add sugar, milk and vanilla, beating until light and fluffy. Stir in toasted pecans.

This cake will be good to the last crumb...

BUTTERMILK GINGERBREAD

1-2/3 cups cake flour
1/4 teaspoon salt
1/2 teaspoon baking soda
1/2 teaspoon cinnamon
3/4 teaspoon ginger
1/2 cup plus 2 tablespoons buttermilk

1/2 teaspoon allspice
1/2 cup butter
1/2 cup sugar
1 egg
1/2 cup molasses

Cream butter and sugar until smooth; add egg and beat until smooth and creamy. Add molasses and beat vigorously until well blended. Add sifted dry ingredients alternately with the buttermilk.

Line bottom of an 8x8x2-inch baking pan with waxed paper; grease paper and sides of pan lightly. Pour batter into pan and bake at 350° F. for 25 to 30 minutes. Serve warm with whipped cream or applesauce.

CARAMEL-PECAN CAKE

3-1/2 cups cake flour
1/4 teaspoon salt
2 sticks butter
1 teaspoon vanilla

3 teaspoons baking powder
2 cups sugar
1 cup milk
5 eggs

Cream together the butter and sugar until light and fluffy. Add eggs, one at a time, beating well after each addition. Add sifted flour, baking powder and salt alternately with the milk and vanilla, blending well. Pour batter into 3 or 4 greased and floured cake pans and bake at 350°F. for 25 to 30 minutes or until the cakes test done. Spread Caramel Pecan Icing between layers and on top and sides.

CARAMEL-PECAN ICING

3 cups sugar
1 teaspoon vanilla extract
1/2 cup sugar
1 cup chopped pecans

1 cup evaporated milk
1 stick butter
1/2 cup boiling water

Combine 3 cups sugar, milk, butter and vanilla in a saucepan and heat to melt butter. Brown 1/2 cup sugar in a heavy skillet until sugar has melted and turned a caramel color. Add boiling water slowly and stir well. Pour melted sugar into the first mixture; slowly bring to a boil and cook until it reaches soft ball stage, stirring occasionally. This should take around 8 or 9 minutes. Remove from heat and cool slightly. Add chopped pecans and then spread immediately on cake layers and on top and sides.

The aristocrat of old-time cakes...

CARROT PUDDING CAKE

1 package (18.5-ounce) yellow cake mix without pudding
1 package (3-3/4 ounce) instant vanilla pudding mix
1/2 teaspoon salt
2 teaspoons cinnamon
4 eggs
1/3 cup milk
1/4 cup wesson oil
3 cups shredded carrots
1 cup finely chopped pecans

Combine first 7 ingredients and beat approximately 2 minutes at medium speed with electric mixer. Stir in carrots and pecans. Pour batter into 3 greased and floured 9-inch cake pans. Bake at

350°F. for 20 minutes or until tests done. Cool in pans for 10 minutes; remove from pans and let cool completely. Spread Orange Cream Frosting between the layers and on sides and top of cake. Garnish top of cake with pecan halves, if desired.

ORANGE CREAM FROSTING

3 tablespoons butter, softened
1 package (8-ounce) cream cheese, softened
1 16-ounce package confectioners sugar, sifted
1 tablespoon fresh orange juice
1 tablespoon grated orange rind

Combine butter and cream cheese, beating until light and fluffy. Add confectioners sugar and juice and rind; beat until smooth. Spread on cake.

Whenever you bake a cake and share it with friends, you are sharing more than cake...

CARROT-WALNUT CAKE

1-1/2 cups finely chopped walnuts
3 cups sifted cake flour
3 teaspoons baking powder
1 teaspoon salt
2 cups brown sugar, packed
4 large eggs or 5 medium
1 cup vegetable oil
1-1/2 teaspoons cinnamon
1 teaspoon nutmeg
1/4 teaspoon cloves
3 tablespoons milk
3 cups grated carrots

Chop 1/2 cup walnuts very fine. Grease 3 9-inch layer cake pans well. Sprinkle each with about 2-1/2 tablespoons to coat. Chop remaining walnuts a little more coarsely; set aside. Resift flour with baking powder and salt. Combine sugar, eggs, oil and spices. Beat at high speed until light and well mixed. Add half of flour mixture; stir until well blended. Add milk, mixing well, then remaining flour, continuing to mix well. Stir in carrots and walnuts. Pour into cake pans and bake at 350°F. for 25 minutes or until cakes test done. Let stand in pans on wire racks 10 minutes. Turn cakes out onto racks to cool. When cold, frost with a butter cream frosting. Decorate with walnut halves, if desired. This makes a large cake.

These cakes make wonderful eating and a sweet way to tell someone Happy Birthday...

CARROT-ORANGE CAKE NO.1

3-1/2 cups sifted cake flour
2 teaspoons baking powder
1 teaspoon baking soda
1/2 teaspoon salt
1 teaspoon cinnamon
1/2 teaspoon nutmeg
1/2 cup butter, softened
2 cups grated carrots

3/4 cup firmly packed
  brown sugar
3 eggs
1/4 cup fresh orange juice
1 tablespoon grated
  orange rind
1 cup chopped pecans

Grease a 10-inch bundt or tube pan; dust lightly with flour, tap out excess. Preheat oven to 350°F. Sift flour, baking powder, baking soda, salt, cinnamon and nutmeg. Beat butter and sugar until light and fluffy; add eggs one at a time beating well after each addition. Add flour alternately with juice, beginning and ending with the flour mixture. Stir in rind, carrots and pecans. Spoon batter into the prepared pan. Bake at 350°F. for 45 minutes or until tests done. Cool in pan for 10 minutes; turn out; cool completely. Spread with Cream Cheese Frosting and garnish with shredded raw carrot and quartered orange slices if desired.

CREAM CHEESE FROSTING

Beat one package (8-ounce) cream cheese, softened; 1/2 cup confectioners sugar and 1 teaspoon vanilla until smooth, light and fluffy.

Get into action and bake this cake...

CARROT-ORANGE CAKE NO. 2

2 sticks butter, softened
1 teaspoon cinnamon
1 tablespoon grated orange rind
3 teaspoons baking powder
3 cups flour
1-1/2 cups grated carrots

2/3 cup chopped pecans
2 cups sugar
1/2 teaspoon nutmeg
4 eggs
1/2 teaspoon salt
1/3 cup fresh orange juice

Preheat oven to 350°F. Grease and flour tube pan.
Cream butter and sugar. Add spices and orange rind. Beat eggs well in a separate bowl. Add to the butter and sugar.
Sift flour, salt and baking powder and add to the batter alternately with the orange juice. Fold in carrots and nuts. Bake 1 hour or until tests done. Cool and turn out. Dust confectioners sugar, if desired, or spread with cream cheese frosting.

CARROT-PECAN CAKE

1-1/4 cups salad oil
2 cups flour
1 teaspoon soda
4 eggs
1 cup finely chopped pecans

2 cups sugar
2 teaspoons baking powder
1 teaspoon salt
2 cups grated carrots
2 teaspoons cinnamon

Combine oil and sugar and mix well. Sift all dry ingredients together and beat into oil and sugar mixture alternately with the eggs, beating well after each addition. Add pecans. Pour into a lightly greased tube pan. Bake at 325° F. for 1 hour and 10 minutes. Cool in pan. Spread Orange Glaze over the cake, if desired.

ORANGE GLAZE

1/4 cup cornstarch
2 tablespoons butter
1 cup sugar

2 tablespoons grated orange peel
1 cup fresh orange juice
1/2 teaspoon salt

Combine sugar and cornstarch in saucepan; add juice slowly and stir until smooth. Cook over low heat until thick and glossy. Cool and spread over Carrot Pecan cake.

CARROT LAYER CAKE

2 cups sugar
1-1/2 cups salad oil
1 teaspoon salt
3 teaspoons cinnamon
2 teaspoons vanilla extract

4 eggs
2 teaspoons baking soda
2 cups sifted flour
3 cups carrots, finely grated

Cream oil and sugar until light and fluffy. Add eggs, one at a time, beating well after each addition. Blend in vanilla. Sift dry ingredients together and add to creamed mixture, blending well. Fold in carrots. Bake in 3 or 4 greased cake pans. Bake at 325° F. for around 40 minutes. Cool and then spread with Cream Cheese Icing.

CREAM CHEESE ICING

1 stick butter
8 ounce package cream cheese
1 box confectioners sugar

1 cup chopped pecans
1 teaspoon vanilla
Pinch of salt

Beat together softened butter and cream cheese until well blended. Add sugar and vanilla and blend well. Fold in pecans. Spread between layers and on top and sides of carrot cake layers.

CARROT LEMON CAKES

1 cup melted butter
4 eggs
2 cups flour
1 teaspoon baking powder
3/4 teaspoon lemon extract
1-1/2 teaspoons lemon extract

1-1/4 cups sugar
1 cup cooked, mashed carrots
1-1/2 teaspoons vanilla extract
2-1/4 cups confectioners sugar
1/4 cup milk

Cream butter and sugar well. Add eggs, one at a time, beating well after each addition. Add carrots, flour and baking powder. Beat 1 minute. Stir in vanilla and 3/4 teaspoon lemon extract. Spoon into a greased 15x10x1-inch jellyroll pan, spreading to edges. Bake at 350°F. for 25 minutes. Cool.

Combine confectioners sugar, milk and 1-1/2 teaspoons lemon extract. Stir until smooth. Pour glaze over cooled cake. Let stand until glaze is firm. Cut into squares.

So simple to make...and never served often enough!

CHRISTMAS CAKE

1/2 cup glace' cherries
1 cup seedless raisins
1 cup currants
1-1/2 cups sultana raisins
1/2 cup mixed candied fruit peel
2 tablespoons finely chopped
   angelica

1 teaspoon salt
1-1/2 cups chopped walnuts
1-1/2 cups butter
1-1/2 cups sugar
7 eggs
4 cups sifted cake flour

Several hours before making the cake: halve the cherries, put all fruits and nuts into a casserole dish. Mix them well together with your hands. Cover loosely with aluminum foil and place in 240°F. oven until the fruit is well heated through; tossing fruit over once or twice. This should be sticky. Let get cold.

Cream butter and sugar well. Add eggs one at a time, beating well after each addition. Add flour and salt mixture, mixing well. Fold cold fruit after you have separated by running fingers through them.

Bake in 10-inch tube pan oiled and lined with heavy paper. Rest an inverted tin plate over the top of the pan.

Bake at 300°F. for 1 hour; reduce to 280°F. Remove the lid after 2 hours and continue baking for another 3 hours, about 6 hours in all. Reduce the heat if baking too fast and keep gradually reducing the heat. Should be golden brown rather than a deep brown on top.

You will like the taste of this rich and elegant cake...

34

CARROT PINEAPPLE CAKE

3 eggs
1-1/4 cups wesson oil
2 teaspoons soda
2 teaspoons cinnamon
1 cup chopped pecans
2 teaspoons vanilla

2 cups sugar
3 cups cake flour
1 teaspoon salt
1-1/2 cups grated carrots
1 (20-ounce) can crushed
    pineapple, well drained

Combine eggs, sugar and oil and beat well. Sift flour, soda, salt and cinnamon; add to sugar mixture and beat well. Stir in carrots, pecans, pineapple and vanilla. Pour into a greased and lightly floured 10-inch tube pan. Bake at 350° F. for 1 hour and 15 minutes or until cake tests done. Cool in pan for 10 minutes. Remove from pan and let cool completely. Serve plain or with butter cream frosting, if desired.

Have a lot of fun today...bake this cake...

CHERRY DESSERT CAKE SQUARES

2 eggs
1 teaspoon vanilla
1 teaspoon baking powder
1/2 cup chopped pecans
3/4 cup sugar
2 Tablespoons cornstarch
Sweetened whipped cream
or Vanilla ice cream

1 cup sugar
1-1/4 cups cake flour
1/2 teaspoon salt
1 (16-ounce) can pitted
    tart cherries
1/2 teaspoon almond extract

Beat eggs until thick and lemon colored; gradually add 1 cup sugar, beating well. Add vanilla and blend well.

Sift together the flour, baking powder and salt. Add to egg mixture and mix thoroughly. Stir in pecans. Pour 2/3 batter into a greased and floured 9-inch square baking pan, spreading evenly.

Drain cherries, reserving juice. Stir cherries into remaining batter. Pour batter evenly over the first layer. Bake at 350° F. for 45 to 50 minutes. Cool. Cut cake into 3-inch squares.

Add water to cherry juice to equal 1 cup. Combine remaining sugar and cornstarch in a saucepan; stir well. Add cherry juice, stirring well. Cook over low heat until clear and thickened. Stir in almond extract.

Serve squares with a dollop of whipped cream or a scoop of ice cream. Spoon cherry topping over each serving.

Get into cake baking and be amazed...

CHERRY UPSIDE-DOWN CAKE

1 cup butter, divided
1 (16-ounce) can pitted
  tart cherries, drained
2-1/2 cups cake flour
1/4 teaspoon salt
1 teaspoon vanilla extract

2 cups sugar, divided
1 cup chopped pecans
2 eggs
1 tablespoon baking powder
2/3 cup milk

Melt 1/3 cup butter in a 10-inch cast iron skillet. Spread 1/2 cup sugar evenly over butter; cook over low heat until sugar is dissolved. Arrange cherries and chopped pecans in skillet; remove from heat and set aside.

Cream remaining 2/3 cup butter; gradually add remaining 1-1/2 cups sugar, beating until light and fluffy. Add eggs one at a time, beating well after each addition.

Sift together flour, baking powder and salt three times. Stir well and add to creamed mixture alternately with the milk, beginning and ending with the flour mixture. Stir in vanilla and blend well.

Spoon batter evenly over cherries and pecans in skillet. Bake at 350°F. for 50 minutes or until cake tests done. Cool in skillet 10 minutes; then invert cake onto a plate. Cool cake completely. Top with sweetened whipped cream and garnish with cherries and pecan halves, if desired.

Try baking a cake...really try it. You will discover for yourself, there's lots of fun in cake baking...

CHERRY CAKE

1 cup butter
1 cup sugar
5 eggs
1 teaspoon grated lemon rind

1/2 teaspoon baking powder
1-1/2 cups glace' cherries
3 tablespoons ground almonds
3-1/2 cups sifted cake flour

Cream together the butter and sugar until soft and fluffy. Add eggs one at a time, beating well after each addition. Stir in the sifted flour and baking powder one half cup at a time, mixing well. Add grated lemon rind, cherries and almonds and blend thoroughly. Bake in a greased tube pan or bundt pan at 300°F. for 1-1/2 hours or until done.

CHOCOLATE CAKE

2 sticks butter
2 cups sugar
5 eggs
1 teaspoon vanilla

3-1/2 cups cake flour
3 teaspoons baking powder
1/4 teaspoon salt
1 cup milk

Cream together softened butter and sugar until light and fluffy. Add eggs one at a time, beating well after each addition. Add vanilla and blend well. Add sifted dry ingredients alternately with milk. Pour into 3 greased and floured 9-inch round cake pans and bake at 350° F. for 20 to 25 minutes or until tests done. Spread chocolate icing over sides and top and in between layers. Add pecans for variation, if desired.

CHOCOLATE ICING

1-1/2 cups sugar
1/4 cup cocoa
6 tablespoons milk

6 tablespoons butter
1 teaspoon vanilla

Combine all ingredients and stir over medium heat until mixture comes to full boil. Cook 1 minute and remove from heat and beat until mixture begins to thicken.

Double the recipe for a thicker icing.

You'll really never bake a better cake than this one...

CHOCOLATE SHEET CAKE

1 cup butter
4 eggs
1/4 teaspoon salt
2/3 cup buttermilk
2/3 cup boiling water

2 cups sugar
2 cups cake flour
1-1/2 teaspoons soda
3 ounces unsweetened chocolate
1 teaspoon vanilla

Cream butter and sugar thoroughly; add eggs, one at a time, beating well after each addition. Sift flour and salt twice. Combine soda and buttermilk. Then add flour alternately to the creamed mixture with the buttermilk, beginning and ending with the flour. Pour boiling water over the chocolate, stirring until smooth. Add to batter. Mix well, add vanilla.

Pour into a well greased and floured 9x13-inch pan and bake in 325° F. oven for 50 minutes to 1 hour.

Frost with your favorite chocolate or fudge frosting.

Have a lot of fun today... bake this cake...

37

CHERRY-PECAN CAKE

2 cups butter
2 cups sugar
6 egg yolks
3/4 pound candied
    cherries

1/4 pound candied pineapple
5 cups chopped pecans
3 cups sifted cake flour
2 tablespoons lemon extract
6 egg whites

Cream butter, add sugar and mix until smooth and light. Add egg yolks one at a time, beating well after each addition. Sift flour over fruit and nuts and toss together until well coated. Stir into the butter and egg mixture. Add lemon extract. Beat egg whites stiff, but not dry and fold into batter. Pour into a well greased tube or bundt pan and bake at 300°F. for 1-3/4 hours. Serve plain or with Lemon Juice Sugar Glaze.

LEMON JUICE SUGAR GLAZE

2 freshly squeezed lemons (juice)
1-1/2 cups confectioners sugar

Heat lemon juice and add confectioners sugar. Pour over warm cake.

A down-to-earth cake...really good!

CHOCOLATE FUDGE CAKE

1 cup butter
2 cups sugar
4 eggs
3 cups cake flour
1/2 teaspoon salt

1-1/2 teaspoons baking soda
1 cup buttermilk
1 teaspoon vanilla
3 ounces unsweetened
    chocolate, grated

Preheat the oven to 325°F. Grease and flour a 9x13x1-1/2-inch pan. Cream the butter and sugar. Add the eggs, one at a time, and beat well after each addition. After the last egg has been added, beat for 1 minute or until the mixture is light and fluffy. Sift the flour with the salt. Mix the baking soda with the buttermilk and add alternately with the flour to the creamed mixture. Add the vanilla.

Melt the chocolate in 2/3 cup boiling water; stir until smooth. Blend the chocolate into the cake mixture. Pour into the prepared pan and bake for 1 hour at 325°F. or until done.

Cool in the pan. Frost while slightly warm with Chocolate Frosting.

CHOCOLATE FROSTING

4 ounces unsweetened chocolate
1/2 cup butter
3 cups sifted confectioners
   sugar

Dash of salt
1 teaspoon vanilla
1/2 to 2/3 cup evaporated
   milk

Melt the chocolate and butter over hot water. Sift the sugar and salt together and add the vanilla and chocolate mixture. Add enough milk to make spreading consistency.

Bake this cake before 10 a.m. and the rest of the day will take care of itself...

CHOCOLATE CHIP FUDGE CAKE

6 ounces butter
6 eggs
3 cups sugar
2 teaspoons vanilla
1-1/2 cups semi-sweet chocolate chips

6 ounces unsweetened
   chocolate
1/2 teaspoon salt
1-1/2 cups flour

Melt butter and unsweetened chocolate over low heat and cool to lukewarm. In a large mixing bowl, beat eggs, sugar, salt and vanilla together just to combine. Blend in the butter-chocolate mixture. Stir in flour and chocolate chips, blending well.

Pour into two 9-inch round, greased cake pans making sure the bottoms are lined with waxed paper. Bake at 350°F. for 30 to 40 minutes. It will be more cake-like and less fudgy if baked for a longer period of time. Frost with Elegant Fudge Frosting.

ELEGANT FUDGE FROSTING

1-1/4 cups sugar
1 cup heavy cream
5 ounces unsweetened chocolate,
   finely chopped

8 tablespoons butter
1 teaspoon vanilla
2 tablespoons instant
   coffee granules

Combine sugar, instant coffee and cream in deep saucepan. Bring to a boil, stirring constantly. Mixture will boil up during cooking. Reduce heat; simmer 6 minutes without stirring. Remove from heat. Add chopped chocolate; stir to blend. Stir in butter and vanilla. Chill until mixture begins to thicken. Beat until thick and creamy. Can be rewhipped next day if left to stand and thicken.

Create a new cake!

CHOCOLATE BEET CAKE

2 cups cake flour
1/2 teaspoon salt
1/3 cup cocoa
1 cup sugar
1/2 cup corn oil
1/4 cup orange juice
1 teaspoon vanilla
1 (6-ounce) package semi-sweet
  chocolate morsels

2 teaspoons baking
  powder
3 eggs
1 cup grated, cooked
  beets
2 teaspoons grated
  orange rind
Powdered sugar
(optional)

Sift flour, baking powder, salt and cocoa together and set aside. Combine oil and sugar and mix thoroughly. Add eggs one at a time beating well after each addition. Add flour mixture alternately with the orange juice and vanilla, mixing well. Add beets, orange rind and mix thoroughly. Then stir in the chocolate morsels.

Pour into a greased square baking pan. Bake at 350°F. for 40 minutes or until cake tests done. Let cool 10 minutes in pan. Remove from pan and cool completely on wire rack. Sprinkle with powdered sugar, if desired.

CHOCOLATE COCONUT CAKE

2 cups cake flour
1 teaspoon soda
1/2 cup butter
2 eggs

2 cups sugar
1 cup water
1/4 cup cocoa
1/2 cup buttermilk

Sift together flour, sugar and soda into a large mixing bowl. Combine water, butter and cocoa in a small saucepan; cook over low heat until mixture comes to a boil; remove from heat and pour over dry ingredients, mixing thoroughly. Add eggs and buttermilk and mix thoroughly.

Spoon batter into a well-greased 13x9x2-inch pan. Bake at 350°F. for 30 minutes or until cake tests done. Cool. Frost with Chocolate Coconut Frosting.

CHOCOLATE COCONUT FROSTING

1 16-ounce package
  confectioners sugar
1 cup chopped pecans
1/3 cup plus 2 teaspoons milk

3 tablespoons cocoa
1 cup shredded coconut
1/2 cup butter

Combine sugar, pecans and coconut. Combine milk, butter and

cocoa and cook over low heat until it comes to a boil. Add chocolate mixture to sugar mixture and beat with electric mixer until frosting is fluffy.

Bake one of these rare and wonderful cakes...

CHOCOLATE MARBLE CAKE

3 cups sifted cake flour
1/2 teaspoon salt
3/4 cup butter
3/4 cup milk
6 egg whites, stiffly beaten
4 tablespoons sugar
1/4 cup boiling water

3 teaspoons baking
powder
2 cups sugar
1 teaspoon vanilla
3 squares unsweetened
chocolate, melted
1/4 teaspoon soda

Sift flour once, measure; add baking powder and salt, and sift together three times. Cream butter thoroughly; add sugar gradually and cream together until light and fluffy. Add flour, alternately with milk, a small amount at a time. Beat after each addition until smooth. Add vanilla. Fold in egg whites. To melted chocolate, add sugar and boiling water, stirring until blended. Then add soda and stir until thickened. Cool slightly. Divide batter into two parts. To one part add chocolate mixture. Put by tablespoons into greased pan, 10x10x2-inch, alternating light and dark mixtures. Bake in 350° F. oven for 55 minutes or until done. Spread Chocolate Seven Minute Frosting on top and sides of cake.

CHOCOLATE SEVEN MINUTE FROSTING

2 egg whites
1/4 teaspoon cream of tartar
Dash of salt
4 or 5 tablespoons cold water
1 square unsweetened chocolate,
melted

1-1/2 cups sugar
1 teaspoon vanilla
3 teaspoons white
corn syrup

Put first 5 ingredients in top of double boiler, then place over boiling water. Beat around 4 or 5 minutes with electric beater until stiff peaks form. Add vanilla and syrup and beat until shiny peaks form. Fold in the chocolate mixture gently. Spread on cake immediately.

This promises to be a wonderful cake!

CHOCOLATE COCA-COLA CAKE

2 sticks butter
1/2 cup wesson oil
1/2 cup miniature
  marshmallows
1 teaspoon soda
2 eggs

2-1/2 tablespoons cocoa
1 cup Coca-Cola
2 cups flour
2 cups sugar
1/2 cup buttermilk
1 teaspoon vanilla

Combine butter, cocoa, oil and cola and bring to a boil. Add the remaining ingredients in order named; beat well. Pour into a large greased and floured sheet cake pan. Bake in 350° F. oven for 45 minutes. Spread Coca-Cola Icing over warm cake.

COCA-COLA ICING

6 tablespoons Coca-Cola
2-1/2 tablespoons cocoa
1 cup chopped pecans

1 stick butter
1 box confectioners sugar
1 teaspoon vanilla

Bring first 3 ingredients to a boil; add remaining ingredients and beat until smooth. Spread over warm cake.

CHOCOLATE CREAM BROWNIE CAKES

1 package German Chocolate
1 3-ounce pkg. cream cheese
1 egg
1/2 teaspoon vanilla
3/4 cup sugar
1/4 teaspoon salt
1/2 cup chopped pecans

5 tablespoons butter
1/4 cup sugar
1 tablespoon flour
2 eggs
1/2 tsp. baking powder
1/2 cup flour
1 teaspoon vanilla

Melt chocolate and 3 tablespoons butter over low heat, stirring constantly. Cool. Blend remaining butter and cheese until softened. Gradually add 1/4 cup sugar, beating well. Blend in 1 egg, 1 tablespoon flour and 1/2 teaspoon vanilla; set aside. Beat 2 eggs until thick and light in color. Gradually add 3/4 cup sugar, beating until thickened. Add baking powder, salt and 1/2 cup flour. Blend in cooled chocolate mixture, nuts, 1 teaspoon vanilla. Spread 1/2 of the chocolate batter in greased 9-inch square pan. Add cream cheese mixture, spreading evenly. Top with remaining chocolate batter by tablespoons. Zigzag a spatula through batter to marbleize. Bake at 350° F. for 35 to 40 minutes. Cool. Cut into serving pieces, as desired.

You will gain a natural kind of joy when you bake these cakes...

CHOCOLATE MARBLE LOAF CAKE

1/3 cup shortening
1 teaspoon vanilla
2 teaspoons baking powder
2/3 cup milk
1 1-ounce square unsweetened
    chocolate, melted

1 cup sugar
1-1/2 cups sifted cake flour
1/4 teaspoon salt
3 stiffly beaten egg whites
1 tablespoon hot water
1/4 teaspoon soda

Cream shortening and sugar together until light and fluffy. Add vanilla. Sift flour, baking powder and salt together 3 times. Add to creamed mixture alternately with the milk. Beat until smooth. Fold in egg whites. Combine chocolate, water and soda. Add to 1/2 the batter.

Alternate light and dark batter by spoonsful in paper-lined 10x5x3-inch loaf pan. Bake in 300°F. oven about 1 hour. Cool and frost with chocolate frosting.

CHOCOLATE FROSTING

1/2 cup milk
1/2 teaspoon vanilla
2 cups sifted,
    confectioners sugar

2 tablespoons butter
2 1-ounce squares
    unsweetened
    chocolate, melted

Combine all ingredients in mixer and beat until smooth. Spread on cake.

CHOCOLATE SPICE CAKE

1/2 cup butter, softened
3 eggs separated
1-3/4 cups flour
3/4 teaspoon baking powder
1 teaspoon cinnamon
1 teaspoon vanilla
1 cup chopped pecans

1-1/2 cups sugar
3/4 cup buttermilk
3/4 teaspoon soda
3/4 teaspoon nutmeg
2 tablespoons cocoa
1 teaspoon lemon extract

Cream butter well; add sugar and beat until light and fluffy. Add egg yolks one at a time, beating well after each addition. Sift all dry ingredients together twice. Add alternately with the buttermilk, blending well. Add flavorings and nuts. Beat egg whites until stiff but not dry and then fold in.

Fold batter into 3 greased and floured cake pans and bake at 350°F. for 25 to 30 minutes or until done. Cool completely and frost with your favorite chocolate frosting.

Bake one of these cakes and you will find new fun in baking...

CHOCOLATE MERINGUE CAKE

2 cups flour
1/4 teaspoon salt
2 cups sugar, divided
1 square (1-ounce) grated
    unsweetened chocolate
3/4 cup milk
8 pecan halves
1 tablespoon baking powder

4 eggs, separated
1 cup finely chopped pecans
1/2 cup butter
1 teaspoon vanilla
2 squares (1-ounce each)
    semi-sweet chocolate, melted
    with 3 tablespoons water

Grease 10-inch tube pan. Line bottom with waxed paper; set aside. Sift together flour, baking powder and salt. Set aside. Beat egg whites until soft peaks form. Gradually beat in 1 cup sugar until stiff, glossy peaks form. Fold in pecans and grated chocolate. Spread mixture on bottom and three quarters up sides of pan as though lining it.

Cream butter and remaining 1 cup sugar until light and fluffy. Beat in egg yolks and vanilla until well blended. Stir in flour mixture alternately with the milk until well blended. Pour cake mixture into pan, making sure it is surrounded by meringue on all sides and lower than top of meringue. Bake in 325°F. oven 65 to 70 minutes or until done.

Do NOT invert pan. Cool on rack 25 minutes or until sides can be loosened easily with metal spatula. Turn out on serving plate. Peel off waxed paper; cool completely. Garnish with melted chocolate mixture and pecans dipped in chocolate mixture.

A cake could be on the way...just bake and look forward to it!

CHOCOLATE STRAWBERRY CAKE

1 package German chocolate
1 teaspoon vanilla
2 cups sugar
3 cups sifted cake flour
1/2 teaspoon salt

1/2 cup water
1 cup butter
4 eggs, separated
1 teaspoon soda
1 cup buttermilk

Melt chocolate in boiling water and cool. Cream butter and sugar until light and fluffy. Add egg yolks one at a time, beating well after each addition. Add sifted dry ingredients alternately with the buttermilk until well blended. Fold in the stiffly beaten egg whites and bake at 350°F. for 25 to 30 minutes. Be sure to grease 2 cake pans and line with waxed paper. Cool completely and spread with the Strawberry Cream Frosting.

STRAWBERRY CREAM FROSTING

1 pint pretty, fresh strawberries   3 tablespoons sugar
1 cup heavy cream

Whip the cream until thickened; add sugar gradually until well blended. Spread 1/2 the cream and half the strawberries on one layer and top with the other half of cream and strawberries.

The reward of baking and serving this cake will be more than worth it...

CHOCOLATE ORANGE CAKE

3 cups cake flour   3/4 cup dutch-type cocoa
3 teaspoons baking powder   Grated rind of 4 large oranges
2 cups sugar   1 pound sweet butter
1-1/2 cups milk   4 eggs

Cream butter until fluffy; add sugar gradually, beating well. Add eggs one at a time, beating well after each addition. Add flour alternately with the milk, blending well. Stir in the grated orange rind. Pour into 3 greased and floured 9-inch round cake pans and bake at 350°F. for 25 to 30 minutes. Frost with your favorite Chocolate Icing.

CHOCOLATE MAYONNAISE CAKE

2 cups flour   1/2 cup cocoa
1 cup sugar   1 teaspoon baking soda
Pinch of salt   1 cup water
1 cup mayonnaise   1-1/2 teaspoons vanilla

Combine flour, cocoa, sugar, soda and salt and mix well. Add water, mayonnaise and vanilla and stir until smooth. Pour batter into a greased and floured 9-inch pan. Bake at 350°F. for 25 to 30 minutes or until done. Cool completely and then spread with Chocolate Frosting.

CHOCOLATE FROSTING

2-3/4 cups sifted confectioners   1/4 cup cocoa
  sugar   2 egg yolks
1/4 cup butter, melted   1 teaspoon
2 tablespoons milk   vanilla
1/8 teaspoon salt

Combine all ingredients; beat until smooth. Spread on cake.

A pleasant surprise awaits you when you bake these cakes!

AMBASSADOR CHOCOLATE CAKE

2 cups sifted cake flour
1/2 teaspoon salt
1-1/2 cups brown sugar,
      firmly packed
4 squares unsweetened chocolate, melted

1 teaspoon soda
1 cup butter
3 eggs, well beaten
2/3 cup water

Sift flour once, measure, add soda and salt and sift together three times. Cream butter thoroughly, add sugar gradually, and cream together until light and fluffy. Add eggs and beat well. Add chocolate and beat until smooth. Add flour, alternately with water a small amount at a time. Beat after each addition until smooth. Bake in two deep greased 9-inch layer pans in 350°F. oven for 30 minutes. Spread Seven Minute Frosting between layers and on top and sides of cake, piling frosting thickly on top. Melt 2 additional squares of unsweetened chocolate with 2 teaspoons butter. When frosting is set, pour chocolate over cake.

SEVEN MINUTE FROSTING

2 egg whites
1/4 teaspoon cream of tartar
Dash of salt
5 tablespoons cold water

1-1/2 cups sugar
1 teaspoon vanilla
3 teaspoons white
      corn syrup

Put first 5 ingredients in top of double boiler, then place over boiling water. Beat with rotary beater 7 minutes or with electric beater 4 minutes or until icing stands in pointed stiff peaks. Remove from heat. Change hot water for cold and replace top in double boiler. Add vanilla and syrup, then continue beating until icing stands in shiny peaks stiff enough to hold shape. Spread on cake immediately.

Bake this cake and it will make you whistle with happiness...

CHOCOLATE VIENNESE LAYER CAKE

1-3/4 cups sifted cake flour
1 teaspoon salt
2 teaspoons baking powder
1-1/2 cups sugar
1/2 cup butter

1-1/4 cups whipping cream
2 eggs
1 teaspoon vanilla
2 squares unsweetened
      chocolate, melted & cooled

Preheat oven to 350°F. Grease 2 9-inch cake pans and dust lightly with flour.

Sift together flour, salt, baking powder and sugar. Cream the butter, sift in the flour mixture. Mix in 1 cup cream, then beat very well. Add the eggs, vanilla, chocolate and remaining cream. Beat very well again. Divide the batter evenly between the two prepared pans. Bake 25 minutes or until done. Cool on a cake rack for 10 minutes before removing from pans. Cool thoroughly before frosting with Rich Chocolate Frosting.

RICH CHOCOLATE FROSTING

4 ounces cream cheese
2 tablespoons heavy cream
2 cups confectioners sugar

3 squares unsweetened
   chocolate, melted
1 teaspoon vanilla

Combine all ingredients, mixing well. Frost cake.

Take a chance... bake this cake and change the atmosphere some place...

CHOCOLATE TEA CAKES

5 (1-ounce) squares unsweetened
   chocolate
2/3 cup butter
5 eggs
2-1/2 cups sugar

2 teaspoons vanilla
1/2 teaspoon salt
1-1/4 cups cake flour
1-1/2 cups chopped pecans

Combine chocolate and butter in a saucepan over low heat; cook until chocolate and butter melt; set aside.

Combine next 4 ingredients; beat until well blended. Stir in flour, chopped pecans and chocolate mixture.

Pour batter into a lightly greased 15x10x1-inch jellyroll pan. Bake at 350° F. for 25 minutes or until done. Cool and frost with chocolate frosting while still warm. Cut into squares; top each square with a pecan half.

CHOCOLATE FROSTING

1/4 cup plus 2 tablespoons butter
1-1/2 (1-ounce) squares
   unsweetened chocolate, melted
3 tablespoons half-and-half

3 cups sifted confectioners
   sugar
2 tablespoons whipping
   cream

Combine first 3 ingredients in saucepan; cook until butter and chocolate melt. Remove from heat and stir in sugar and whipping cream.

Arrange at least a little time to bake a cake...

RICH CHOCOLATE CAKE

2-1/2 cups sifted cake flour
1/2 teaspoon salt
1 teaspoon baking soda
1/4 pound sweet chocolate
1/2 cup brewed coffee

1 cup butter
1-3/4 cups sugar
4 egg yolks
1 cup buttermilk
4 egg whites, stiffly beaten

Sift together the flour, salt and baking soda. Combine the chocolate and coffee in top of a double boiler; place over hot water until melted. Cool. Cream the butter; gradually beat in the sugar until light and fluffy. Add 1 egg yolk at a time, beating well after each addition. Mix in the melted chocolate. Add flour mixture alternately with the buttermilk, beating until smooth after each addition. Fold in egg whites. Pour into 3 greased and floured cake pans. Bake 35 minutes or until done at 350° F. Cool 20 minutes on cake rack. Frost with Seven Minute Frosting, Cream Frosting or with sweetened Whipped Cream.

GERMAN CHOCOLATE CAKE

1 (4-ounce) package German
  chocolate
1/2 cup water
1 cup butter
4 eggs, separated
1 teaspoon soda

1 cup buttermilk
1 teaspoon vanilla
2 cups sugar
3 cups sifted cake flour
1/2 teaspoon salt

Melt chocolate in 1/2 cup boiling water and cool. Cream butter and sugar gradually until light and fluffy. Add egg yolks one at a time beating well after each addition. Add sifted dry ingredients alternately with the buttermilk. Fold in stiffly beaten egg whites and pour into 3 greased and floured 9-inch cake pans. Bake for 25 to 30 minutes at 350° F. or until done. Frost with Coconut Pecan Frosting.

COCONUT PECAN FROSTING

1-1/3 cups evaporated milk
4 egg yolks
1-1/2 teaspoons vanilla
1-1/3 cups chopped pecans

1-1/3 cups sugar
2/3 cup butter
1-1/3 cups grated
  coconut

Combine milk, sugar, egg yolks and butter in heavy saucepan; bring to a boil and cook over medium heat for 12 minutes, stirring constantly. Add vanilla, coconut and pecans; stir until frosting is cool and of spreading consistency.

Make someone happy... bake this scrumptious cake!

WHITE CHOCOLATE LAYER CAKE

1 cup butter
2 cups sugar
4 eggs
1/4 pound white chocolate,
  melted in 1/2 cup boiling water

3 cups cake flour
1 teaspoon soda
1 cup buttermilk
1 teaspoon vanilla

Cream butter and sugar until light and fluffy. Add eggs, one at a time, beating well after each addition. Cool the melted chocolate in the water and add to the egg mixture. Add sifted dry ingredients alternately with the buttermilk. Stir in the vanilla. Pour into 3 well greased and floured layer cake pans and bake for 30 minutes at 350° F. or until done.

You may vary by folding in the egg whites; folding in 1 cup finely chopped pecans and 1 cup grated coconut.

Frost with your favorite chocolate icing or with coconut icing, as desired.

SOUR CREAM DEVIL'S FOOD CAKE

2 cups sifted cake flour
1/2 teaspoon salt
1-1/4 cups sugar
3 squares unsweetened chocolate,
  melted
3/4 cup sweet milk

1 teaspoon soda
1/3 cup butter
1 egg
1 teaspoon vanilla
1/2 cup thick sour cream

Sift flour once, measure, add soda and salt, and sift together three times. Cream butter thoroughly, add sugar gradually and cream together well. Add egg and beat thoroughly, then add chocolate and vanilla and blend. Add about 1/4 of the flour and beat well; then add sour cream and beat thoroughly. Add remaining flour, alternately with milk, in small amounts, beating well after each addition until smooth. Bake in two greased 9-inch cake pans at 350° F. for 30 minutes, or until done. Spread Chocolate Butter Frosting between layers and on top of cake.

CHOCOLATE BUTTER FROSTING

1 stick butter, melted
4 tablespoons cocoa
6 tablespoons milk

1 teaspoon vanilla
1 box confectioners sugar
chopped pecans, optional

Blend together all ingredients in mixer. Blend well and ice cake.

Make these cakes your cakes...put some OOMPH into them!

COCOA CAKE

2 cups flour
2 cups sugar
3/4 cup cocoa (Ideal or Droste,
   if you can locate)
2 teaspoons baking soda

1 teaspoon baking powder
1/2 cup butter, melted
1 egg
1 cup boiling water
1 cup milk

Preheat oven to 350°F. Sift dry ingredients together. Add the remaining ingredients and beat 2 minutes with electric mixer. Bake for 35 minutes (or more, if necessary) at 350°F.

Bake in greased and lightly floured tube pan or bundt pan. Serve plain or dust with confectioners sugar or with sweetened whipped cream.

DEVIL'S FOOD CAKE

2-1/2 cups flour
1 teaspoon baking soda
1 teaspoon baking powder
1/2 cup cocoa
1 teaspoon vanilla

2 sticks butter
2 cups sugar
5 eggs
1 cup buttermilk

Sift together flour, soda, salt, baking powder and cocoa three times. Cream together butter and sugar until light and fluffy. Add eggs, one at a time, beating well after each addition. Add flour mixture alternately with the buttermilk, blending well. Stir in vanilla. Grease and flour 3 9-inch round cake pans. Pour into the pans and bake at 350°F. for 25 minutes. Frost with Chocolate Icing, Seven Minute Icing or Creole Icing.

CHOCOLATE ICING

3 cups sugar
1/2 teaspoon salt
13 large marshmallows,
   cut up
1 cup evaporated milk

1/2 stick butter
3 ounces unsweetened
   chocolate
1 teaspoon vanilla

Cook sugar, salt, marshmallows and milk about 5 minutes, stirring constantly. Add butter and chocolate and stir until it melts. Beat until cool. Add vanilla and blend well. If icing is too thick to spread, add a little cream or milk.

Another exquisite cake!

CREOLE ICING

4 egg whites
1/4 teaspoon salt
3/4 cup white granulated
  sugar
Pecans, chopped

1/4 cup white Karo syrup
1-1/2 cups light brown sugar
1 tablespoon vanilla extract
1 cup water

Combine syrup, sugars and water and dissolve. Bring mixture to a boil, stirring until it begins to boil. Then cook, without stirring, until it spins a thread. Beat the egg whites and salt until stiff but not dry. Pour the syrup over the whites in a very thin stream, beating constantly, until thick enough to spread. Add the vanilla. Sprinkle finely chopped pecans on top of frosting, if desired.

The attractive finish makes the icing look difficult... but it is easy to make... and so delicious!

CHOCOLATE PUDDING CAKE

3/4 cup sugar
2 tablespoons cocoa
1/4 teaspoon salt
3 tablespoons butter
1/2 cup sugar
1/4 cup cocoa
1-1/2 cups water
1-1/4 cups cake flour

2 teaspoons baking powder
1/2 cup milk
1 teaspoon vanilla
1/2 cup firmly packed
  brown sugar
1 cup sweetened
  whipped cream, optional

Sift 3/4 cup sugar, flour, 2 tablespoons cocoa, baking powder and salt into a 9-inch square pan. Stir in milk, butter, and vanilla and spread mixture evenly in pan.

Combine next 3 ingredients and sprinkle over batter: 1/2 cup sugar, brown sugar and 1/4 cup cocoa. Pour water over top. Bake pudding at 350° F. for 40 minutes. Serve with sweetened whipped cream, if desired.

Go ahead... use your talent and bake that cake!

CONGO BARS

Melt 2/3 cup butter or margarine; add and blend 1 box light brown sugar. Lightly beat 3 eggs and then beat into mixture. Add 2-2/3 cups sifted flour, 2-1/2 teaspoons baking powder and 1/2 teaspoon salt. Add 1 cup chocolate drops and 1 cup chopped pecans. Pour into a lightly greased baking dish and bake at 350° F. for around 45 to 50 minutes. Cut into bars when cooled.

CHOCOLATE CANDY CAKE

8 milk chocolate Hershey bars
2 cans chocolate syrup, small
2 cups sugar
1 cup buttermilk
1/2 teaspoon soda

2-1/2 cups cake flour
2 teaspoons vanilla
2 sticks butter
1 cup chopped pecans
5 eggs

Preheat oven at 350°F. Melt candy and syrup in double boiler. Add vanilla and cool. Cream butter and sugar until soft and fluffy. Add eggs, one at a time, beating well after each addition. Add chocolate mixture and beat well. Mix soda and flour and sift twice; add alternately with buttermilk and continue to beat until well blended. Add pecans and bake in tube pan for 1 to 1-1/2 hours or until done.

Use your favorite chocolate icing and top with pecan halves, if desired.

CHOCOLATE CHIFFON CAKE

1/2 cup cocoa
1-3/4 cups flour
1-1/2 teaspoon soda
1/2 cup Wesson oil
2 teaspoons vanilla

3/4 cup boiling water
1-3/4 cup sugar
1 teaspoon salt
8 eggs, separated
1/2 teaspoon cream of tartar

Mix cocoa and boiling water and set aside to cool.

Sift together flour, sugar, baking soda and salt. Make a well in the center. Add oil, egg yolks, vanilla and cocoa mixture. Beat well (about 3 minutes).

Beat egg whites and cream of tartar until stiff. Fold into batter. Pour into ungreased 10-inch tube pan. Cut through with spatula.

Bake in 325°F. oven for 55 minutes; increase temperature to 350°F.; bake 10 minutes or until tests done. Frost with your favorite chocolate frosting.

Keep in a good humor and spirit--bake a cake today and share it!

MILK CHOCOLATE CAKE

8 (1-7/8 ounce) chocolate-covered malt-caramel
  candy bars (MILKY WAY)
2 cups sugar
1/2 cup butter, softened
4 eggs
1-1/4 cups buttermilk

3 cups cake flour
1 cup chopped pecans
1 teaspoon vanilla
1/2 teaspoon soda

Combine candy bars and 1/2 cup melted butter in a saucepan;

place over low heat until candy bars are melted, stirring constantly; cool.

Cream 1/2 cup softened butter, gradually adding sugar and beat until light and fluffy. Add eggs, one at a time, beating well after each addition; stir in the vanilla.

Combine buttermilk and soda; add to creamed mixture alternately with flour, beating well after each addition; stir in candy bar mixture and pecans.

Pour batter into a greased and floured 10-inch tube pan. Bake at 325° F. for 1 hour and 20 minutes or until tests done.

Let cool in pan for 1 hour; remove and completely cool, then frost: Use Milk Chocolate Frosting.

MILK CHOCOLATE FROSTING

2-1/2 cups sugar
1 cup evaporated milk
1 (6-ounce) package
semi-sweet chocolate pieces

1 cup marshmallow cream
1/2 cup melted butter

Combine sugar, milk and butter in heavy saucepan; cook over medium heat until a small amount dropped in cold water forms a soft ball.

Remove from heat; add chocolate pieces and marshmallow cream, stirring until melted.

If necessary, add a small amount of milk to make spreading consistency.

Hope you have a reason to bake and serve this super cake soon...

CHOCOLATE CREAM CAKE

4 eggs
2 cups whipping cream
2 teaspoons vanilla
2-1/2 cups sifted cake flour

1/2 teaspoon salt
2 cups sugar
1/2 cup cocoa
3 teaspoons baking powder

Beat eggs thoroughly in a large mixing bowl (about 5 minutes.) Gradually beat in cream and vanilla, mixing well.

Sift flour, sugar, cocoa, baking powder and salt. Add to egg mixture; beat until smooth. Pour into 2 greased 9x5x3-inch loaf pans.

Bake at 350° F. for 45 minutes. Cool 10 minutes. Remove from pans. Dust with confectioners sugar. Cool on racks. Also, good with sweetened strawberries and sweetened whipped cream.

CHOCOLATE SAUERKRAUT CAKE

2-1/2 cups cake flour
1 teaspoon soda
1 teaspoon baking powder
1-1/2 cups sugar
1/2 cup cocoa
2/3 cup sauerkraut, chopped,
  rinsed and drained

2/3 cup butter
3 eggs
1-1/4 teaspoons vanilla
1/4 teaspoon salt
1 cup buttermilk

Cream together sugar and butter until light and fluffy. Add eggs one at a time, beating well after each addition. Add vanilla and blend well. Sift together the flour, salt, soda, baking powder and cocoa. Add the flour mixture alternately with the buttermilk. Fold in the sauerkraut by hand. Bake in either a greased and floured sheet cake pan or in 2 9-inch cake pans, at 350°F. for 25 to 30 minutes or until the cake tests done. Frost with either a cream cheese frosting or a mocha frosting.

CREAM CHEESE FROSTING

1 (8-ounce) package cream cheese
1 package confectioners sugar

milk to soften

Combine these ingredients, blending until soft and creamy.

MOCHA CREAM FROSTING

1 (8-ounce) package cream cheese
1 package confectioners sugar

2 tablespoons strong
  coffee

Combine these ingredients, blending until soft and creamy.

A pleasant way to sneak sauerkraut into the diet...

COCONUT CREAM CAKE

3 cups sugar
1 cup whipping cream
1/2 pound butter
2 teaspoons vanilla

6 eggs
1 teaspoon lemon extract
3 cups cake flour

Cream butter and sugar until light and fluffy. Add eggs one at a time, beating well after each addition. Add sifted flour a little at a time alternately with the whipping cream and flavorings. Pour into 3 greased and floured 9-inch cake pans and bake in 350°F. oven for about 25 minutes or until done. Cool and frost.

COCONUT CREAM FROSTING

4 tablespoons butter
3-1/2 cups confectioners
    sugar
2 tablespoons milk

1 package (8-ounces) cream cheese
2 cups shredded coconut
1/2 teaspoon vanilla

Melt 2 tablespoons butter in skillet; add coconut, stirring constantly until golden brown. Spread coconut on paper towel to cool. Cream remaining butter with the cream cheese; add sugar and milk alternately, beating well. Add vanilla. Stir in 1-1/4 cups of the coconut. Spread on layers, top and sides of cake. Sprinkle remaining coconut over top. You may add chopped pecans to the frosting if you want to.

Prove you can bake a cake and make someone happy!

COCONUT MARBLE CAKE

3 cups cake flour
1 teaspoon salt
2 cups sugar
1 cup milk
1/2 cup chocolate malted milk powder

2 teaspoons
    baking powder
1 cup butter
4 eggs
1 teaspoon vanilla

Cream butter and sugar until soft and fluffy. Add eggs one at a time, beating well after each addition. Sift together the flour, baking powder and salt, then add alternately with the milk, beating well. Stir in the vanilla, blending well. Pour half of the batter into a bowl; blend in the malted milk powder, mixing until smooth.

Spoon plain and malted batters alternately into well greased and floured 10-inch tube or bundt pan. Bake at 350°F. for 60 to 70 minutes or until done. Remove from oven and cool in pan on wire rack for 15 minutes. Invert onto oven-proof serving plate and cool completely. Spread with Broiled Coconut Frosting and bake at 500°F. 2 to 5 minutes, until frosting browns lightly.

BROILED COCONUT FROSTING

1/4 cup butter
1 cup chopped or
    flaked coconut

1/2 cup firmly packed brown sugar
1/4 cup heavy cream

Melt butter; while still warm, add brown sugar, coconut and cream and stir until sugar is partially melted and mixture is well combined. Spread evenly over cake. Bake at 500°F. for 2 to 5 minutes or until lightly browned.

Follow the directions --- there's the key, and you will be rewarded with a wonderful cake...

55

COCONUT CAKE

3/4 cup butter
3 cups sifted cake flour
6 egg yolks
3 egg whites
1 teaspoon vanilla

2 cups sugar
3 teaspoons baking powder
Dash of salt
1 cup milk

Cream butter and sugar until light and fluffy. Add egg yolks, one at a time, beating well after each addition. Sift together the flour and baking powder; add alternately with the milk. Beat egg whites until stiff along with the salt; fold into batter. Add the vanilla flavoring and bake at 350° F. for 30 minutes or until done. Frost with Coconut Frosting of your choice.

COCONUT FROSTING

2 cups sugar
1/4 cup white syrup
2 coconuts grated (or large
    package fresh-frozen grated coconut)

1 cup water
1 teaspoon vanilla
3 egg whites
Dash of salt

Boil sugar, water and syrup until it spins a thread. Beat egg whites and salt until stiff. Gradually add hot syrup, beating all the time. Add vanilla flavoring and cool until stiff enough to spread. Frost between and on top of layers with frosting and layers of coconut. Or add the coconut to the frosting and spread evenly over cake.

What a glorious cake...

OLD FASHIONED COCONUT ICING

Cook in separate saucepans; put in one ten minutes ahead of the other:

First saucepan	Second saucepan
1-1/2 cups sugar	2 egg whites
2 cups coconut juice or juice	1 cup sugar plus 3
of 2 coconuts and water	tablespoons water
to equal 2 cups	1/2 teaspoon cream of tartar
	Pinch salt
	1 teaspoon vanilla extract
Cook until it begins to thicken; add 2 handsful of fresh grated coconut; cook 1 minute longer.	Cook over hot water, beating constantly for 3 minutes until it stands in peaks.

Put one layer of cake on dish, then layer of juice with coconut and some white frosting, if desired. Stack all layers the same way, then cover cake with white egg frosting; hold hand to catch coconut and cover frosting with grated coconut.

A very old, old family recipe. The icing will seep down into the cake, making the cake very moist and delicious!

CRANBERRY-ORANGE CAKE

1 cup cut-up dates
1 cup halved cranberries
1 teaspoon baking powder
1/4 teaspoon salt
1 cup sugar
2 tablespoons grated
 orange rind
2/3 cup sugar
1 cup chopped walnuts
1/2 cup sifted cake flour
1 teaspoon soda
1/2 cup butter
2 eggs
1 cup buttermilk
2/3 cup orange juice
2 cups cake flour

Combine dates, walnuts, cranberries and one-half cup flour. Set aside. Sift together 2 cups flour, baking powder, baking soda and salt and set aside.

Cream butter and 1 cup sugar until light and fluffy. Add eggs, one at a time, beating well after each addition. Add orange rind, blending well.

Add dry ingredients alternately with the buttermilk, beating well after each addition. Stir in fruit-nut mixture. Turn batter into greased 9-inch springform pan.

Bake in 350°F. oven for 1 hour or until tests done. Cool 10 minutes. Remove from pan. Cool on rack. Heat orange juice and 2/3 cup sugar until dissolved. Pour over cake.

Let cake stand for 12 hours before slicing.

CRANBERRY CAKE

1 (1 lb. 3 oz.) package
 Lemon Cake Mix
1 (3-ounce) package cream
 cheese, softened
3/4 cup milk
4 eggs
1-1/4 cups ground cranberries
1/2 cup ground walnuts
1/4 cup sugar
1 teaspoon mace

Blend cake mix, cream cheese and milk; beat with mixer for 2 minutes at medium speed. Add eggs, one at a time, beating for 2 additional minutes.

Thoroughly combine cranberries, walnuts, sugar and mace; fold into cake batter.

Pour into a well greased and floured 10-inch tube pan or bundt pan. Bake in 350°F. oven for 1 hour or until done. Cool for 5 minutes. Remove from pan and dust with confectioners sugar, if desired.

CRUMB CAKE

1 cup butter
2 cups dark brown sugar
3-1/2 cups cake flour
2 teaspoons cinnamon
1 teaspoon cloves
1/2 cup chopped pecans

1 cup buttermilk
1 teaspoon vanilla
1/4 teaspoon salt
1 teaspoon baking soda
1 teaspoon baking powder
2 eggs

Cream sugar and butter until light and fluffy. Add sifted flour and spices until a crumbly mixture forms. Reserve 1 cup of the mixture. Add the rest of the dry ingredients and then add alternately with the buttermilk, beating well after each addition. Add eggs, one at a time, beating well. Fold in the pecans. Pour into a large tube pan (well greased). Sprinkle the reserved crumbs on top.

Bake at 325°F. for 50 minutes or until done.

Make good things happen today... bake a cake...

COCONUT CAKE SUPREME

1 cup butter
2 cups sugar
3 cups cake flour
4 eggs

1-1/2 cups buttermilk
1 teaspoon baking soda
1 tablespoon vanilla
1/2 teaspoon salt

Cream butter and sugar; add eggs one at a time, beating well. Add salt and vanilla. Stir soda into buttermilk. Now add 1/2 cup flour, then 1/2 cup buttermilk, continuing until all is used, being sure to end with flour.

Grease 3 9-inch cake pans, then cut waxed paper to fit bottom. Pour in batter and bake at 350°F. for 30 minutes, or until cake tests done. Cool and then spread filling between layers and on top and sides.

COCONUT FILLING

3 cups sugar
2 packages frozen coconut or 1
  large coconut, freshly grated

1-1/2 cups milk
1/4 pound butter
1 teaspoon vanilla

Cook sugar and milk together until it changes color from white to oyster white. Remove from heat and add butter, mix, then add vanilla, mix well. Stir in fresh or defrosted coconut. Cool to lukewarm and put between layers and on sides and top of cake. This will seep down into cake and make it very moist and good.

You will have a hard time finding a better cake...

COCONUT PINEAPPLE CAKE

1 cup butter, softened
4 eggs
2 teaspoons baking
  powder
1 cup milk
1 teaspoon vanilla extract
Pineapple Filling
Heavenly Frosting

1-1/3 cups flaked coconut
2 cups sugar
3-1/2 cups cake flour
1 teaspoon salt
1 teaspoon lemon juice
1/2 teaspoon almond
  extract

Cream butter; gradually add sugar, beating until light and fluffy. Add eggs, one at a time, beating well after each addition.

Sift together the flour, baking powder and salt; add to creamed mixture alternately with milk, beginning and ending with the flour mixture. Beat on low speed just until blended. Stir in lemon juice and flavorings.

Pour batter into 3 greased and floured 9-inch cake pans. Bake at 350°F. for 25 to 30 minutes or until done. Cool in pans 10 minutes; remove from pans.

Spread Pineapple Filling between warm layers; let cool. Spread top and sides of cake with Heavenly Frosting; sprinkle with coconut.

PINEAPPLE FILLING:

3 tablespoons cake flour
1 (20-ounce) can crushed
  pineapple, drained

1/2 cup sugar
2 tablespoons butter
1/8 teaspoon salt

Combine flour, sugar and salt in saucepan. Add pineapple and butter. Cook over medium heat, stirring constantly, until thickened.

HEAVENLY FROSTING:

1-1/2 cups sugar
Pinch of salt
1/2 cup water

1 teaspoon vinegar
3 egg whites

Combine all ingredients except egg whites in a heavy saucepan. Cook over medium heat, stirring constantly, until mixture is clear. Cook without stirring until the syrup spins a thread 4 x 6 inches.

Beat egg whites until soft peaks form. Continue beating while slowly adding syrup mixture; beat until stiff peaks form and frosting is thick enough to spread.

It's fun to bake cakes...especially this one!

CUT-A-RIBBON CAKE

8 eggs, separated
2 cups sugar
8 teaspoons lemon juice
2 packages unflavored gelatin
1/2 cup cold water

grated rind of 2 lemons
2 packages ladyfingers
1 cup whipping cream,
   whipped
fresh fruit

Combine egg yolks, sugar and lemon juice in top of a double boiler. Cook, stirring constantly, until thickened. Dissolve gelatin in cold water. Remove mixture from stove; add lemon rind and dissolved gelatin. Cool to room temperature. Beat egg whites until stiff peaks form. Fold into cooled mixture.

Line a springform pan with single ladyfingers in an unbroken row around the sides and like spokes of a wheel in the bottom. Pour in lemon mixture and let set overnight in the refrigerator. Remove sides of pan and invert cake on a large plate. Decorate with whipped cream in spaces between ladyfingers (cream may be flavored with a little lemon rind) and fresh fruit. (Strawberries or peaches).

Tie a ribbon around circumference of cake to be cut by the guest of honor!

DUTCH OATMEAL CAKE

1-1/2 cups boiling water
1/2 cup crisco
1 cup firmly packed brown
   sugar
1 teaspoon baking soda
1/2 teaspoon salt
1 cup quick cooking oats,
   uncooked
2 eggs

2 cups cake flour
1 teaspoon cinnamon
Topping:
1/2 cup firmly packed
   brown sugar
1/2 cup chopped pecans
1/2 cup butter, melted
1/2 teaspoon vanilla
1 cup coconut

Combine boiling water and oats, stirring well, let cool.

Cream shortening; add sugar and beat until light and fluffy. Add eggs, one at a time, beating well after each addition.

Sift flour, soda, cinnamon and salt and add to creamed mixture, beating well. Stir in the oats mixture until blended well.

Pour into a greased and floured 13x9x2-inch baking pan.

Combine the remaining ingredients and spoon over batter. Bake at 350° F. for 40 minutes or until done.

A versatile cake...delicious as is...

DAISY CAKE

2-1/2 cups self-rising flour
1/2 cup shortening
3 whole eggs, lightly beaten

1-1/2 cups sugar
1 cup milk
1 teaspoon vanilla

Combine flour and sugar and set aside.

Measure shortening into bowl, mix to soften; sift flour and sugar mixture into creamed mixture. Stir in eggs and 1/4 cup milk until flour and sugar are dampened. Then beat vigorously for 2 minutes.

Stir in remaining milk and vanilla and beat 1/2 minute.

Pour batter into 3 greased and floured 9-inch round cake pans. Bake at 350° F. approximately 15 to 20 minutes or until lightly browned and cake begins to turn loose from sides of pan.

Spread with desired icing.

The Daisy Cake can be made in minutes... top with your very favorite icing for a real treat!

DATE-ORANGE CAKE

3-1/2 cups cake flour
1/2 teaspoon salt
1 cup butter
2 cups sugar
4 eggs
1/2 cup buttermilk
1 teaspoon soda

1/2 cup orange juice
1/2 cup confectioners sugar
1 pound candy orange slices, chopped
1 (8-ounce) package chopped dates
2 cups chopped pecans
1 (3-1/2-ounce) can flaked coconut

Combine flour and salt; stir and set aside.

Combine orange slices, dates, pecans, and coconut; stir in 1/2 cup flour mixture. Set aside.

Cream butter; gradually add sugar, beating until light and fluffy. Add eggs, one at a time, beating well after each addition.

Combine buttermilk and soda, mixing well. Add remaining 3 cups flour mixture alternately with buttermilk to creamed mixture, beginning and ending with flour. Add candy mixture; stir until well blended.

Spoon batter into a greased and floured 10-inch tube pan. Bake at 300° F. for 2 hours or until cake tests done.

Combine orange juice and powdered sugar. Punch holes in top of cake using a toothpick; while cake is still hot, spoon glaze over top. Let cake cool before removing from pan.

A good and different cake...

DATE PECAN CAKE

1 quart chopped pecans
1 cup flour
2 teaspoons baking powder
1 cup sugar

2 (7-ounce) package dates, cut up
4 eggs
1 teaspoon vanilla

Chop nuts and cut dates with scissors. Sift together flour and baking powder. Add this to the pecans and dates and dredge thoroughly.

Beat eggs, sugar and vanilla. Add egg mixture to nuts and dates mixture and mix well. Bake in lightly greased tube pan for 1 hour at 300° F. or until tests done.

A delicious cake...don't skimp on the ingredients...

DREAM CAKE

First mixture: 1 cup flour
1/2 cup butter
1/4 teaspoon salt

Mix together and spread in 9-inch square cake pan.

Second mixture: 2 eggs
1 cup brown sugar
1 teaspoon baking powder
1 teaspoon vanilla

1/2 cup coconut
1/2 cup dates, cut up
1/2 cup candied cherries
1 cup chopped pecans

Mix and pour over first mixture. Bake slowly at about 325° F. for around 40 minutes or until tests done. Spread butter icing or lemon butter icing on top if you wish and then cut into squares before serving.

BUTTER CREAM ICING

4 tablespoons butter, softened
2 cups sifted confectioners sugar

3 tablespoons milk
1 teaspoon vanilla

Cream butter well, then add sugar and milk alternately, a little at a time, stirring until smooth after each addition. Stir in vanilla. When smooth, pour over cake and let stand until set before cutting.

LEMON CREAM ICING

4 tablespoons butter, softened
2 cups sifted confectioners sugar
1 teaspoon white corn syrup

3 tablespoons lemon juice

Cream butter, then add sugar and juice alternately, a little at a time, stirring until smooth. Stir in the white corn syrup until smooth and shiny. When icing has set, cut the cake for serving.

Try this cake...it's deliciously different...

DOLLEY MADISON'S LAYER CAKE

3/4 cup butter
2-1/2 cups sugar
1 cup milk
2-1/2 teaspoons vanilla

3 cups cake flour
3/4 cup cornstarch
8 egg whites, stiffly beaten

Cream butter and sugar together until light and fluffy. Add sifted dry ingredients alternately with the milk and vanilla. Beat the egg whites until stiff peaks form, adding about 3 tablespoons sugar. Fold in the egg whites gently but thoroughly.

Pour batter into 4 greased and floured 9-inch round cake pans and bake at 350° F. for 20 to 25 minutes or until tests done. Spread with DOLLEY MADISON'S CARAMEL ICING.

DOLLEY MADISON'S CARAMEL ICING

3-1/2 cups light brown sugar
4 tablespoons butter

1 cup heavy cream
1 teaspoon vanilla

Heat sugar, cream and butter in a double boiler; cook for about 15 to 20 minutes. Add vanilla and then decorate cake.

DOLLEY MADISON'S PECAN CAKE

1/2 cup butter
1 cup sugar
1 cup milk
1/2 teaspoon vanilla
2 cups cake flour

2 teaspoons baking powder
1-1/2 cups chopped pecans
*4 egg whites, stiffly
beaten*

Cream together butter and sugar, beating thoroughly; add sifted dry ingredients alternately with the milk and vanilla. Beat egg whites until soft peaks form and add 3 tablespoons sugar until stiff peaks form. Then fold in the pecans and finally the egg whites.

Bake in a loaf pan (greased and floured) for around 50 minutes at 350° F.

If you want something really luxurious...these cakes are worth the price!

FIG CAKE

1 cup butter
3-1/2 cups sifted cake flour
2 teaspoons baking powder
1 teaspoon vanilla extract

2 cups sugar
1 teaspoon salt
1 cup milk
8 egg whites

Cream butter and sugar together until light and fluffy. Sift dry ingredients together two times; add to creamed mixture alternately with milk. Add vanilla extract. Fold in egg whites which have been beaten stiff but not dry. Pour batter into three 9-inch cake pans which have been greased and floured. Bake at 350°F. for 20 to 25 minutes. Spread between layers of cake the FIG FILLING and frost sides and top with Seven Minute Frosting.

FIG FILLING

2 cups dried figs
3 cups water
2 cups sugar

1 cup crushed pineapple
1/4 teaspoon salt

Rinse figs in hot water and drain. Clip off stems and cut figs into thin strips. Combine with pineapple and water and cook about 10 minutes. Add salt and sugar and cook, stirring occasionally, until figs are tender and mixture is very thick, about 10 to 15 minutes. Cool. Filling for 3 (9-inch) layers.

SEVEN MINUTE FROSTING

1-1/2 cups sugar
2 egg whites
1/4 teaspoon salt

1/3 cup water
1/4 teaspoon cream of tartar
1 teaspoon vanilla

Combine all ingredients except vanilla in top of double boiler. Beat until thoroughly mixed. Place over rapidly boiling water and beat constantly for 7 minutes or until icing will hold a peak. Remove from heat and add vanilla. Beat until cool and thick enough to spread. Quickly cover sides and top of cake.

A most attractive and tasty cake...

FIG PRESERVES CAKE

1 cup salad oil
2 cups sugar
3 eggs
2 cups flour
1 teaspoon baking soda
1 teaspoon allspice

1 teaspoon cinnamon
1 teaspoon nutmeg
2/3 cup buttermilk
1 cup fig preserves,
   undrained
1 cup chopped pecans

Combine oil and sugar in large mixing bowl and beat until

light and well blended. Add eggs, one at a time, beating well after each addition. Add sifted dry ingredients alternately with the buttermilk, blending well. Fold in the preserves and pecans well.

Pour batter into a greased and floured tube pan and bake at 350° F. for 1 hour or until tests done. Dust with confectioners sugar.

FRUIT COCKTAIL CAKE

2 eggs	1/3 cup evaporated milk
2 cups sugar	2 teaspoons baking soda
2-1/2 cups cake	1 can (17-ounce) fruit
flour	cocktail, undrained

Beat together eggs, evaporated milk, sugar, salt, baking powder, flour and fruit cocktail. Pour into a greased and floured 13x9x2-inch baking pan. Bake at 350° F. for 30 minutes. Cool 30 minutes, then turn out onto serving tray. Spread glaze over top and sides of cake.

GLAZE

3/4 cup sugar	1/3 cup evaporated milk
1/3 cup butter, melted	1 teaspoon vanilla
1/2 cup chopped pecans	

Combine all ingredients well and pour over cake while still warm.

Both of these cakes have a little different flavor...but very well liked...

GINGER CAKES

1/4 cup lard	3/4 cup sugar
1/4 cup butter	3/4 cup molasses
1/2 cup buttermilk	1 cup nuts, chopped fine
1/2 pound raisins, chopped	3 cups cake flour
2 eggs	1 teaspoon cinnamon
1 teaspoon allspice	1/2 teaspoon ginger
1 teaspoon baking powder	1 teaspoon soda

Sift all dry ingredients together and set aside. Beat butter and lard together; add sugar, beating until light and fluffy. Add eggs, one at a time, beating well after each addition. Add dry ingredients and milk and syrup alternately, blending well. Add the nuts and raisins, stirring.

You may spoon the mixture on a greased cookie sheet for ginger cakes or if you wish to make gingerbread men, add a little flour so you can roll out dough and cut the men. Press a few raisins on each cake, if desired. Bake at 350° F. until done.

FRUIT PRESERVES CAKE

3 cups sifted cake flour
1/2 teaspoon cinnamon
1/2 teaspoon cloves
2 cups brown sugar,
  firmly packed
1/2 cup buttermilk
2/3 cup apricot preserves
1 cup chopped pecans

1 teaspoon baking soda
1/2 teaspoon nutmeg
3/4 cup butter
4 eggs, separated
1 teaspoon vanilla
2/3 cup strawberry preserves
2/3 cup pineapple preserves

Sift together flour, soda, cinnamon, nutmeg and cloves.

Cream together butter and brown sugar until light and fluffy. Add egg yolks, beat well. Add vanilla. Then add dry ingredients alternately with buttermilk, beating well after each addition. Stir in preserves and pecans. Beat egg whites until stiff and fold into batter.

Pour into greased 10-inch tube pan and bake in 350° F. oven for 1 hour and 30 minutes or until cake tests done.

Cool 10 minutes in pan and remove. Continue cooling on wire rack.

Interesting in texture and color... delectable!

GINGERBREAD CAKE

1/4 cup butter
1/4 cup lard
1/2 cup sugar
1 egg, beaten
1 cup dark molasses
2-1/2 cups cake flour

1-1/2 teaspoons soda
1/2 teaspoon salt
1/2 teaspoon cloves
1 teaspoon ginger
1 teaspoon cinnamon
1 cup hot water

Cream butter, lard and sugar, then add the egg, followed by the molasses. Now add the dry ingredients and finally the hot water. Beat in an electric mixer for several minutes. Pour into a buttered baking dish and bake at 325° F. for around 30 minutes. Top with Applesauce Topping.

APPLESAUCE TOPPING

8 tart apples
2 drops red vegetable coloring

Juice of 1 lemon

Peel apples and cut into little pieces. Put in a saucepan and add lemon juice. Cover and simmer until apples are soft, but be careful not to let the apples burn. Then put through a sieve. Add vegetable coloring.

Will keep fresh as long as it lasts...

HAWAIIAN CAKE

1-1/2 cups sifted cake flour
1/2 cup butter
1 teaspoon vanilla
2 eggs
1/2 cup chopped unsalted
   macadamia nuts

1-1/2 teaspoons baking powder
1 cup sifted confectioners
   sugar
1 cup milk
1/2 cup coconut
1 cup glace' pineapple

Slice the pineapple into small pieces and set aside. Sift together the flour and baking powder.

Cream butter and sugar until light and fluffy. Add eggs, one at a time, beating well after each addition. Stir in the vanilla. Add flour mixture alternately with the milk, beating just until smooth. Fold in the pineapple, nuts and coconut. Pour into a butter-greased and floured Bundt pan. Bake at 350° F. for around 45 minutes or until cake tests done. Loosen edges and turn out on wire rack and then cool completely.

HOT MILK CAKE

1 cup milk
1 stick butter
4 eggs, well beaten
2 cups sugar

2 cups sifted flour
2 teaspoons baking powder
1/2 teaspoon salt
1 teaspoon vanilla

In small saucepan, bring milk and butter to a boil. Combine other ingredients and mix well. Mix the two mixtures together and bake immediately in tube pan for 35 to 40 minutes at 350° F. or in three 8-inch layer pans (grease and flour pans). Serve warm or cold. Good served with Hot Fudge Sauce.

HOT FUDGE SAUCE

3/4 cup sugar, 3 tablespoons cocoa, 2 tablespoons water, dash of salt - Put these ingredients in saucepan and blend until cocoa dissolves. Add 1 small can evaporated milk; bring to boil gently (3 to 4 minutes) stirring constantly. Do not use high heat. Remove from heat and stir in 2 tablespoons butter and 1 teaspoon vanilla. Pour over cake or ice cream while sauce in still hot.

DEE-LICIOUS!

These cakes are also delicious with ice cream or coffee...

GRAHAM CRACKER CAKE

3/4 cup butter
5 eggs, separated
2 teaspoons baking powder
3 cups graham cracker crumbs
1 teaspoon vanilla extract

1-1/2 cups sugar
1/2 cup flour
1/4 teaspoon salt
1-1/4 cups milk

Cream butter and sugar until light and fluffy. Add egg yolks, beating well. Sift together flour, baking powder and salt; combine with graham cracker crumbs. Add alternately with the milk, beating well after each addition. Stir in vanilla. Beat egg whites until stiff; fold into batter.

Pour batter into 3 greased and floured 9-inch cake pans; bake at 350°F. for 25 to 30 minutes. Cool completely. Spread filling between layers and Brown Sugar Frosting on sides and top of cake.

Filling: 1/4 cup cake flour
1/2 teaspoon salt
2 eggs, slightly beaten

1 cup sugar
2 cups milk, scalded
1 teaspoon vanilla

Combine flour, sugar and salt in a saucepan. Slowly stir in milk; cook over low heat 15 minutes or until thickened, stirring constantly. Add a small amount of the hot mixture to yolks. Stir yolk mixture into hot mixture. Remove from heat and stir in vanilla. Cool and spread between layers of cake.

Brown Sugar Frosting: 1 cup firmly packed
light brown sugar

1/4 cup water
2 egg whites

Combine sugar and water in a heavy saucepan; cook over low heat to soft ball stage (234°F. to 240°F.). Beat egg whites until soft peaks form. Continue beating and gradually add syrup mixture; beat well. Frost sides and top of cake.

A great favorite...delicate...sweet and good!

SOUTHERN SPECIAL JAM CAKE

1 cup butter
3 eggs
3 cups flour
1 teaspoon each cinnamon,
   nutmeg, allspice, ginger
1-1/2 cups chopped pecans

2 cups sugar
1 cup blackberry jam
1/2 teaspoon salt
1 teaspoon soda
1 cup buttermilk

Cream butter and sugar until light and fluffy; add eggs, one at a time, beating well after each addition. Sift together flour, salt and spices. Stir soda into buttermilk. Add dry ingredients alternately with buttermilk to the creamed mixture, beginning and ending with the dry mixture.

Fold in 1 cup pecans and jam. Grease and flour 3 9-inch cake pans and pour batter into them. Bake at 350° F. for 30 to 35 minutes or until done.

Frost only between layers and on top of cake with Butter Cream Frosting. Sprinkle remaining pecans over top.

BUTTER CREAM FROSTING

2 cups sugar   1/2 cup whipping cream
1 cup butter

Combine all ingredients and cook without stirring until mixture reaches soft-ball stage or 230° F. Beat until spreadable and quickly spread on layers.

This cake is highly prized in the "Southern Country"...

HERMIT CAKE

1 cup butter
1-1/2 cups brown sugar
3 egg yolks
2-1/2 cups flour
3 egg whites, stiffly
    beaten
1/2 pound English walnuts,
    chopped

2 teaspoons vanilla
1/2 teaspoon nutmeg
1/2 teaspoon cinnamon
1-1/2 teaspoons baking powder
Juice of 1/2 fresh lemon
1 pound pitted dates,
    cut up

Cream butter until light and fluffy; add sugar gradually, beating well. Add egg yolks, one at a time, beating well after each addition. Stir in vanilla. Add sifted dry ingredients 1/2 cup at a time, mixing thoroughly. Then pour the lemon juice over the dates and walnuts and combine well. Dredge them in 1/2 cup flour and fold in the creamed mixture. Then fold in the stiffly beaten egg whites.

Pour batter into a greased and floured tube pan and bake at 250° F. for 2-1/2 to 3 hours (put pan of water on bottom rack for first 2 hours of baking).

HUMMINGBIRD CAKE

3 cups cake flour
2 cups sugar
1 teaspoon salt
1 teaspoon soda
1 teaspoon cinnamon
3 eggs, beaten
2 cups chopped bananas

1-1/2 cups salad oil
1-1/2 teaspoons vanilla
1 (8-ounce) can crushed
 pineapple, undrained
2 cups chopped pecans,
 divided

Combine dry ingredients; add eggs and salad oil, stirring until dry ingredients are moistened. Do not beat. Stir in vanilla, pineapple, 1 cup chopped pecans and bananas. Spoon batter into 3 well-greased and floured 9-inch pans. Bake at 350°F. for 25 to 30 minutes. Cool in pans 10 minutes; remove and cool completely. Spread frosting between layers and on top and sides. Sprinkle with 1 cup pecans.

CREAM CHEESE FROSTING

2 (8-ounce) packages cream cheese
1 16-ounce package confectioners sugar
2 teaspoons vanilla extract

1 cup butter

Combine cream cheese and butter, beating until light and smooth. Add sugar and vanilla and blend well.

Hummingbird cake may also be baked in a tube pan or bundt pan. You will only need one-half of the Cream Cheese Frosting.

Both of these cakes are delicious...may be frozen...

ITALIAN CREAM CAKE

1/2 cup butter
1/2 cup Crisco
2 cups cake flour
1 cup buttermilk
1 teaspoon vanilla extract
5 egg whites, stiffly beaten

2 cups sugar
5 egg yolks
1 teaspoon soda
1 small can coconut
1 cup chopped pecans

Cream butter and Crisco until light and fluffy; add sugar, gradually, and beat well. Add egg yolks, one at a time, beating well after each addition. Stir together the flour and soda and add alternately with the buttermilk, beating well.

Stir in vanilla, then the coconut and pecans. Fold in beaten egg whites.

Grease and flour 3 9-inch round cake pans. Bake in 350°F. oven for about 25 minutes or until lightly browned. Cool. Frost with Cream Cheese Frosting.

CREAM CHEESE FROSTING

1 package (8-ounce) cream cheese
1 box confectioners sugar
1 cup chopped pecans

1/4 stick butter
1 teaspoon vanilla

Mix all ingredients together until smooth. Spread between layers and over top of cake.

A luxury cake...even the crumbs are delicious!

JAM CAKE

1-1/2 cups sugar
1 cup butter
Pinch salt
1 tablespoon cinnamon
1 tablespoon allspice
1 tablespoon nutmeg
1 cup pecans, chopped

4 eggs
3 cups cake flour
1 teaspoon soda
3/4 cup buttermilk
1 teaspoon vanilla
1 cup strawberry preserves

Cream butter until fluffy; add sugar, gradually, beating until light and creamy. Add eggs, one at a time, continuing to beat well, after each addition. Combine the dry ingredients and sift 2 or 3 times. Add alternately with the buttermilk until well blended. Stir in the pecans and fold in the preserves.

Pour batter into 3 (9-inch) round cake pans that have been greased and floured. Bake at 350°F. for 25 to 30 minutes or until the cakes tests done. Spread Caramel Icing between layers and over top and sides.

CARAMEL ICING

3 cups sugar
1 cup evaporated milk
1 stick butter

1 teaspoon vanilla
1/4 cup sugar
1/4 cup boiling water

Combine first 4 ingredients in a saucepan and heat to melt butter. Put remaining sugar in a heavy skillet and cook on medium high until sugar has melted and turned a caramel color. Add boiling water, slowly, and stir well. Pour melted sugar into milk mixture in saucepan. Bring to a slow boil and boil until it reaches soft ball stage, stirring occasionally. This should take around 8 to 10 minutes. Remove from heat and cool slightly, then beat to spreading consistency.

Treat yourself to this ultra delicious cake...

LANE CAKE

2 sticks butter
2 cups sugar
3 cups sifted cake flour
3 teaspoons baking powder
1/2 teaspoon salt

4 eggs
1 cup evaporated milk
1 teaspoon vanilla extract
1/2 teaspoon almond extract

Cream butter; gradually add sugar, creaming until light and fluffy. Add eggs, one at a time, beating well after each addition. Sift flour, baking powder and salt together and add alternately with milk and flavorings, beating until smooth.

Grease and flour 4 (9-inch) round cake pans. Pour batter into pans and bake at 350° F. for 25 to 30 minutes or until done. Spread Lane Frosting between layers and on top and sides of cake.

LANE FROSTING

Grind coarsely: 2 pounds English walnuts
2 pounds Brazil nuts
1 quart shelled pecans
2 pounds seedless raisins
2 large coconuts

Beat: 6 eggs to lemon color

Add: 2 cups sugar
2 sticks butter
2 cups evaporated milk

Cook and stir over medium heat until thickened, about 12 minutes. Add fruits and nuts. Cool until thick enough to spread, beating occasionally.

Batter can be made into two cakes by using 8-inch round cake pans and dividing equally. Layers will be thin.

This cake will appeal to the eye as well as the palate...

A family recipe, at least 60 years old...enjoyed over and over again, especially at Christmas time!

LADY BALTIMORE CAKE

1 cup butter
3 cups sugar, sifted
4 teaspoons baking powder
1/2 teaspoon salt
8 egg whites
(add 1/8 teaspoon salt)

1 cup milk
1/4 teaspoon almond extract
1 teaspoon vanilla
3-1/2 cups cake flour

Cream butter and sugar until light and fluffy. Add eggs, one at a time, beating well after each addition. Stir in flavorings. Then add sifted dry ingredients, blending thoroughly. Beat egg whites until soft peaks form. Fold into the creamed mixture. Pour into 3 greased and floured 9-inch cake pans and bake at 350° F. for 30 to 35 minutes or until done. Spread White Icing between layers and on top and sides.

WHITE ICING

2 cups sugar
1 cup water
2 egg whites

1/8 teaspoon cream of tartar
1/8 teaspoon salt
1 teaspoon vanilla

Boil sugar and water until a bit of the syrup forms a soft ball when dropped into cold water. Beat egg whites, cream of tartar and salt until frothy, adding syrup in a thin stream, beating constantly. Add vanilla. Ice cake immediately.

Make this simple but luscious cake...

SOUTHERN LANE CAKE

1 cup butter
2 cups sugar
1 teaspoon vanilla
3-1/2 cups sifted cake flour

3 teaspoons baking powder
3/4 teaspoon salt
1 cup milk
8 egg whites

Cream butter; add sugar gradually, beating until light and fluffy. Add vanilla, then sifted dry ingredients alternately with milk, beating until smooth. Beat egg whites until stiff but not dry. Fold in egg whites. Pour batter into 4 round (9-inch) cake pans lined on the bottom with waxed paper and then greased. Bake in 350° F. oven for about 25 minutes or until cakes tests done. Spread with Southern Lane Frosting.

SOUTHERN LANE FROSTING

8 egg yolks
1-1/2 cups sugar
1/2 cup butter
1 cup evaporated milk

1 cup chopped pecans
1 cup finely chopped raisins
1 cup fresh grated coconut
1 cup finely cut candied cherries

Beat egg yolks slightly; add sugar and butter and evaporated milk and cook over medium heat, stirring constantly until sugar has dissolved and mixture is slightly thickened. Remove from heat and add remaining ingredients. Let stand until cold before spreading on cake.

This recipe belongs in the top bracket of delicious cakes...

LAYER CAKE NO. 1

2 sticks butter
2 cups sugar
5 eggs
3-1/2 cups sifted flour
1 teaspoon vanilla

3 teaspoons baking
   powder
1/2 teaspoon salt
1 cup milk

Cream the butter and sugar until light and fluffy. Add eggs, one at a time, beating well after each addition. Sift the dry ingredients together and add alternately with the milk and vanilla. Pour into 3 or 4 greased and lightly floured cake pans and bake at 350°F. for 20 to 25 minutes. Cool and frost with your favorite frosting.

LAYER CAKE NO. 2

1-1/2 cups butter
2 cups sugar
4 eggs
3 cups sifted cake flour

3 teaspoons baking powder
1/2 teaspoon salt
1 cup milk
1 teaspoon vanilla

Cream butter and sugar until light and fluffy. Add eggs, one at a time, beating well after each addition. Add sifted dry ingredients alternately with the milk and vanilla. Pour into 3 or 4 greased and floured cake pans and bake at 350°F. for 20 to 25 minutes. Cool and frost with your favorite frosting.

LAYERED DESSERT CAKE

1-1/2 sticks butter
1 cup flour

1 cup chopped pecans

Melt butter; add flour and pecans. Work together well. Spread over bottom of large pyrex dish, 13-1/2x9 inches. Bake at 325°F. until very light brown.

2 8 ounce packages cream cheese
1 small carton Cool Whip
   (9-ounces)

1-1/2 cups confectioners
   sugar

Cream together the cream cheese and sugar. Fold in the Cool Whip. Spread over first layer.

2 boxes instant chocolate pudding mix (or lemon, butterscotch or vanilla). Go by directions on package to mix except use 3-1/2 cups milk. Spread over second layer.

1 large carton Cool Whip. Spread on top of final layer. Sprinkle with cut pecans and chocolate curls.

This dessert is better made one day and served the next. Serves 15 to 18.

LEMON CAKE

1 cup butter
1/2 cup crisco
2 cups sugar
3 eggs
3 cups flour
1/2 teaspoon baking soda

1/2 teaspoon salt
1 cup buttermilk
2 tablespoons grated lemon rind
1/2 cup plus 1 tablespoon
   lemon juice
3 cups confectioners sugar

Beat 1/2 cup butter, crisco and granulated sugar until light and fluffy. Add eggs, one at a time, beating well after each addition. Sift together flour, baking soda and salt and add alternately with buttermilk. Stir in one tablespoon of lemon rind and 1 tablespoon lemon juice. Pour into a greased tube pan and bake 1 hour and 15 minutes at 325° F. or until cake tests done.

Mix remaining butter (1/2 cup) and confectioners sugar until creamy. Add remaining lemon rind and enough lemon juice to give pouring consistency. Pour over the warm cake.

You must taste this cake to believe how good it really is...

LEMON CAKE SUPREME

1/3 cup butter
2/3 cup crisco
2 cups sugar
3-1/2 cups sifted cake flour

3 teaspoons baking powder
1 cup milk
6 egg whites
1 teaspoon vanilla

Cream butter and crisco until light; gradually add sugar, beating until light and fluffy. Add vanilla and then the sifted dry ingredients alternately with the milk. Fold in the stiffly beaten egg whites.

Pour into 3 greased and floured 9-inch cake pans and bake at 350° F. for 25 to 30 minutes or until done. Spread Lemon Jelly Filling between layers and on top and sides.

LEMON JELLY FILLING

1 cup sugar
3 tablespoons cornstarch
1/2 cup hot water

2 lemons (juice and grated rind)
1 stick butter
6 egg yolks

Combine sugar, cornstarch, hot water and lemon rind and lemon juice in top of double boiler over hot water. Beat egg yolks until fluffy and add, gradually, to mixture in boiler. Add butter. Cook over simmering, not boiling water, stirring constantly until thick enough to hold shape in spoon. Remove from heat and cool. Spread on layers of cake.

A refreshing and delicate cake...

LEMON CHEESE CAKE NO. 1

1 cup butter
2 cups sugar
3-1/2 cups sifted cake flour
1 teaspoon salt

2 teaspoons baking powder
1 cup milk
1 teaspoon vanilla extract
5 egg whites

Cream butter and sugar together until light and fluffy. Sift dry ingredients together two times; add to creamed mixture alternately with milk. Add vanilla extract. Fold in egg whites which have been beaten stiff but not dry. Pour batter into three 9-inch cake pans which have been greased and floured. Bake at 350°F. for 20 to 25 minutes. Spread with Lemon Cheese Filling No. 1.

LEMON CHEESE FILLING NO. 1

5 egg yolks
1 cup sugar,
  plus 2 tablespoons

1 stick butter
Juice of 3 lemons
Grated rind of 1/2 lemon

Beat egg yolks in mixer; add sugar gradually, mixing well. Add butter and mix until creamy, then add the juice and rind and cook until just slightly thickened in top of double boiler. Spread between layers and on top and sides of cake. (Refrigerate uneaten portion.)

For variation, you may wish to use the Lemon Cheese Filling on the layers and a white Seven Minute Frosting on the top and sides of the cake. See Index for Seven Minute Frosting.

An heirloom recipe you will prize!

LEMON CHEESE CAKE NO. 2

2-1/2 cups self-rising flour,
  sifted
1-1/2 cups sugar
1/2 cup crisco

1 cup milk
3 whole eggs, slightly beaten
1 teaspoon lemon flavoring

Cream shortening and sugar; add eggs. Then add to moist mixture alternately the sifted flour and milk and flavoring. Grease and flour three 9-inch cake pans. Bake at 350°F. for 25 to 30 minutes or until cakes tests done. Spread with Lemon Cheese Filling No. 2.

LEMON CHEESE FILLING NO. 2

2 cups sugar
Juice of 3 lemons
Rind, grated, of 2 lemons

3 whole eggs
1/3 stick melted butter
Pinch salt

Combine ingredients and mix well. Cook in a double boiler (not aluminum) on medium heat, stirring often until the mixture drops in flakes from spoon. Ice between layers and on top and sides. (Refrigerate uneaten portion.)

An old family recipe...delicious!

LEMON LOAF

6 tablespoons butter
1 cup sugar
1 teaspoon baking powder
2 beaten eggs
1/2 cup milk
1-1/2 cups chopped pecans (fine)

1-1/2 cups flour
1/4 teaspoon salt
Grated rind of 1 lemon
Juice of 2 lemons combined
   with 1/2 cup sugar

Cream butter and sugar until soft and fluffy. Add beaten eggs, then milk and rind. Sift dry ingredients and blend in quickly. Add pecans. Spoon batter into greased loaf pan. Bake at 350° F. for 1 hour and 5 minutes. The second you remove from oven, pour over the lemon juice-sugar mixture.

LEMONADE CAKE

1/2 cup butter
3/4 cup sugar
4 eggs, separated
2 tablespoons grated lemon
   rind

1/4 cup lemonade concentrate
1-1/2 cups sifted cake flour
2-1/2 teaspoons baking powder
1/8 teaspoon salt

Cream butter and sugar until light and fluffy. Add egg yolks, one at a time, beating well after each addition. Add lemon rind and lemonade concentrate. Gradually add sifted dry ingredients, blending well. Add salt to egg whites and beat until stiff; gently fold them into the batter.

Pour mixture into a well buttered and lightly floured square baking pan. Bake at 350° F. for 30 to 35 minutes, or until done. Do not overbake. Cool. Dust top generously with confectioners sugar or top with lemon flavored and sweetened whipped cream.

A different and delightful cake...

SWISS LEMON CAKE

1 pound butter	3 cups sugar
2 ounces lemon extract	1-1/2 teaspoons baking powder
6 eggs	1 pound bleached raisins
1 pound pecans, chopped	3-1/2 cups flour

Cream together the butter and sugar until light and fluffy. Add eggs, one at a time, beating well after each addition. Add lemon extract, blending well. Sift together the flour and baking powder. Add to the first mixture, blending thoroughly. Add raisins and pecans. Pour into a greased tube pan. Bake at 300° F. for 2 hours or until it tests done and is a light tan color.

These practical and proven cake recipes show you how to bake a successful cake... thrilling things happen when you follow the directions...

LEMON PUDDING CAKE

1 cup sugar	1/4 cup lemon juice,
5 tablespoons flour	freshly squeezed
2 tablespoons melted	grated lemon rind of
butter	1/2 lemon
1 cup milk	3 egg yolks, beaten
pinch salt	3 egg whites, stiffly beaten

Combine sugar and flour and set aside. Blend the egg yolks and flour-sugar mixture together. Add the melted butter and blend well. Then add the milk, lemon juice and rind, mixing together thoroughly. Beat the egg whites and salt until stiff peaks form. Fold into the first mixture. Put into pan lightly greased with margarine. Place pan in another pan of hot water. Bake 45 minutes at 350° F. (Turn out so pudding side will be up.)

An old family recipe. Takes only minutes to prepare but very delicious!

MANDARIN ORANGE CAKE

1 package Yellow Cake Mix	1 (11-ounce) can
4 eggs	Mandarin Oranges
1/4 cup vegetable oil	

Combine cake mix, mandarin oranges, eggs, and oil. Beat 2 minutes at highest speed of electric mixer. Reduce speed to low; beat 1 minute. Pour batter into 3 greased and floured 9-inch round cake pans. Bake at 350° F. for 20 to 25 minutes or until tests done. Cool in pans for 5 to 10 minutes; remove layers from pans and let cool completely. Spread with the following icing.

ICING FOR MANDARIN ORANGE CAKE

1 large (13-ounce) carton frozen whipped topping, thawed
1 large can crushed pineapple (drain and save juice)

1 5-1/2 ounce package vanilla pudding

Combine all ingredients; beat 2 minutes at medium speed with electric mixer; let stand 5 minutes; add enough pineapple juice for spreading consistency. Spread mixture between layers and on top and sides of cake. Chill at least 2 hours before serving. Store in refrigerator.

This unusual cake has delicious flavor and attractive color...

MANY FLAVORS CAKE

Bake your favorite white cake. Make 6 or 7 thin layers and ice each one with a different icing. You will be pleasantly surprised!

MAPLE SUGAR CAKE

2 cups cake flour
2 teaspoons baking powder
1/4 teaspoon baking soda
1 teaspoon cinnamon

1/4 teaspoon nutmeg
2 eggs
1 cup soft maple sugar
1 cup sour cream

Grease two 8-inch cake pans. Sift flour, baking powder, soda and spices 4 times. Beat eggs until light and fluffy. Add maple sugar gradually mixing well. Add flour mixture and sour cream alternately beginning and ending with the flour mixture. Bake in 350° F. oven for 20 minutes or until done. Frost with Maple Frosting and decorate with pecans between layers and on top of cake.

MAPLE FROSTING

2/3 cup maple syrup
1/3 cup sugar

2 egg whites

Stir together the maple syrup and sugar. Cook slowly to the soft ball stage - 234° F.

Beat the egg whites to soft peaks. Pour the cooked syrup into them in a thin, steady stream, beating all the time with an electric beater. Keep beating until the frosting starts to cool. Put pecan halves on one layer and cover it with frosting; then put frosting on the top layer and decorate with pecans.

Surprisingly good! Fluffy, flavorful and nutritious...

MISSISSIPPI MUD CAKE NO. 1

1-1/2 sticks butter (3/4 cup)
1/2 cup heavy cream
1/2 cup cold coffee
4 eggs
1-1/2 cups sugar
1/2 cup cocoa

1-3/4 cups cake flour
1 teaspoon baking powder
1/2 teaspoon salt
1 teaspoon vanilla
4 bars milk chocolate
    (1.2 ounces each)

Grease and flour an 11-3/4x7-1/2x1-3/4-inch baking pan. Preheat oven to 350° F. Cream butter and sugar until light and fluffy. Add eggs, one at a time, beating well after each addition. Add vanilla and blend well. Then add sifted dry ingredients alternately with the cream and coffee. Pour into prepared pan. Bake for 40 minutes or until done.

Break chocolate into pieces and place on hot cake and let stand 1 minute, then spread softened chocolate to frost cake. Cool before serving.

This is a very good cake!

MISSISSIPPI MUD CAKE NO. 2

1 cup Wesson oil
1/3 cup cocoa
4 eggs
2 cups chopped pecans

1-3/4 cups sugar
1-1/2 cups self-rising flour
3 teaspoons vanilla

Grease and flour oblong baking pan. Beat eggs until fluffy; add sugar gradually, blending well. Add Wesson oil. Then add cocoa and flour (combined and sifted) alternately with the vanilla. Blend in pecans and bake at 300° F. for 40 to 45 minutes. Cover with miniature marshmallows while still warm and pour over:

Combine: *1-1/2 sticks butter   1/3 cup cocoa*
        1 teaspoon vanilla   1/2 cup whipping cream
        1 box confectioners sugar 1-1/2 cups chopped pecans
Cool and then serve.

This is a moist cake, appealing in color and flavor...

MELT-IN-YOUR-MOUTH CAKE

1-1/2 cups softened butter
3-1/2 cups powdered sugar
6 eggs

3-1/2 cups sifted cake flour
1 tablespoon vanilla extract

Cream butter until smooth. Add sugar gradually and beat until light and fluffy. Add eggs one at a time, beating well after each addition. Add cake flour and vanilla and beat well. Spoon batter into a greased 10 inch tube pan. Bake at 325° F. for 45 minutes or until done.

ORANGE FLORIDA-STYLE CAKE

CAKE

1 cup butter
1-1/2 cups sugar
4 eggs
2-1/2 cups cake flour
2 teaspoons baking powder

1/2 teaspoon salt
1 tablespoons grated
   orange rind
1/4 cup freshly squeezed
   orange juice

FILLING

3 tablespoons flour
2 tablespoons cornstarch
1/2 cup sugar
1 cup orange juice
1 teaspoon grated orange rind

1 teaspoon unflavored gelatin
1 tablespoon water
2 egg yolks, lightly beaten
1/4 cup butter
1/2 cup heavy cream, whipped

FROSTING

2 egg whites
1-3/4 cups sugar

1 tablespoon light corn syrup
5 tablespoons orange juice

Cake: Cream butter with sugar; add eggs, one at a time. Add sifted flour, baking powder and salt alternately with the juice and rind. Pour mixture into two greased and floured 9-inch cake pans and bake at 325° F. for around 30 minutes or until tests done.

Filling: Combine flour, cornstarch and sugar in small pan. Add orange juice and orange rind and mix well. Soak gelatin in water. Bring the orange juice mixture to a boil, stirring constantly. Cook 2 minutes. Spoon a little of hot mixture into the egg yolks and mix. Add the rest of the orange mixture. Cook 1/2 minute longer. Add the soaked gelatin and the butter. Stir to dissolve. Cool and chill, stirring occasionally. Fold in whipped cream just before spreading on the cake layers.

Frosting: Place all ingredients in top of double boiler over rapidly boiling water. Beat with electric mixer for approximately 7 minutes or until soft, stiff peaks form.

A fancy, delicious cake... made from the simplest ingredients..

ORANGE CAKE

1 Navel orange
1/2 cup pitted dates
2 cups cake flour
1 teaspoon baking soda
1-1/2 cups sugar
1/2 cup buttermilk

1/2 cup plumped raisins
1/2 cup ground pecans
1 teaspoon salt
1/2 cup butter
3 eggs

Squeeze the juice and grind 1/4 cup of the orange rind; now blend together. Grind pecans, dates, raisins. Stir orange juice and rind into ground mixture. Set aside.

Cream butter and sugar together until light and fluffy. Add eggs, one at a time, beating well after each addition. Sift the flour, soda and salt together and add alternately with the buttermilk. Beat in the ground mixture very well. Grease and flour a tube pan or Bundt pan. Bake at 325° F. for around 1 hour and 15 minutes or until it tests done. Cool completely and then spread with Orange Butter Cream Frosting.

ORANGE BUTTER CREAM FROSTING

1-1/2 cups butter, softened
2 tablespoons orange juice
1 tablespoon grated orange rind

4-1/2 cups confectioners sugar
(1 box)

Combine butter and sugar, creaming until well blended. Add orange juice and beat until smooth. Stir in orange rind. Spread on cake immediately.

Delicate orange flavor and color--very good!

OLD FASHIONED PLAIN CAKE

1 stick margarine
1/2 cup shortening
2 cups cake flour
2 teaspoons flavoring
  (1 teaspoon lemon and
  1 teaspoon vanilla or almond)

5 large eggs
2 cups sugar
2 tablespoons fresh
  orange juice or diluted
  frozen

Beat margarine, shortening and sugar until light and creamy. Add eggs, one at a time, beating well after each addition. Sift flour three times (one time before measuring, two after). Add flour and then juice and flavorings alternately, blending well. Pour batter into a greased and floured Bundt pan. Bake at 325° F. for 1 hour and 5 minutes or until tests done. Let cool in pan for

10 minutes, then turn out on rack. Drizzle sifted confectioners sugar and lemon juice combined over cake, if desired.

Expect a delightful flavor and fragrance...especially good warm! Another Heirloom recipe...over 80 years old...

ORANGE SOUR CREAM CAKE

1 cup butter	1 cup sour cream
1-1/2 cups sugar	Grated rind of one orange
3 eggs, separated	1/2 cup chopped pecans
2 cups flour	1/2 cup fresh orange juice
1 teaspoon baking powder	2 tablespoons slivered
1 teaspoon baking soda	almonds, blanched

Cream together the butter and 1 cup sugar until light and fluffy. Beat in the egg yolks. Sift flour, baking powder, baking soda and add alternately with sour cream. Stir in the orange rind and nuts. Beat egg whites and fold into the batter. Bake in greased 9-inch tube pan for around 50 minutes at 325° F.

Combine the orange juice and remaining sugar and mix well. Spoon over hot cake. Decorate with almonds. Let cake cool before removing from pan.

Try to bring out the best in this delicious cake...

PEACH CRUMB CAKE

1-1/2 cups sifted cake flour	1/2 cup sugar
1/2 cup sugar	3 tablespoons quick
Dash of salt	cooking tapioca
1/2 cup softened butter	1 tablespoon lemon juice
4 cups sliced, peeled fresh peaches	

Combine flour, 1/2 cup sugar and salt. Cut in butter until mixture resembles coarse crumbs. Measure 3/4 cup and set aside. Press remaining flour mixture over bottom and about 3/4 inch up sides of a 9-inch spring form pan. Bake crust at 425° F. for 5 to 10 minutes or until lightly browned. Cool.

Meanwhile, mix peaches, 1/2 cup sugar, tapioca and lemon juice. Arrange in bottom of crust. Bake at 425° F. for 20 minutes; then sprinkle with the reserved flour mixture. Continue baking 20 to 25 minutes longer or until top is golden brown. Serve warm or cold with sweetened whipped cream, if desired.

Alternate baking pan: may also be baked in a 9-inch flan ring but do not pre-bake the crust.

Unusual...delicious as is, but topped with ice cream, it's tops!

ORANGE BUTTERMILK CAKE

1 cup butter
2 cups sugar
4 eggs
1-1/3 cups buttermilk
1 teaspoon baking soda

4 cups cake flour
2 tablespoons grated
orange rind
1 cup dates (cut)
1 cups pecans, chopped

Cream butter and sugar. Beat in eggs, one at a time. Dissolve soda in buttermilk. Add sifted flour alternately with the buttermilk. Beat until smooth after each addition. Add orange rind, dates, nuts, which have been floured. Bake in tube pan about 1-1/2 hours at 325° F. When cake is done, pour sauce over cake and cool in the pan.

SAUCE FOR ORANGE BUTTERMILK CAKE

2 cups sugar
1 cup orange juice, freshly squeezed

2 tablespoons orange rind

Stir and beat in electric mixer until sugar is dissolved. Do not heat. This makes a large cake and is delicious served with whipped cream.

Every bite will be a delight!

PEACH SOUR CREAM CAKE

1 (18.5-ounce) package butter
flavor cake mix
1-1/2 cups sugar
4 tablespoons cornstarch
4 cups chopped fresh peaches
1/2 cup water

2 cups whipping cream
2 to 3 tablespoons
confectioners sugar
1 cup sour cream
Fresh sliced peaches
(optional)

Prepare cake according to package directions, using two (8-inch) cake pans. Cool, then split each layer.

Combine sugar and cornstarch in a saucepan. Add peaches and water; cook over medium heat, stirring constantly, until smooth and thickened. Cool mixture completely.

Combine whipping cream and powdered sugar in a medium mixing bowl; beat until stiff peaks form.

Spoon 1/3 of peach filling over split layer of cake; spread 1/3 sour cream over filling. Repeat procedure with remaining cake layers, peach filling, and sour cream, ending with remaining cake layer. Frost with sweetened whipped cream, and garnish with fresh peach slices.

PEACH MARSHMALLOW CAKE

1 tablespoon butter
1/4 cup sugar
1/4 teaspoon salt
1 egg
2 cups cake flour
2 teaspoons baking powder

1/4 cup milk
6 peach halves
1/4 cup brown sugar
1 teaspoon cinnamon
1 tablespoon butter
6 marshmallows

Cream 1 tablespoon butter; add sugar and salt and mix well. Add egg and beat until light and smooth. Sift flour, baking powder and add to first mixture alternately with the milk. Pour into greased 10x7-inch pan. Arrange peaches, cut side up over batter. Sprinkle brown sugar and cinnamon. Dot with butter. Bake at 350° F. for 30 minutes. Place marshmallow in each peach and return to oven. Brown just lightly.

Make one of these peach cakes during peach season--you will love them...

ORANGE MARMALADE CAKE

3/4 cup butter, softened
1 cup sugar
3 eggs
1 cup orange marmalade
4-1/4 cups cake flour
1-1/2 teaspoons baking soda
1 teaspoon salt

1/2 cup fresh orange juice
1/2 cup evaporated milk
1 teaspoon vanilla
1 tablespoon grated
orange rind
1 cup chopped pecans

Cream butter and sugar thoroughly. Add eggs, one at a time, beating well after each addition. Add marmalade, mixing well. Sift together the flour, baking soda and salt. Add this alternately with the milk and orange juice. Stir in vanilla, grated orange rind and pecans well.

Pour batter into a greased and floured 10-inch tube pan. Bake at 350° F. for 1 hour and 5 minutes or until cake tests done. Cool in pan for 10 minutes; remove and cool completely. Frost cake with Whipped Orange Topping.

WHIPPED ORANGE TOPPING

1 cup whipping cream
2 tablespoons sugar

1 tablespoon grated orange rind

Beat whipping cream until foamy; gradually add the sugar, beating until soft peaks form. Stir in rind.

Tastes perfectly wonderful...

ORANGE PECAN CAKE

1/2 cup butter, softened
1/4 cup shortening
1-1/2 cups sugar
3 eggs
3 cups cake flour
1-1/2 teaspoons baking soda
3/4 teaspoon salt

1-1/2 cups buttermilk
1-1/2 teaspoons vanilla
1 cup golden raisins, chopped
1 cup finely chopped pecans
1 tablespoon grated orange rind

Cream together the butter, shortening and sugar. Add eggs, one at a time, beating well after each addition. Add sifted flour, soda, and salt alternately with the buttermilk and vanilla; mix just until blended and then beat at high speed with electric mixer for 3 minutes.

Stir raisins, pecans and orange rind into batter and pour into 3 greased and floured cake pans. Bake at 350°F. for 30 to 35 minutes or until tests done. Cool 5 to 10 minutes in pans; remove and cool completely.

Spread Orange Buttercream Frosting between layers and on top and sides of cake.

ORANGE BUTTERCREAM FROSTING

1-1/2 cups butter, softened
4-1/2 cups confectioners sugar

1 tablespoon orange juice
1 tablespoon grated orange rind

Combine butter and sugar, creaming until light and fluffy. Add orange juice; beat until spreading consistency. Stir in orange rind.

An interesting, very good cake....

ORANGE SHORTCAKE

12 to 16 medium oranges
3/4 cup sugar
1/3 cup butter
1 tablespoon cornstarch

3/4 cup water
1-1/2 teaspoons lemon juice
1/2 teaspoon grated orange rind

Peel and section enough oranges to make 5 cups of orange sections; drain, reserving 3/4 cup juice. Set aside 1 cup of sections for topping.

Combine sugar, butter, orange juice, cornstarch, water, lemon juice, and orange rind in a medium saucepan. Cook over low heat, stirring constantly, until slightly thickened and bubbling. Remove from heat; stir in 4 cups orange sections.

SHORTCAKE PASTRY ROUNDS:

3 cups all-purpose flour
1 tablespoon sugar
2 teaspoons salt

1 cup vegetable oil
1/4 cup milk

Combine dry ingredients; add oil and milk, stirring until mixture forms a ball. Roll dough out on a lightly floured surface to 1/8-inch thickness. Cut into rounds with a 2-1/2-inch biscuit cutter. Using a metal spatula, lift rounds and place on a lightly greased baking sheet. Bake at 350° F. for 18 to 20 minutes or until lightly browned (pastry will be very fragile.) Cool on wire racks.

Place 1 pastry round on each serving dish; cover each with 1/3 cup orange sauce. Top with remaining pastry rounds. Spoon remaining orange sauce over each. Garnish with a dollop of whipped cream and an orange section.

PEANUT GRAHAM CAKE

2 cups cake flour
1 cup dark brown sugar
1 teaspoon baking powder
1/2 teaspoon cinnamon
2/3 cup butter
3 eggs
1 cup graham cracker crumbs

1/2 cup granulated sugar
1 teaspoon baking soda
1/3 cup creamy peanut butter
1 cup orange juice
1 cup chopped roasted
   cocktail peanuts

Cream together the sugars, softened butter and peanut butter until light and fluffy. Add eggs, one at a time, beating well after each addition. Add the sifted dry ingredients alternately with the orange juice, blending well. Stir in the peanuts. Turn into a greased and floured 10-inch tube pan or 12 cup Bundt pan. Bake in 350° F. oven for 50 minutes or until cake tests done.

Cool in pan for around 15 minutes. Remove to wire rack; glaze.

PEANUT GLAZE

2 tablespoons dark brown sugar
2 tablespoons milk
1 tablespoon butter
2 teaspoons creamy peanut
   butter

1 cup confectioners sugar
1/2 teaspoon vanilla
1/4 cup chopped roasted
   cocktail peanuts

In saucepan, combine first 4 ingredients; heat until melted. Stir in remaining ingredients and beat until smooth.

PEANUT CAKE

1-1/2 cups sifted cake flour
1 teaspoon baking soda
1/3 cup shortening
1 egg
1 teaspoon vanilla
1 cup sugar

1 cup sour cream
1 (6-1/2-ounce) can salted Spanish
  peanuts, chopped (1 cup)
1 6-ounce package chocolate pieces
  (sweet milk chocolate)

Sift together flour and baking soda. Cream together shortening and sugar until light and fluffy. Add egg, beat well. Add vanilla. Add dry ingredients alternately with the sour cream. Stir in peanuts. Pour into a greased 9-inch square pan. Bake at 350° F. for 30 minutes. Sprinkle chocolate pieces over top and place cake in oven until they begin to melt. Remove and spread chocolate over top. Cool in pan on rack.

PEANUT BUTTER CAKE

3/4 cup butter
2 cups firmly packed
  brown sugar
3 eggs
1/2 teaspoon salt
1/2 cup chopped peanuts

3/4 cup creamy peanut butter
1 teaspoon vanilla
2-1/2 cups cake flour
1 tablespoon baking powder
1 cup milk

Combine butter and peanut butter and cream well. Add sugar and cream until light and fluffy. Add eggs, one at a time, beating well after each addition. Add vanilla. Sift together flour, baking powder and salt; add to creamed mixture alternately with milk, beating well. Spoon into a greased 13x9x2-inch baking pan. Bake at 350° F. for 45 to 50 minutes or until cake tests done. When cool, spread with chocolate frosting, and sprinkle with the chopped peanuts.

CHOCOLATE FROSTING FOR CAKE

1 (6-ounce) package
  semisweet chocolate morsels

1/3 cup evaporated milk
1-1/2 cups confectioners sugar

Combine chocolate morsels and milk in a medium saucepan and place over low heat, stirring, until melted. Stir in sugar and beat until smooth.

Another sure-to-be-eaten cake!

PECAN CAKE

3 eggs
1 cup sugar
1 cup chopped pecans
1 teaspoon baking powder

1 teaspoon vanilla
Pinch of salt
2-1/2 cups vanilla wafers,
    rolled into crumbs

Beat eggs until thick; add sugar gradually; add nuts, vanilla, and salt. Add crumbs and baking powder. Line cake pan with wax paper. Grease pan and paper. Bake at 275°F. for 25 minutes. Cool. Put layers together with whipped cream sweetened with brown sugar and some chopped pecans. Top with whipped cream and whole pecans.

PECAN CAKE/MISSISSIPPI

1/2 cup butter
1 teaspoon vanilla
3 egg yolks
3 teaspoons baking powder
1 cup milk

2 cups sugar
1 egg
3/4 teaspoon salt
3 cups flour
Pecan Mixture (below)

Grease 10-inch tube pan and line bottom only with wax paper.

Cream butter and sugar until light and fluffy; add egg and yolks one at a time, beating well after each addition. Add vanilla. Sift together the dry ingredients and add alternately with the milk, blending well. Pour 1/2 batter into pan. Drop pecan mixture by spoonsful on batter, then top with remaining batter. Bake at 325°F. for 1 hour and 25 minutes or until tests done. Cool in pan on rack; turn out.

PECAN MIXTURE

Combine 3 egg whites, 1/4 teaspoon salt and 1/4 cup water. Beat at high speed until stiff but not dry. Stir together 1/2 cup sugar, 2 tablespoons all-purpose flour and 1 teaspoon baking powder. Gradually beat into whites until stiff. Fold in 1 pound (4 cups) pecans, ground.

A wonderful cake -- will leave a lingering memory of the delicious flavor...

PEAR CAKE

2 cups sugar
3 eggs, well beaten
1-1/2 cups salad oil
3 cups cake flour
1 teaspoon baking soda

1 teaspoon salt
1 teaspoon vanilla
2 teaspoons cinnamon
3 cups thinly sliced pears
Powdered Sugar Glaze

Combine sugar, eggs, and oil; beat well. Combine flour, soda and salt; add to sugar mixture, 1 cup at a time, mixing well after each addition. Stir in vanilla, cinnamon and pears. Spoon batter into a well-greased 10-inch Bundt pan. Bake at 350° F. for 1 hour. Allow to cool and top with Powdered Sugar Glaze.

POWDERED SUGAR GLAZE

1-1/4 cups sifted powdered sugar
2 to 4 tablespoons milk

Blend these ingredients well and pour over cooled cake.

This recipe belongs in the top bracket of delicious cakes!

PECAN SPICE CAKE

1 cup shortening
2 cups sugar
4 beaten eggs
3 cups sifted flour
1 teaspoon baking powder

1 teaspoon baking soda
1-1/2 teaspoons cinnamon
1/2 teaspoon ground cloves
1 cup buttermilk
2 cups chopped pecans

Cream shortening and sugar until light and fluffy. Add beaten eggs and blend well. Sift the dry ingredients together 3 times and add alternately with the buttermilk, blending well. Stir in the pecans. Grease a tube pan and pour batter into it. Bake at 350° F. for 1 hour. Cake needs no frosting.

PECAN SUPREME LOAF

1 8-ounce package
   cream cheese, softened
1-1/4 cups sugar
1 cup butter
1 teaspoon grated orange peel
1/2 teaspoon orange extract

4 eggs
2-1/2 cups cake flour
3/4 cup, chopped finely, pecans
2 teaspoons baking powder
1/2 teaspoon salt

Cream together the cream cheese, butter and sugar, beating until very light and fluffy. Add eggs, one at a time, beating well after each addition. Add the orange peel and extract and blend well. Add the sifted dry ingredients and blend in well. Stir in the pecans just until blended. Bake in a 9 x 5 inch loaf pan, greased and floured at 325° F. for 1 hour and 10 minutes.

Any bride can make these cakes and the groom will think they are just like mother made...

PERFECT CAKE

3-1/2 cups cake flour	1 cup butter
2 cups sugar	5 eggs
1 cup milk	2-1/2 teaspoons baking powder
1/4 teaspoon salt	1 teaspoon vanilla extract

Cream butter and sugar until light and fluffy. Add eggs, one at a time, beating well after each addition. Blend in vanilla. Sift the flour, baking powder and salt together and then add alternately with the milk, blending thoroughly. Pour batter into 3 or 4 9-inch round cake pans. Bake at 350° F. for 20 to 25 minutes or until cake tests done. Frost top, sides and layers with Perfect Cake Icing.

PERFECT CAKE ICING

2 cups sugar	1 cup water
1/4 cup white Karo syrup	3 egg whites, stiffly beaten
1 teaspoon vanilla extract	

Boil sugar, water and syrup together until it spins a thread. Pour slowly and in a very thin stream over stiffly beaten, but not dry, egg whites, beating constantly. Beat until stiff enough to hold its shape. Blend in the vanilla extract and then add the following:

1 fresh coconut, grated	1 small bottle maraschino
1 small can pineapple,	cherries, chopped
crushed and well drained	in small pieces
1 cup chopped pecans	

After blending, spread immediately on cake. You may also use a Seven Minute Frosting instead of the cooked frosting; however, I prefer the cooked frosting since the frosting will hold its shape on the cake until it is all eaten.

A beautiful heirloom cake...and delicious!

PETIT FOURS

4 eggs	1/2 stick butter
1/2 cup granulated sugar	1 cup flour
1 teaspoon grated lemon rind	

Cream butter and sugar together until well blended. Add eggs, one at a time, beating well after each addition. Blend in flour and then the rind. Bake in a greased and floured sheet pan at 350°F. 20 to 25 minutes. Cool and then with a sharp knife, cut shapes neatly, then spread tops and sides thinly with the Fondant and let set.

FONDANT FOR PETIT FOURS

1-1/4 cups water	4 cups sugar
1/2 cup white corn syrup	

Boil water and sugar together for 5 minutes, then add corn syrup and bring to boiling point again. Pour over Petit Fours. You may want to add a little food coloring to tint the Fondant.

Delicate...glamorous...good...

PINEAPPLE CREAM CHEESE CAKE

3-1/2 cups cake flour	1 teaspoon almond extract
2 cups sugar	1 (8-ounce) can crushed
1 teaspoon baking soda	pineapple, undrained
1 teaspoon salt	1 cup chopped toasted almonds
1 teaspoon ground cloves	2 cups mashed banana
3 eggs, beaten	Cream Cheese Frosting
1-1/4 cups vegetable oil	

Combine first 5 ingredients in a large mixing bowl; add eggs and oil, stirring until dry ingredients are moistened. Do not beat. Stir in almond extract, pineapple, almonds, and banana.

Spoon batter into a greased and floured 10-inch tube pan. Bake at 300°F. for 1 hour and 15 minutes. Cool in pan 10 minutes; remove cake from pan and cool completely. Frost with Cream Cheese Frosting.

CREAM CHEESE FROSTING

1/2 cup butter, softened	1 tablespoon
1 (8-ounce) package cream cheese, softened	instant tea
1 (16-ounce) package	1/8 teaspoon
confectioners sugar	salt

Cream butter and cream cheese; gradually add sugar, tea and salt, beating until very light and fluffy.

Make this your famous cake...sweetly delicious.

PINEAPPLE CAKE

1 15-ounce can sweetened
   condensed milk
Juice and grated rind of 1 lemon
1-1/2 cups crushed pineapple
   drained

3 eggs, separated
1/4 cup butter
20 graham crackers,
   rolled fine
2 tablespoons sugar

Melt butter over low heat. Crush graham crackers into fine crumbs. Add sugar and melted butter to crumbs and mix well. Pat half the mixture in bottom of 8-inch spring form pan.

Beat egg yolks until light yellow in color. Add condensed milk, lemon juice, grated rind and crushed pineapple, blending well. Beat egg whites until they hold a peak. Carefully fold them into pineapple-condensed milk mixture. Spoon gently into crumb-lined pan. Sprinkle remaining crumbs on top.

Bake for 1 hour in 325°F. oven. Cool. Serve with sweetened whipped cream.

PINEAPPLE CARROT CAKE

3 cups cake flour
1 teaspoon baking powder
1 can (8-ounce) crushed pineapple
1-1/2 cups Wesson oil
2 cups sugar
confectioners sugar

1/2 teaspoon salt
1 teaspoon cinnamon
3 eggs
2 cups finely shredded
   carrots

Beat together the oil and sugar until well blended. Add eggs, one at a time, beating well after each addition. Sift the dry ingredients and blend in well. Add the pineapple and carrots and pour into a greased and floured 13-inch x 9-inch x 2-inch pan. Bake at 350°F. for around 45 minutes. Cool in pan. Sprinkle with confectioners sugar and cut into squares.

A perfect dessert!

PINEAPPLE LOAF

3 sticks butter
1-1/2 boxes confectioners sugar
6 eggs
1 teaspoon vanilla

1 teaspoon lemon juice
1 sugar box of cake flour
1 large can crushed
   pineapple, well drained

Cream butter and sugar until light and fluffy. Add eggs, one at a time, beating well after each addition. Add vanilla and lemon juice. Stir in flour, mix well. Add drained pineapple. Spoon into a greased and floured 10-inch tube pan. Bake in 350°F. oven for 1-1/2 hours. No frosting needed.

PINEAPPLE MUFFINS

1 (8-ounce) can crushed pineapple
1/2 cup all-purpose flour
1/3 cup firmly packed brown sugar
1/4 teaspoon ground cinnamon
1/2 cup butter, melted and divided
2 cups all-purpose flour

1/2 cup sugar
1 tablespoon baking
  powder
1/2 teaspoon salt
1 egg, beaten
3/4 cup milk

Drain pineapple, reserving 1/4 cup juice. Combine 1/2 cup flour, brown sugar, cinnamon, and 1/4 cup butter; stir well. Combine next 4 ingredients. Combine egg, milk, remaining 1/4 cup butter, and reserved pineapple juice; stir well. Make a well in center of dry ingredients; add liquid ingredients, stirring just until the dry ingredients are moistened.

Spoon batter into greased and floured muffin pans, filling half full. Spoon pineapple over batter, and sprinkle with cinnamon mixture. Bake at 375° F. for 30 minutes.

Easy to make -- has a wonderful flavor...

PINEAPPLE CREAM ROLL

3/4 cup sifted cake flour
1 teaspoon vanilla
3/4 teaspoon baking powder
1/4 teaspoon salt
4 eggs

3/4 cup sugar
confectioners sugar
Pineapple Cream Filling
(Recipe follows)

Sift flour, baking powder and salt. Beat eggs until light and lemon-colored (about 10 minutes). Gradually add sugar, beating well after each addition. Add vanilla. Fold in dry ingredients. Spread batter in wax-paper-lined 15-1/2 x 10-1/2 x 1-inch Jelly Roll Pan. Bake at 375° F. for 13 minutes.

Turn out on dish towel dusted with confectioners sugar. Roll up starting at long side. Cool for 10 minutes. Unroll cake and spread with Pineapple Cream Filling to within 1/2 inch of edges. Start rolling up cake from long end. Cool thoroughly. Refrigerate until serving time.

PINEAPPLE CREAM FILLING

Combine 1/2 cup sugar, 2 tablespoons cornstarch, 2 tablespoons flour and 1/4 teaspoon salt in small saucepan. Stir in 2 cups milk. Cook, stirring constantly, until mixture thickens. Mix some of the hot mixture with 2 egg yolks. Then stir egg mixture into hot mixture. Cook for 1 minute. Add 1 (8-1/2-ounce) can crushed pineapple, drained; 8 maraschino cherries, quartered; and 1 teaspoon vanilla. Cool.

Take it slow and easy when you make this cake...it's delicious!

PLUM CAKE

2 cups self-rising flour
2 cups sugar
1 teaspoon ground cinnamon
3/4 cup Wesson oil
3 eggs

1 cup chopped dates (or 1 8-ounce package), cut up
1 cup chopped pecans
2 small jars of plum baby food

Mix all ingredients together in electric mixer until well blended. Grease and flour a Bundt pan. Pour mixture into pan and bake for 1 hour at 350°F. or until cake tests done. Spread with Confectioners Sugar Icing.

CONFECTIONERS SUGAR ICING

1 cup confectioners sugar   Lemon juice, 1 lemon

Add enough lemon juice for a thin frosting. Spread over cake while still warm. Prick cake for icing to go through.

Excellent flavor...stays moist!

PINEAPPLE UPSIDE DOWN CAKE

3 tablespoons butter, melted
1 cup firmly packed brown sugar
1 (15-1/2-ounce) can sliced pineapple, drained
1/2 cup shortening
1 cup sugar

2 eggs
1-1/2 cups all-purpose flour
2 teaspoons baking powder
1/2 teaspoon salt
2/3 cup milk
1 teaspoon vanilla extract

Melt butter in a 10-inch cast-iron skillet. Spread brown sugar evenly over butter. Arrange pineapple on sugar.

Combine shortening and sugar, creaming until light and fluffy. Add eggs, one at a time, and mix well.

Stir in remaining ingredients; beat 2 minutes or until batter is smooth and fluffy. Spoon batter evenly over pineapple slices. Bake at 350°F. for 50 to 55 minutes or until cake tests done. Cool 5 minutes, and invert cake onto plate.

Bake this outstanding cake with exceptionally good flavor!

POPPY SEED CAKE

3/4 cup poppy seeds
2 cups flour
2 tablespoons baking powder
4 egg whites

3/4 cup milk
1-1/2 cups sugar
1 teaspoon vanilla
1/2 cup butter

Soak seeds in milk 5 to 6 hours. Cream butter and sugar until light and fluffy. Add seeds and blend well. Add sifted flour and baking powder alternately with the milk; then fold in stiffly beaten egg whites and vanilla. Pour into 3 greased and floured cake pans and bake at 350° F. for 30 minutes or until done. Spread Filling between layers and Frosting on top and sides of cake.

PECAN FILLING

4 egg yolks
1 cup sugar
1 cup chopped pecans

2 cups milk
3 tablespoons cornstarch
1/4 teaspoon salt

Mix cornstarch and sugar. Beat egg yolks, add milk and then combine with sugar mixture. Cook in double boiler, stirring constantly, until thick. Remove from heat; add pecans and cool. Spread between layers.

COCOA FROSTING

1/2 cup butter
4 tablespoons cocoa

3 cups confectioners sugar
2 teaspoons vanilla

Cream butter and sugar; add cocoa and vanilla. Moisten with enough cold, strong coffee to spread over top and sides of cake.

Moist -- delicate texture -- good!

PRUNE CAKE

1-1/2 cups dried prunes
1 teaspoon grated lemon rind
2 cups sifted all-purpose flour
1 teaspoon baking powder
1 teaspoon baking soda
1/2 teaspoon salt
3 eggs
1 cup sugar

1/2 cup light brown sugar
1 cup butter, softened
1 cup sour cream
1 teaspoon vanilla
1/2 cup light brown sugar
1 tablespoon cinnamon
1/2 cup chopped pecans

Prepare dried prunes as directed on package. Drain, pit, and dice. Sprinkle over lemon rind and set aside. Grease and flour a 9-inch tube pan or Bundt pan. Sift together the flour, baking powder, soda and salt. Take out 1/4 cup of mixture and toss with the diced prunes.

Cream butter and the sugars, beating until light and fluffy. Add eggs, one at a time, beating well after each addition. Stir in vanilla. Add sifted dry ingredients alternately with the sour cream. Fold in prunes.

Combine the 1/2 cup of light brown sugar with the cinnamon and nuts.

Pour 1/3 of the batter into pan. Sprinkle over 1/2 of the cinnamon-nut mixture, 1/3 batter, remaining cinnamon-nut mixture, topping with remaining batter.

Bake in 350° F. oven for about 55 minutes or until cake tests done. Cool in pan for 10 minutes; remove, pour over cake a glaze made of the juice and grated rind of 1 lemon and 1 cup of confectioners sugar.

Rich in flavor and attractive...

PRALINE ICE CREAM CAKE

2 cups cake flour	1 pint vanilla ice cream,
1 cup sugar	softened
1 cup graham cracker crumbs	2 eggs, beaten
1 tablespoon baking powder	Topping (recipe follows)
1/2 teaspoon salt	1/2 cup chopped pecans
1/2 cup butter	

Combine first 5 ingredients and set aside.

Melt butter over low heat and remove. Add ice cream, flour mixture, and eggs; stir until batter is smooth.

Pour batter into a lightly greased 13x9x2-inch baking pan; spoon 1/3 cup topping over batter. Bake at 350° F. for 30 minutes or until cake tests done.

Stir pecans into remaining 2/3 cup topping; spread over hot cake. Cool on wire rack.

BROWN SUGAR TOPPING

1 cup firmly packed brown	2 tablespoons butter
sugar	2 teaspoons cornstarch
1/2 cup sour cream	1/2 teaspoon vanilla extract

Combine first 4 ingredients in a small saucepan over low heat; cook over medium heat until thickened and bubbly, stirring constantly. Remove from heat and stir in vanilla.

Delicious with ice cream or with coffee...

PUMPKIN CAKE

1 teaspoon salt
2 cups sugar
1 (16-ounce) can pumpkin
(or 2 cups cooked, mashed)
1 cup vegetable oil
4 eggs, beaten
2 cups all-purpose flour

2 teaspoons baking soda
2 teaspoons baking powder
2 teaspoons ground cinnamon
1/2 cup flaked coconut
1/2 cup chopped pecans
Frosting (recipe follows)

Combine sugar, pumpkin, oil, and eggs; beat 1 minute at medium speed of electric mixer. Combine next 5 ingredients; add to pumpkin mixture. Beat 1 minute at medium speed. Stir in coconut and pecans. Pour batter into three greased and floured cake pans. Bake at 350° F. for 25 minutes or until cakes test done. Cool in pans 10 minutes; remove from pans, and cool completely. Spread frosting between layers and on top of cake.

CREAM CHEESE FROSTING

1/2 cup butter, softened
1 (8-ounce) package cream
cheese, softened
1 (16-ounce) package confectioners
sugar

2 teaspoons vanilla extract
1/2 cup chopped pecans
1/2 cup flaked coconut

Combine butter and cream cheese; beat until light and fluffy. Add sugar and vanilla, mixing well. Stir in pecans and coconut.

Good cake for any occasion...

PUMPKIN BREAD

Delicious! Tastes like cake.

2 cups sugar
4 eggs
1 teaspoon nutmeg
1 teaspoon cinnamon
1-1/2 teaspoons salt

1 cup salad oil
1 cup canned pumpkin
2/3 cup water
2 teaspoons baking soda
3 cups sifted flour

Blend together spices, eggs, salt and oil. Then stir in the pumpkin, water, baking soda and flour. Blend well. Fill 3 greased and floured 1 pound coffee cans one-half full of batter. Bake in 350° F. oven for 50 to 55 minutes.

RED VELVET CAKE NO. 1

2-1/2 cups sifted flour
1 teaspoon baking soda
1 cup buttermilk
1 teaspoon vinegar
2 eggs
1 bottle red food coloring (1-ounce)

1-1/2 cups sugar
1 teaspoon cocoa
1 cup butter flavored
    Wesson oil and 1/2 cup
    regular Wesson oil
1 teaspoon vanilla extract

Sift together dry ingredients. Cream oil and sugar together until well blended. Add eggs, one at a time, beating well after each addition. Add food coloring, vinegar and extract; mix well. Add dry ingredients alternately with the buttermilk. Bake in 3 round cake pans which have been greased and floured at 350°F. for 25 minutes. Cool completely and frost with cream cheese frosting.

RED VELVET CAKE NO. 2

3 cups sifted cake flour
1 teaspoon baking soda
1 cup buttermilk
4 eggs
1 bottle red food coloring (1-ounce)
1 teaspoon vinegar

2 cups sugar
1-1/2 teaspoons cocoa
1 stick butter
1 cup Wesson oil
1 teaspoon vanilla extract

Cream butter, oil and sugar together until very light and fluffy. Add eggs, one at a time, beating well after each addition. Add vanilla and blend well. Add red food coloring and vinegar and mix thoroughly. Add sifted dry ingredients alternately with the buttermilk. Bake in 4 greased and floured cake pans at 350°F. for around 25 minutes or until the cakes test done. Cool completely and frost with Cream Cheese Frosting.

CREAM CHEESE FROSTING

1 stick butter
1 box confectioners
    sugar

1 8-ounce package cream cheese
1/2 teaspoon vanilla extract
1 cup chopped pecans

Cream softened cream cheese and butter well. Add confectioners sugar and vanilla and blend well. Fold in pecans and spread on cooled cake.

Distinctive in appearance... this cake has glamour... turns out perfectly and is perfectly delicious!

RAISIN CAKE

1 (15-ounce) package raisins
2 cups sugar
1 cup butter
2 cups boiling water
2 tablespoons baking soda
1/4 cup warm water
2 eggs, slightly beaten

4-1/2 cups all-purpose flour
1/2 teaspoon baking powder
1 tablespoon ground allspice
2 teaspoons ground cinnamon
1 teaspoon ground cloves
2 cups chopped pecans or walnuts

Combine raisins, sugar, butter, and boiling water in a large saucepan; bring to a boil and boil for 5 minutes. Allow to cool to lukewarm.

Dissolve baking soda in warm water; add to raisin mixture. (Mixture will foam.) Stir in eggs. Combine dry ingredients; gradually add to raisin mixture, stirring after each addition. Stir in pecans, if desired.

Spoon batter into a lightly greased 10-inch Bundt pan or tube pan. Bake at 350° F. for around an hour or until cake tests done.

RASPBERRY CAKE

1 cup butter
2 cups sugar
4 cups sifted cake flour
2-1/2 teaspoons baking powder
1/2 teaspoon salt
1/2 cup milk

2 tablespoons orange rind
4 tablespoons shaved citron
7 egg whites, beaten stiff
1/4 teaspoon salt
Raspberry whipped cream
7 egg yolks, unbeaten

Cream butter thoroughly with sugar. Add egg yolks, one at a time, beating well after each addition. Alternately add sifted dry ingredients with milk and beat until smooth. Add grated orange rind; citron must be in very fine shreds. Shave or shred on fine grater. Add to the butter mixture and blend well. Fold egg whites into batter. Pour batter into 3 9-inch greased and floured cake pans. Bake at 350° F. for 25 to 30 minutes. Cool and spread with Raspberry whipped cream between layers and over top and sides of cake. Sprinkle generously with shaved citron.

RASPBERRY WHIPPED CREAM

Beat 1 pint heavy sweet cream. Fold in 3 tablespoons raspberry jelly, only once or twice, giving a marbled effect. Spread over cake immediately.

Two-tone in color, delicate in texture...

SCRIPTURE CAKE

3-1/2 cups I Kings 4:22   *Flour*
1 cup Judges 5:25 (last clause)   *Butter*
2 cups Jeremiah 6:20   *Sugar*
2 cups I Samuel 30:12   *Raisins*
2 cups Naham 3:12   *Figs*
2 cups Numbers 17:8   *Almonds*
1/2 cup Judges 4:19 (last clause)   *Milk*
2 tablespoons I Samuel 14:25   *Honey*
2 teaspoons Amos 4:5 (leavening)   *Baking Powder*
Season to taste with II Chronicles 9:19   *Spices**
A pinch of Leviticus 2:13   *Salt*
Six of Jeremiah 17:11   *Eggs*

*I use 1 tablespoon each of Allspice, Cinnamon & Nutmeg

This is a fun cake to make but also a very delicious one if the directions are followed.

Cream together the butter and sugar until light and very fluffy. Add the sifted flour, baking powder, salt and spices alternately with the milk and the honey. Dredge the raisins and figs in a very small amount of flour and then stir in along with the almonds. I chop the almonds very fine. This makes a large cake, so pour into a tube pan that you have greased and floured and bake at 300° F. for around an hour and 30 minutes or until it tests done.

SILVER CAKE (WHITE CAKE)

3 cups sifted cake flour   1-1/2 cups sugar
1/2 cup butter   1 cup milk
1/2 teaspoon lemon extract   4 egg whites, stiffly beaten
3 teaspoons baking powder

Sift flour once, measure, add baking powder, and sift together three times. Cream butter thoroughly, add sugar gradually, and cream together until light and fluffy. Add flour, alternately with milk, a small amount at a time. Beat after each addition until smooth. Add lemon extract. Fold in egg whites and bake in three greased 9-inch cake pans in 350° F. oven for 25 to 30 minutes. Spread with your favorite frosting.

SILHOUETTE CAKE

2-1/3 cups cake flour, sifted
1/4 teaspoon salt
1 egg and 2 egg yolks, well beaten
2-1/4 teaspoons baking powder

1/2 cup butter
3/4 cup milk
1 cup sugar
1 teaspoon vanilla

Chocolate Mixture:

2-1/2 squares unsweetened
  chocolate, melted
3 tablespoons sugar
1/4 teaspoon salt

1/2 teaspoon baking soda
2 tablespoons melted butter
1/4 cup boiling water

Sift flour once, measure; add baking powder and salt and sift together 3 times. Cream butter thoroughly; add sugar gradually, creaming until light and fluffy. Add egg and egg yolks and beat well after each addition.

Prepare chocolate mixture by combining melted chocolate, soda, sugar, butter, salt and water. Mix well. Put aside.

Add flour to first mixture alternately with milk blending well after each addition. Pour 1/3 of batter into a greased round layer pan. Add chocolate mixture to remaining batter, blend, pour into two greased layer pans. Bake all 3 layers at 350° F. for 20 to 25 minutes or until cakes test done. Frost with Harvest Frosting. Put chocolate layer on bottom, plain layer next, then top layer, chocolate.

HARVEST FROSTING

4 egg whites, unbeaten
2 cups brown sugar,
  firmly packed
Dash of salt

1/4 cup water
1 teaspoon vanilla
3/4 cup almonds, blanched,
  chopped, toasted

Combine egg whites, sugar, salt and water in top of double boiler, beating with rotary beater until thoroughly mixed. Place over rapidly boiling water beating constantly, and cook for 7 minutes. Remove from heat, add vanilla and beat until thick enough to spread. Add nuts. You may also melt 2 additional squares of chocolate and pour over the top of the cake, for decoration, if desired.

SEVEN UP-CAKE

1 box lemon supreme cake mix   3/4 cup vegetable oil
1 box instant pineapple pudding   10 ounce bottle or can of 7 Up
4 eggs

Beat eggs thoroughly; add oil and blend. Add 7 Up, pudding and cake mix and blend thoroughly. Pour batter into three greased and floured round cake pans and bake at 350° F. for around 30 minutes or until the cakes test done. Cool layers completely and then ice with Pineapple-Coconut Icing.

PINEAPPLE-COCONUT ICING

1 cup crushed pineapple   1 cup coconut
1 stick butter   1 teaspoon vanilla extract
1 cup sugar   1 cup chopped pecans
1 tablespoon flour

Combine all ingredients and cook and stir for 5 minutes. Spread on cooled cake layers.

This cake is a pleasing adventure in baking...

SHORT CAKES

1-1/4 sticks butter   Jelly
1/4 cup sugar   Powdered sugar icing
1-1/2 cups cake flour

Cream together butter, sugar, flour. Roll out to 1/4-inch thickness on lightly floured board; cut in small rounds. Bake in 300° F. oven until light brown. While still hot put 2 rounds together with your favorite jelly, then lightly ice with a powdered sugar icing. Place a pecan half on top of each round, if desired.

SILVER MOON CAKE (WHITE CAKE)

3 cups sifted cake flour   1-3/4 cups sugar
1/2 teaspoon salt   1 cup milk
3 teaspoons baking powder   1 teaspoon vanilla
2/3 cup butter   5 egg whites, stiffly beaten

Cream butter and sugar together until light and fluffy. Add sifted dry ingredients alternately with the milk. Add vanilla. Fold in the egg whites. Pour into three greased and floured round cake pans and bake at 350° F. for around 30 minutes. Spread with icing of your choice.

Expect the best when you bake this white cake...

SOCK-IT-TO-ME CAKE

1 package Golden Butter Cake Mix
1 cup sour cream
1/2 cup vegetable oil

1/4 cup sugar
1/4 cup milk
4 eggs

Filling:

1 cup chopped pecans
2 tablespoons brown sugar

2 teaspoons cinnamon

Blend together the cake mix, sour cream, oil, 1/4 cup sugar, milk, and eggs. Beat at high speed for 2 minutes. Pour 2/3 of the batter into a greased and floured tube pan or Bundt pan. Sprinkle filling ingredients, that have been combined, over. Spread remaining batter evenly and bake at 350° F. for about 25 minutes. Drizzle glaze over cake when cake has finished baking.

Glaze: Blend 1 cup confectioners sugar and 2 tablespoons milk together thoroughly.

A glazed beauty and delicious!

SOUR CREAM CAKE

3 cups sifted cake flour
1-1/2 teaspoons baking soda
1/2 teaspoon cream of tartar
1 teaspoon salt
1/2 cup butter, softened

1-1/2 cups sugar
2 eggs
1 teaspoon vanilla
1-1/2 cups sour cream

Cream butter and sugar together until light and fluffy. Add eggs, one at a time, beating well after each addition. Add sifted dry ingredients alternately with the sour cream. Add vanilla. Bake at 350° F. for 20 minutes or until cakes test done. Spread with Strawberry 7-Minute Frosting.

STRAWBERRY 7 MINUTE FROSTING

7 tablespoons strawberry puree'
2 egg whites
1 teaspoon cream of tartar

Dash of salt
1-1/2 cups sugar
2 teaspoons white corn syrup

Combine first 5 ingredients in top of double boiler. Beat with electric beater until mixture stands in peaks. Remove from heat. Replace hot water with cold, add syrup and beat until mixture is cool and stiff.

A blushing, beautiful cake! Luscious...

SOUR CREAM CUSTARD CAKE

2 tablespoons cold water   1 cup sour cream
1 cup cornstarch   1/2 cup sugar

Mix cornstarch and water to a smooth paste. Heat cream, adding sugar and cornstarch mixture. Cook 15 minutes over low heat, stirring constantly. Cool.

1-1/2 cups sifted cake flour   1 egg, beaten
1/2 teaspoon salt   1/2 cup milk
2 teaspoons baking powder   1/2 teaspoon vanilla
2/3 cup sugar   1/2 teaspoon cinnamon
1/4 cup melted shortening

Sift flour, salt, baking powder, and sugar together. Combine butter, egg, milk, vanilla. Add to dry ingredients, beating 1 minute until smooth. Pour into 9-inch springform pan. Make an indentation in center of batter and pour custard into it slowly. Cake batter will be pushed toward edges of pan and custard in center. As it bakes, cake will rise partly over custard; sprinkle with cinnamon. Bake at 350° F. for 25 minutes or until done.

A delightful climax to any meal...

SOUR CREAM FUDGE CAKE

2 cups sifted cake flour   3 (1-ounce) squares unsweetened
1-1/2 cups sugar   chocolate, melted
1 teaspoon baking soda   2 eggs
1 teaspoon salt   1 teaspoon vanilla
1/3 cup solid shortening   1/4 cup hot water
1 cup sour cream

Grease the bottom of a 13x9x1-1/2-inch pan; line with waxed paper, then grease the paper. Sift together the flour, sugar, soda and salt. Cut in shortening, then add sour cream, beating 2 minutes. Add remaining ingredients, beating additional 2 minutes.

Turn batter into pan, bake in 350° F. oven for around 25 to 30 minutes. Cool cake in pan for 5 minutes and then turn out on rack and remove paper. Frost as desired, serving in squares. This cake is especially good with a 7 Minute Frosting.

The goodness of this cake is unforgettable... incredibly good!

SPONGE CAKE

6 eggs, separated
1 teaspoon vanilla
1/2 teaspoon salt
1/2 teaspoon baking powder
1/2 cup sugar

1/4 cup water
1 cup sugar
1-1/2 cups cake flour
1 teaspoon cream of tartar

Beat egg yolks at high speed of electric mixer until thick and lemon colored. Add water and vanilla and blend well. Beat until thoroughly blended and thickened; then gradually beat in 1 cup sugar and salt. Sift together the flour and baking powder. Sprinkle about one-fourth at a time over yolk mixture and carefully fold in. Set aside.

Beat egg whites until foamy and add cream of tartar. Then beat until soft peaks form. Gradually add 1/2 cup sugar, 2 tablespoons at a time, beating until stiff peaks form. Gently fold egg whites into yolk mixture. Pour batter into an ungreased 10-inch tube pan. Bake at 350° F. for 50 minutes or until tests done.

Remove from oven and invert pan and cool completely before removing from pan.

Golden, delicious butter-flavored cake...

SPICE CAKE

1-1/2 cups boiling water
1-1/2 cups sifted flour
1 teaspoon cinnamon
1/2 teaspoon salt
1/2 cup shortening
1/2 cup sugar
1 teaspoon vanilla

1 cup quick rolled oats
1 teaspoon baking soda
1 teaspoon nutmeg
1/4 teaspoon allspice
1 cup brown sugar, firmly packed
2 eggs
1/2 cup chopped walnuts or pecans

Pour water over oats; let stand until cool.

Mix together shortening and sugars until light and fluffy. Beat in eggs, one at a time, beating well after each addition. Stir in oats mixture and vanilla. Mix in dry ingredients that have been sifted together and blend well. Stir in nuts. Spread mixture in greased and floured 9-inch square pan.

Bake in 350° F. oven 45-50 minutes. Cool in pan on rack. Spread with Lemon Butter Frosting.

LEMON BUTTER FROSTING

Cream together 1/4 cup butter and 1/4 cup shortening. Gradually beat in 2 cups confectioners sugar. Add 1 tablespoon milk, 1 teaspoon grated lemon rind, 1/2 teaspoon lemon extract and dash of salt. Whip until light and creamy.

SPICE-SURPRISE CAKE

2 cups sifted flour
2 teaspoons baking powder
1 teaspoon nutmeg
1/2 teaspoon salt
2 cups sugar
1 cup unseasoned mashed
   potatoes
1 cup chopped pecans
1/2 cup cocoa
1 teaspoon ground cinnamon
1 teaspoon cloves
1 cup butter
4 eggs
1/2 cup whipping cream
1 (8-1/2-ounce) can crushed
   pineapple, drained

Sift together flour, cocoa, baking powder, salt and spices. Cream butter and sugar until light and fluffy. Add eggs, one at a time, beating well after each addition. Beat in mashed potatoes. Add dry ingredients alternately with the cream, beating well after each addition. Stir in pineapple and pecans. Pour into a greased and floured 13x9x2-inch cake pan. Bake at 350° F. for around 45 minutes. Cool in pan on rack. Frost with Cream Cheese Frosting.

CREAM CHEESE FROSTING

Beat together 1 (8-ounce) package cream cheese and 1/4 cup butter. Slowly beat in 2 cups sifted confectioners sugar and 2 teaspoons vanilla; beat until light and fluffy.

Elegant and expensive... but worth the cost...

STRAWBERRY CAKE

2 sticks butter
1 small package strawberry jello
3 teaspoons baking powder
6 egg whites, stiffly beaten
2 cups sugar
3-1/2 cups sifted cake flour
1 cup milk
1/2 cup strawberries, cut up

Preheat oven at 350° F. Cream together butter, sugar and jello until well mixed and light and fluffy. Add sifted flour and baking powder alternately with the milk. Fold in the stiffly beaten egg whites. Pour into three or four greased and floured 9-inch round cake pans and bake around 25 minutes or until cakes test done. Spread layers, top and sides with Strawberry Icing.

STRAWBERRY ICING

1 stick butter, softened
1/2 cup strawberries, cut up
1 box confectioners sugar

Blend all ingredients well and spread on cake when cool.

Appreciated more today than when developed so many years ago!

SPICE CARAMEL CAKE

1-3/4 cups sugar
3/4 cup soft shortening
1/2 teaspoon nutmeg
3 eggs
1 cup buttermilk
3/4 cup chopped pecans

1 cup cold mashed potatoes
1 teaspoon cinnamon
1/2 teaspoon salt
1 teaspoon baking soda
2-1/4 cups flour

Preheat oven 350° F. Combine sugar, potatoes, shortening. Cream well. Add eggs, one at a time, beating well after each addition. Sift together the dry ingredients and add alternately with the buttermilk beginning and ending with the flour mixture. Turn into a greased and floured 13x9x2-inch pan. Bake 50-60 minutes. Cool and frost with Quick Caramel Frosting.

QUICK CARAMEL FROSTING

Melt 1/4 cup butter in saucepan, stir in 3/4 cup firmly packed brown sugar. Continue cooking over low heat for 2 minutes. Add 3 tablespoons milk. Bring to a FULL boil; cool to lukewarm without stirring. Add 2 cups confectioners sugar. Beat until smooth and of spreading consistency.

SPICE-SOUR CREAM CAKE

1 cup butter, softened
6 eggs, separated
4 cups all-purpose flour
1 teaspoon allspice
1 teaspoon cloves
1 (8-ounce) carton sour cream

1 cup sugar
1 cup molasses
1 teaspoon salt
1 teaspoon cinnamon
1 teaspoon nutmeg
1 teaspoon baking soda

Cream butter and sugar together until light and fluffy. Add egg yolks, one at a time, beating well after each addition. Add molasses and beat well.

Combine flour, salt, and spices and sift together. Combine sour cream and baking soda and mix well. Add flour mixture to creamed mixture alternately with sour cream mixture, beginning and ending with flour mixture.

Beat egg whites until stiff peaks form; gently fold into batter. Pour into a greased and floured 10-inch tube pan. Bake at 300° F. for 1 hour and 40 minutes or until tests done. Cool in pan for 10 minutes; remove from pan and cool completely. Sprinkle with confectioners sugar.

An aristocratic, delicious, rich dessert...

STRAWBERRY MERINGUE CAKE

1/2 cup sugar
1/2 cup butter
4 egg yolks
Whipped cream, sweetened

1/4 cup milk
2-1/2 cups sifted flour
1 teaspoon baking powder
1/4 teaspoon salt

Cream sugar and butter; add beaten yolks; beat until light and fluffy. Sift dry ingredients; add to mixture alternately with milk. Pour into greased long cake pan; set in cool place.

4 egg whites
1 cup sugar
1 tablespoon vanilla

chopped pecans
strawberries

Beat egg whites; add sugar gradually until soft peaks form. Beat in vanilla. Spread on cake batter; sprinkle with chopped pecans. Bake in 325° F. oven for 20 to 25 minutes. Cool. Put fresh strawberries on top. Serve with sweetened whipped cream.

STRAWBERRY SHORTCAKE

2 cups plain flour
1/2 teaspoon salt
1/2 cup butter
1 quart strawberries, halved
and sweetened to taste

3 teaspoons baking powder
1/2 cup sugar
3/4 cup milk or light cream
1 cup whipping cream, whipped
and sweetened to taste

Sift flour, baking powder, salt and sugar together. Cut in butter until mixture looks like coarse breadcrumbs. Stir in milk. (Don't overmix.) Turn dough out on floured board, knead quickly to distribute ingredients evenly.

With floured rolling pin, roll out dough about 3/4-inch thick. Cut in circles with a 3-inch cookie cutter or a glass dipped in flour. Place 2 inches apart on ungreased cookie sheet and bake about 10 to 15 minutes or until golden brown in a 400° F. oven. Split crosswise while warm, butter both halves. Spoon sweetened berries over bottom half; put on top, spoon on more strawberries. Top with whipped cream and a whole berry.

Has genuine old-time flavor...

STRAWBERRY CREAM CAKE

2 packages (10-ounce) frozen
strawberries or 1 quart fresh
strawberries, sweetened and
cut up
2 cups all-purpose flour
1 teaspoon baking powder
1/2 teaspoon baking soda
1/2 teaspoon salt
1-1/4 cups sugar

1 cup butter, softened
2 eggs
1 cup (8-ounce carton)
sour cream
1/3 cup firmly packed
light brown sugar
1/2 cup chopped pecans
1 teaspoon cinnamon

Drain strawberries and reserve juice for glaze. Sift together flour, baking powder, baking soda and salt and set aside.

Combine 1-1/4 cups sugar and butter in a large mixing bowl, creaming well. Add eggs, beating until smooth. Slowly mix in the sour cream. Add flour mixture and stir in well.

Combine brown sugar, pecans and cinnamon; set aside for topping. Pour half of batter into a lightly greased 13x9x2-inch baking pan. Spoon strawberries over batter; sprinkle with half of topping mixture. Top with remaining batter and sprinkle with remaining topping. Bake at 350° F. for 30 to 35 minutes or until cake tests done. Let cool; cut into squares (around 15). Top each square with Strawberry Glaze and whipped, sweetened cream.

STRAWBERRY GLAZE

Reserved strawberry juice, 1 tablespoon plus 1 teaspoon cornstarch, 2 teaspoons lemon juice, freshly squeezed.

Combine strawberry juice and cornstarch in a small saucepan; cook over medium heat, stirring constantly until thickened. Remove from heat and stir in lemon juice. Serve warm over cake.

STRAWBERRY SPONGE CAKE

Cake:
1 cup flour
5 eggs
5 tablespoons butter
2 teaspoons grated lemon
peel

1 teaspoon baking powder
3/4 cup sugar
1/4 cup heavy cream
1 teaspoon lemon extract
1 teaspoon vanilla extract

Filling and Topping:
1 quart strawberries, hulled
and halved
(Reserve a few whole and
unhulled for garnish)

1/2 cup sugar
1-1/2 cups heavy cream, whipped

Cake: Sift flour and baking powder together and set aside. Beat eggs and sugar together in large mixing bowl. In small saucepan over low heat melt butter in cream; set aside to cool slightly. Fold flour mixture into egg mixture, then fold in cream mixture, peel and extracts. Bake in two 9-inch greased and floured round cake pans at 350°F. for 20 - 25 minutes.

Filling and Topping: Gently toss berries with sugar. Let stand at room temperature until juice forms (about 1 hour). Place one layer of cake on serving plate. Spoon one half berries and juice over; top with whipping cream. Place second layer of cake on top, then top with remaining berries and juice. Mound remaining whipped cream in center. Garnish with whole berries.

STRAWBERRY YUM YUM

3/4 cup butter
1 cup sugar
2 envelopes Dream Whip

2 cups graham cracker crumbs
1 8-ounce package cream cheese
1 quart fresh strawberries*

Melt butter and mix with graham cracker crumbs. Put half in bottom of serving dish. Cream sugar and cream cheese together. Beat Dream Whip as directed on package. Mix cream cheese mixture with Dream Whip until smooth. Put half on top of cracker crumbs, then fresh strawberry glaze or pie filling. Add rest of cream cheese mixture, then other half of cracker crumbs.

*1 can strawberry pie filling may be used. If using fresh strawberries, get Continental Strawberry Glaze and mix with berries according to package instructions.

Don't let anyone tell you fresh strawberries won't make a delicious cake...

VANILLA WAFER CAKE

2 sticks butter
2 cups sugar
6 eggs
1 box (12-ounce) vanilla wafers

1/2 cup milk
7 ounce can angel
flake coconut
1 cup chopped pecans

Cream butter and sugar until light and fluffy. Add eggs, one at a time, beating well after each addition. Crush wafers with a rolling pin until crumbs are fine. Add wafer crumbs and milk alternately to the creamed mixture. Add coconut, then fold in pecans. Grease and flour a tube pan; pour in batter and bake at 300°F. for 1 hour and 15 minutes or until done. Important to let cool in pan before removing.

A notable cake with unaffected goodness...

SUGAR PLUM CAKE

3/4 cup butter
1-3/4 cups sugar
4 eggs
4 cups flour
3/4 pound candied orange
  slices, cut finely
  with scissors
1 8-ounce package dates,
  cut small

1 (3-1/2-ounce) can flaked coconut
1/8 teaspoon salt
1 teaspoon baking soda
2/3 cup buttermilk
1 tablespoon lemon juice
1 teaspoon orange extract
1-1/2 cups coarsely chopped pecans

Preheat oven to 300° F. Cream butter and sugar until light and fluffy. Add eggs, one at a time, beating well after each addition. Sift 1/2 cup flour over the orange slice bits, pecans, dates and coconut and mix well.

Sift remaining flour with the salt and baking soda. Add alternately with the buttermilk. Stir in lemon juice and orange extract. With hands mix in the dredged fruits. Fill two greased and floured 9x5x3-inch loaf pans and bake 1 hour and 40 minutes. Start testing for doneness after 1 hour and 15 minutes. Let cake rest for 5 minutes, then prick all over with skewer or ice pick. Spoon glaze over.

ORANGE GLAZE

2 cups confectioners sugar
2 teaspoons grated orange rind

1 cup orange juice

Blend all ingredients together thoroughly for glaze.

Serve this cake and it will produce a sense of complete satisfaction...

SWEET POTATO CAKE

1-1/2 cups salad oil
2 cups sugar
4 eggs, separated
4 tablespoons hot water
2-1/2 cups cake flour
3 teaspoons baking powder
1 teaspoon vanilla extract

1/4 teaspoon salt
1 teaspoon cinnamon
1 teaspoon nutmeg
1-1/2 cups grated raw sweet
  potatoes
1 cup chopped pecans
Coconut Filling

Combine oil and sugar in a large mixing bowl and beat until smooth. Add egg yolks and beat well. Stir in hot water. Combine dry ingredients and sift together; blend into sugar mixture, continuing to mix thoroughly. Stir in potatoes, pecans and vanilla. Beat egg whites until stiff peaks form; fold into batter.

Spoon mixture into three greased 8-inch cake pans. Bake at 350° F. for 25 to 30 minutes. Remove from pans; cool and spread Coconut Filling between layers and on top of cake. Garnish with whole pecans, if desired.

COCONUT FILLING

1 (13-ounce) can evaporated milk
1 cup sugar
1/2 cup butter
3 tablespoons flour
1 teaspoon vanilla
1 (3-1/2-ounce) can coconut

Combine milk, sugar, butter, flour and vanilla in a saucepan. Cook, stirring constantly, over medium heat; stir in coconut. Beat until thickened and cooled.

A luscious cake to get enthused about!

TROPICAL CHIFFON CAKE

2-1/4 cups sifted cake flour
3 teaspoons baking powder
3/4 teaspoon salt
1-1/2 cups sugar
1/2 cup salad oil
6 large eggs, separated
2 large ripe bananas, sieved
1-1/2 teaspoons grated
  orange rind
1/3 cup orange juice
1/2 teaspoon cream of tartar

Sift dry ingredients into mixing bowl. Make well in center of dry ingredients and fill with salad oil, egg yolks, bananas, grated orange rind and orange juice. Beat, using wooden spoon, until smooth.

Put egg whites in large bowl, add cream of tartar and beat until peaks are formed. Fold into batter, mixing well. Pour into ungreased 10-inch tube pan and bake at 325° F. about 1 hour and 10 to 15 minutes. Invert pan and cool completely. Frost with your favorite cream cheese frosting or a glaze.

WALNUT CAKE

1 cup butter
3-1/2 cups sifted cake flour
1/2 teaspoon salt
5 eggs
1 teaspoon vanilla

2 cups sugar
1 tablespoon baking powder
2 cups chopped walnuts
1 cup milk

Cream butter and sugar until light and fluffy. Add eggs, one at a time, beating well after each addition. Add vanilla and blend well. Add sifted dry ingredients alternately with the milk. Stir in the nuts. Pour into 2 lightly greased loaf pans and bake at 350° F. for around 45 to 50 minutes. Let cakes cool and then spread with Chocolate-Nut Frosting.

CHOCOLATE-NUT FROSTING

2 squares unsweetened
  chocolate
5 egg yolks
1 cup sugar

2 tablespoons strong coffee
1/4 teaspoon salt
1 cup butter
1 cup chopped walnuts

Melt chocolate in very hot coffee, stirring often. Set aside. Beat egg yolks until light lemon color, then add the sugar and salt and beat until smooth. Spoon the chocolate mixture into the yolk mixture and then add the butter and cook over medium heat until the mixture thickens slightly and becomes spreadable. Add the nuts and spread over cake as quickly as possible.

WALNUT-COCONUT CAKE

1/2 cup butter
2 cups sugar
1 cup buttermilk
2-1/2 cups cake flour
1-1/2 cups chopped walnuts
1/2 teaspoon cream of tartar

1/2 cup shortening
5 eggs, separated
1 teaspoon baking soda
1 teaspoon vanilla
1 (3-1/2-ounce) can
  flaked coconut

Cream butter and shortening; gradually add sugar, beating until light and fluffy. Add egg yolks, one at a time, beating well after each addition. Add sifted dry ingredients alternately with the buttermilk. Stir in vanilla. Add chopped walnuts and coconut, blending well. Beat egg whites with cream of tartar until stiff peaks form. Fold egg whites into batter. Pour batter into 3 greased and floured 9-inch round cake pans and bake at 350° F. for 30 minutes or until done. Cool completely and frost with Cream Cheese Frosting and sprinkle with chopped walnuts.

CREAM CHEESE FROSTING

3/4 cup butter, softened
6-3/4 cups confectioners sugar
    sugar
1-1/2 teaspoons vanilla

1 (8-ounce) package cream
    cheese, softened
1 (3-ounce) package cream
    cheese, softened

Cream butter and cream cheese; gradually add sugar, beating until light and creamy. Stir in vanilla.

Oh's and Ah's are sure to greet you when you serve this delectable creation...

WALNUT TORTE

3-1/4 cups ground walnuts
1 tablespoon chopped walnuts
3-1/2 tablespoons cake
    flour
1 cup sugar

1 teaspoon baking powder
1/2 teaspoon salt
1 cup whipping cream,
    sweetened
6 eggs, separated

Beat egg yolks and sugar until thick and lemon colored. Gently fold in ground walnuts, then yolk mixture into beaten egg whites.
Pour batter into two 8-inch greased cake pans that have been lined with wax paper and greased again. Bake at 350° F. for 25 to 30 minutes. Cool cakes in pans on wire racks for 5 minutes. Remove from pans and gently remove wax paper. Cool cakes completely and then spread top of cakes with whipped cream and chopped nuts.

WASHINGTON CAKE

1 pound butter
2 cups sugar
8 eggs
4-1/2 cups cake flour
1 teaspoon cinnamon and
    cloves, mixed

1/2 cup whipping cream
1/4 cup wine
1 pound raisins, chopped fine
1 pound currants
1 nutmeg, grated

Cream butter and sugar together until light and fluffy. Add eggs, one at a time, beating well after each addition. Add sifted remaining dry ingredients alternately with the cream and wine. Bake at 300° F. for around 1 hour and 30 minutes. Batter should be poured into a large and lightly greased tube pan. Serve plain or with your favorite glaze.

ZUCCHINI CAKE

3 eggs, beaten
2 cups sugar
2-1/2 cups cake flour
2 teaspoons baking soda
1/2 teaspoon baking powder

1 cup salad oil
1 tablespoon vanilla
3 teaspoons cinnamon
1/2 teaspoon salt
2 cups grated raw zucchini

Beat oil and sugar until well blended. Add beaten eggs and blend thoroughly. Add sifted remaining dry ingredients, mixing well. Stir in the zucchini and the vanilla. Pour batter into a greased and floured 10-inch Bundt pan or tube pan. Bake at 350°F. for 55 to 60 minutes. Cool before removing from pan.

Pour glaze over top.

CONFECTIONERS SUGAR GLAZE

1 cup confectioners sugar   3 teaspoons (approximately) milk

Combine and mix well the sugar and enough milk to make a glaze.

ZUCCHINI CHOCOLATE CAKE

1/2 cup butter
1/2 cup salad oil
2-1/2 cups cake flour
1/2 cup sour milk (put 1
    tablespoon vinegar in cup,
    add milk to 1/2 cup line)
2 cups grated raw zucchini

1-3/4 cups sugar
2 eggs
1 teaspoon baking powder
1 teaspoon baking soda
1 cup chopped pecans
1/3 cup cocoa
1/2 teaspoon salt

Beat together butter and oil. Add sugar and blend well. Then add 2 beaten eggs; beat and then sift together the flour, baking powder, salt, cocoa and baking soda. Add alternately with the sour milk. Stir by hand the grated zucchini and pecans. Grease and flour a Bundt or tube pan or 2 loaf pans. Pour batter in pan and bake at 325°F. for around 45 to 50 minutes.

Bake a cake...it will lead you to an exciting adventure...

Angel and
Angel Food Cakes

ANGEL FOOD CAKE

1-1/3 cups sugar
1 cup cake flour
1-1/4 teaspoons cream of tartar
1 teaspoon pure vanilla
    extract

1/2 teaspoon salt
1-1/2 cups egg whites
    (about 12)
1/2 teaspoon almond
    extract

Preheat oven to 350° F. Combine in a sifter 1/4 cup of the sugar, the cake flour and salt. Sift the mixture 3 times. Put the whites into the bowl of an electric mixer and beat until foamy. Add the cream of tartar. Continue beating until the whites hold soft peaks. While still beating, gradually add the remaining sugar, 1 tablespoon at a time. Fold in the vanilla and almond extracts. Sift approximately one-fourth of the flour mixture over the batter. Fold this in with a rubber sptaula. Continue adding the flour mixture one-fourth at a time; fold in after each addition.

Pour batter into an ungreased tube pan. Bake 45 minutes or until the top of the cake springs back when lightly touched.

Immediately turn the pan upside down, suspending if necessary, the tube part over the neck of a funnel or bottle. Let the cake stand in the pan until cold, about 1-1/2 hours.

FILLING FOR ANGEL FOOD CAKE

1 pint whipping cream (whipped)
1 package instant vanilla pudding
1 can peaches (mashed) drained
    (or pineapple)

1 envelope gelatin
    (unflavored)
3/4 cup sugar

Mix all dry ingredients together; add peaches or pineapple and let stand while whipping cream. Fold whipped cream into mixture and spread over 3 layers of the Angel Food Cake. (Slice cake in 3 layers in advance.)

HEAVENLY TOPPING FOR
ANGEL FOOD CAKE

Split the cake lengthwise and place a layer of ice cream between. Return top layer, wrap in foil and freeze.

1 cup drained crushed
    pineapple
1/4 cup chopped pecans
1 package whipped topping
    (Cool Whip or 1 pint whipping
    cream)

1 cup sliced ripe
    strawberries
1 cup miniature
    marshmallows

Combine the fruits, nuts and marshmallows; fold into the whipped topping and chill for at least 2 hours. To serve, slice the cake, spread with the topping. Looks pretty if topped with a maraschino cherry or with a strawberry halved.

MOCHA ANGEL FOOD CAKE

1 cup sifted cake flour
2 cups sugar
1/2 cup unsweetened cocoa -
1 tablespoon instant coffee
1-1/2 cups egg whites (from
  12 large eggs)

1/2 teaspoon salt
1-1/2 teaspoons cream
  of tartar
1-1/2 teaspoons vanilla
Mocha Cream, see recipe

Sift together cake flour, 1 cup of sugar, cocoa and coffee. Beat together egg whites, salt and cream of tartar until whites hold straight peaks when the beater is slowly withdrawn. Add remaining 1 cup sugar and vanilla and beat until whites hold peaks that tilt slightly when the beater is slowly withdrawn. Gradually fold in flour mixture until blended. Turn into an ungreased 10-inch angel-cake pan. Bake at 375° F. for 35 minutes or until done. If top browns too much toward end of baking period, cover loosely with foil. Invert pan and cool for 1 hour. Loosen edges and ease from pan. Cut in 3 layers with a serrated knife. Fill and frost with Mocha Cream. Refrigerate.

MOCHA CREAM

Whip together 2 cups heavy cream, 1 cup milk-chocolate flavor hot cocoa mix and 2 tablespoons instant coffee until cream is stiff.

MARBLE ANGEL FOOD CAKE

3/4 cup sifted cake flour, sifted 3 times with 1/2 cup sugar. Beat 1-1/4 cups egg whites (9 to 11 medium) with 1/4 teaspoon salt and 1-1/4 teaspoons cream of tartar until foamy. Sprinkle 3/4 cup additional sugar, 2 tablespoons at a time over egg whites. Beat well after each addition. Continue beating until stiff, straight peaks form when beater is raised. Add 1 teaspoon vanilla and 1/4 teaspoon almond extract. Sift in dry ingredients gradually, folding carefully but thoroughly. Divide batter in half. Sift together 2 tablespoons cake flour and 2 tablespoons sugar; fold into half of batter. Sift together 3 tablespoons cocoa, 2 tablespoons sugar; fold into remaining batter. Pour light and dark batters alternately into ungreased 9-inch tube pan. Bake in slow oven (325° F.) for 50 to 60 minutes. Cool in inverted pan for 1 hour.

CHOCOLATE ANGEL FOOD CAKE

3/4 cup sifted cake flour
4 tablespoons cocoa
1-1/4 cups egg whites
1/4 teaspoon salt

1 teaspoon cream
of tartar
1-1/4 cups sifted sugar
1 teaspoon vanilla

Sift flour, cocoa and sugar together 6 times. Beat egg whites until foamy throughout; add salt and cream of tartar and continue beating until eggs are stiff enough to hold a peak but not dry. Fold in vanilla. Sift 2 or 3 tablespoons dry ingredients at a time over egg whites and fold in lightly until all is used. Bake in 350°F. oven 50 to 70 minutes. Invert pan and let cake hang in pan until cool.

MERINGUE ANGEL FOOD CAKE

1-1/2 cups sugar
1/2 cup water
1-1/4 cups egg whites
1 teaspoon cream of tartar
1/4 teaspoon salt

1 teaspoon vanilla
1/4 teaspoon almond
extract
1 cup sifted cake
flour

Cook sugar and water to 242°F. or until syrup spins a long thread. Beat egg whites until frothy throughout. Add cream of tartar with salt and continue beating until egg whites hold a peak. Pour syrup slowly over beaten egg whites and continue beating until mixture is cold. Add flavorings. Fold in flour. Cut through batter with spatula to remove large air bubbles. Bake in ungreased tube pan in 350°F. oven for 45 minutes. Invert pan and let hang in pan until cool.

You can be enthusiastic about serving these delicious and elegant angel food cakes!

ANGEL GINGER CAKE

2 cups sifted cake flour
1 teaspoon baking soda
1 teaspoon ginger
1/4 teaspoon salt
6 tablespoons butter

1/2 cup sugar
2 eggs, well beaten
1/2 cup molasses
1/2 cup buttermilk

Sift flour, soda, ginger and salt together 3 times. Cream butter with sugar until fluffy. Add molasses, eggs and milk and beat well. Fold in sifted dry ingredients; beat thoroughly and pour into greased pan. Bake at 350°F. for 35 to 40 minutes. Makes 1 (8x10-inch) cake.

ANGEL CUSTARD CAKE

6 egg yolks, beaten
3/4 cup sugar
3/4 cup freshly squeezed lemon
  juice
1/2 teaspoon grated lemon rind
1 tablespoon unflavored gelatin

1/4 cup water
6 egg whites,
  beaten
3/4 cup sugar
1 large angel
  food cake

Make a custard of egg yolks, 3/4 cup sugar, lemon juice, and lemon rind. Cook over hot, not boiling water, until mixture coats a spoon. Remove from heat; add gelatin, softened in 1/4 cup water, and stir until gelatin is dissolved. Fold in egg whites, beaten with the remaining 3/4 cup sugar. Tear angel food cake into bite-size pieces; place in tube pan, oiled with salad oil. Pour custard over cake. Chill until firm; unmold. Fill center with whipped cream. Garnish with fresh cherries or maraschino cherries and green gumdrops if desired.

Really put yourself into the making of these cakes and you will be richly rewarded!

ANGEL LEMON CAKE

2 envelopes unflavored gelatin
6 large eggs, separated
1 angel food cake, cut into
  pieces
Yellow food coloring

1 cup lemon juice
2 cups sugar, divided
1 cup whipping cream
1/4 cup powdered sugar

Soften gelatin in lemon juice and let stand 5 minutes.

Beat egg yolks until thickened. Combine yolks, 1 cup sugar and gelatin in a small saucepan; cook over low heat until thickened. Set aside to cool.

Beat egg whites until soft peaks form. Gradually add 1 cup sugar; continue beating until peaks are stiff and glossy. Fold lemon mixture into egg whites.

Gently fold cake pieces into lemon mixture, coating all pieces well. Spoon into a lightly greased 10-inch tube pan; chill overnight.

Remove cake from pan by gently running knife between sides of cake and edge of pan; invert onto cake plate.

Combine whipping cream and powdered sugar; beat until soft peaks form. Add a few drops of yellow food coloring, mixing well. Spread on top and sides of cake. Store in refrigerator until serving time.

Different...delicious...sure to give a lot of eating pleasure!

ANGEL ICE CREAM CAKE

1 angel food cake
1 quart strawberry ice cream,
 softened
1 pint vanilla
 ice cream,
 softened

2 cups whipping cream
1/4 cup confectioners sugar
1/4 teaspoon almond
 extract
1/4 cup slivered almonds,
 toasted

Bake and completely cool angel food cake. Then split the cake horizontally into 4 layers.

Place bottom layer of cake on a cake plate and spread half of the strawberry ice cream; freeze. Add second layer and spread with vanilla ice cream; freeze. Repeat with third layer and remaining strawberry ice cream. Place remaining layer, cut side down, on top of cake. Cover and freeze cake several hours or overnight.

Beat whipping cream until foamy; gradually add the confectioners sugar and almond extract, beating until stiff peaks form. Frost sides and top of cake with whipped cream. Sprinkle with the toasted almonds, if desired.

A very unique cake... and very good!

ANGEL SHERRY PUDDING CAKE

2-1/2 cups milk
1/8 teaspoon salt
1 cup thick cream, whipped
2 tablespoons gelatin
3 eggs, separated

1/2 cup sugar
1 cup broken pieces of either
 Angel Food cake or Ladyfingers
1/2 cup Sherry

Put gelatin in 1/2 cup of the milk; let stand 5 minutes. Mix the egg yolks, sugar and remaining milk; cook over low heat until it begins to thicken. Remove from heat; stir in dissolved gelatin and sherry; mix well. Let cool. Beat egg whites. Pour cooled mixture over whites. Just before mixture begins to set, fold in whipped cream and cake pieces. Put into individual compotes or large mold. Let chill in refrigerator. Serves 6.

If you're looking for a conversation piece... here it is... turns out beautifully!

Cheesecakes

ALMOND CHEESECAKE

CRUST:

2 cups sliced almonds
2 teaspoons melted butter
1/2 teaspoon vanilla

4 tablespoons brown sugar
1 tablespoon water

Grind almonds in food processor until fine; add melted butter, brown sugar, vanilla and water while processor is going. Continue processing until mixture begins to fall from side of processor. Press into a 9-inch pie pan.

CAKE:

2 8-ounce packages cream cheese
2/3 cup sugar
3 tablespoons milk

3 eggs
1/8 teaspoon almond
extract

Beat cheese until light and creamy. Add eggs, one at a time, beating after each addition. Add sugar and almond extract. Beat until thick and lemon colored (about 5 minutes). Add milk, blending well. Pour into pie crust (unbaked). Bake 50 minutes at 325° F. Cool for 20 minutes.

TOPPING:

2 cups sour cream
2 teaspoons vanilla

3/4 cup sugar

Beat together the sour cream, sugar and vanilla. Spoon over cheesecake and spread smooth. Sprinkle with sliced almonds. Return to oven for 15 minutes at 325° F. Cool completely before serving. Better still, overnight.

An elegant cheesecake...for special occasions!

FABULOUS CHEESECAKE

2 packages (8-ounce) cream cheese
1 pound creamed cottage cheese
1-1/2 cups sugar
4 eggs, slightly beaten
3 tablespoons cornstarch
Fresh strawberries, blueberries,
peaches or pineapple

1 teaspon vanilla
1/2 pound butter, melted
1 pint sour cream
3 tablespoons flour
2 tablespoons lemon juice

Beat cream cheese and cottage cheese until smooth and creamy. Gradually beat in the sugar, then one egg at a time until well combined. At low speed, beat in cornstarch, flour, lemon juice and vanilla. Add melted butter and sour cream, beating just until smooth. Pour into prepared pan: 2 cups graham cracker crumbs, 2 tablespoons sugar, 1/2 cup softened butter mixed together well (use a springform pan). Bake at 325° F. for 1 hour and 10 minutes or until firm around the edges. Turn off oven; let cool completely in oven for 2 hours. Remove from oven and continue cooling; then refrigerate for several hours or until well chilled.

Serve with fresh, sweetened to taste strawberries, blueberries or peaches or with pineapple, as desired.

CHERRY CHEESECAKE

1 cup graham cracker crumbs
3 tablespoons butter, melted
3 (8-ounce) packages cream
  cheese, softened
2 teaspoons lemon juice
5 eggs
1-1/2 cups sour cream
1/2 teaspoon vanilla

3 tablespoons sugar
1/4 teaspoon cinnamon
1 cup sugar
1/4 teaspoon salt
2 tablespoons sugar
1 (21-ounce) can cherry
  pie filling

Combine graham cracker crumbs, 3 tablespoons sugar, butter and cinnamon; mix well. Press into a 10-inch springform pan; set aside. Beat cream cheese and lemon juice in a large mixing bowl until soft and creamy. Add 1 cup sugar, and mix well; add eggs one at a time, mixing well; add salt; beat on medium speed for 10 minutes. Pour mixture into crust and bake at 350° F. for 45 minutes. Remove to wire rack and let stand for 20 minutes. Combine sour cream, 2 tablespoons sugar and vanilla; stir well. Spread over cheesecake. Bake at 350° F. for 10 minutes; cool. Chill before removing sides from pan, top with cherry pie filling. Delicious!

"Isn't that beautiful?" is what you'll hear when you serve this cheesecake. Start looking for joy in baking cakes and you'll find it!

CHEESECAKE

1-1/2 cups graham cracker crumbs   2 tablespoons butter
2 tablespoons sugar   1/2 cup sugar
2 tablespoons flour   1/4 teaspoon salt
2 (8-ounce) packages cream cheese   1 teaspoon vanilla
4 egg yolks   1 cup whipping cream
4 stiffly beaten egg whites

Blend graham cracker crumbs with butter and 2 tablespoons sugar. Press into bottom of spring form pan.

Blend 1/2 cup sugar with flour, salt and cream cheese, mixing well. Add vanilla, stir in egg yolks and mix well. Add cream slowly and blend thoroughly. Fold in egg whites and pour mixture into crumb crust. Bake at 325°F. about 1 hour and 15 minutes or until center is set. When cooled, spread with whipped, sweetened cream.

LARRY'S FAMOUS CHEESECAKE

1-1/2 cups graham cracker crumbs   3/4 cup sugar
1/4 cup, plus 2 tablespoons   2 tablespoons sugar
   melted butter   1-1/2 teaspoons cinnamon
3 (8-ounce) packages cream   1 cup sugar
   cheese, softened   4 eggs
1 teaspoon vanilla   6 or 7 tablespoons milk
1 pint sour cream

Combine crumbs, 2 tablespoons sugar, butter, and cinnamon, mixing well. Press into a 10-inch springform pan; set aside.

Beat cream cheese in a large mixing bowl until soft and creamy. Gradually add 1 cup sugar, beating until soft and fluffy. Add eggs, one at a time, beating well after each addition. Add 6 or 7 tablespoons milk and blend well. Pour mixture into crust; bake at 350°F. for 25 to 35 minutes or until cake is set. Let cheesecake cool for around 30 minutes.

Beat sour cream and then add 3/4 cup sugar and the vanilla. Beat until thoroughly blended. Spread over cheesecake and bake for 10 minutes longer at 350°F. Cool completely or better still, chill 8 hours or overnight.

It's fun to bake cakes... especially these... enjoy life and try baking a cake now!

CREAMY CHEESECAKE

1/4 cup butter, melted
1/4 cup sugar
2 (8-ounce) packages cream
cheese, softened
1 (14-ounce) can Eagle Brand
Sweetened Condensed Milk
3 eggs

1/4 cup fresh lemon juice
1 cup graham cracker
crumbs
1/4 teaspoon salt
1 (8-ounce) carton
sour cream

Combine butter, crumbs and sugar well; pat firmly on bottom of buttered 9 or 10-inch springform pan. Set aside. Beat cream cheese until light and fluffy. Beat in Eagle Brand milk well, add eggs one at a time, beating well after each addition; add salt and beat until smooth. Stir in lemon juice. Pour into prepared pan. Bake 50 to 55 minutes at 300° F. Cool to room temperature; chill. Spread sour cream on cheesecake. Garnish as desired. Leftovers may be refrigerated for future use.

CHEESECAKES SUPREME

Makes 3 cheesecake pies or 1 very large cheesecake.

3-3/4 cups graham cracker crumbs
3/4 cup butter
2-3/4 cups sugar
3 tablespoons flour
1-1/2 teaspoons grated orange
rind
1 teaspoon grated lime rind
5 eggs
1/4 cup whipping cream
3/4 cup sugar

5 8-ounce packages
cream cheese, softened
1-1/2 teaspoons grated
lemon rind
1/4 teaspoon vanilla
2 egg yolks
Fresh strawberries
and whipped cream, for
topping (optional)

Combine graham cracker crumbs, 3/4 cup sugar and butter; stir well. Press mixture into 3 (9-inch) pie plates or 1 large springform pan. Beat cream cheese until soft and creamy. Gradually add 1-3/4 cups sugar, beating until fluffy. Add flour, citrus rind, and vanilla. Mix well. Add eggs, one at a time, and egg yolks, beating well after each addition. Stir in whipping cream. Pour into prepared crusts; bake at 400° F. for 5 minutes. Reduce heat to 250° F. and bake 30 minutes or until set. Cool. Two of the cheesecakes may be covered securely with plastic wrap and frozen for future use. Chill remaining cheesecake for 8 hours or overnight. If desired, spread sweetened fresh strawberries over cheesecake and top with dollops of sweetened whipped cream.

Have a lot of fun today...bake one of these cakes...

CHOCOLATE CHEESECAKE

Crust:

2 cups graham cracker crumbs
1/2 cup melted butter

1/4 cup sugar
1/8 teaspoon cinnamon

Filling:

4 eggs separated
1 pound cream cheese
1/2 cup hot strong coffee
1 teaspoon vanilla
1/8 teaspoon salt

1 cup sugar
2 packages (6-ounces
each) semi-sweet
chocolate bits

Topping:
1 cup heavy whipping cream
4 tablespoons sugar

Preheat oven to 350°F. Butter bottom and sides of a 9-inch springform pan. Blend crust ingredients and pat mixture to bottom and sides of pan. Set aside. Prepare filling by beating softened cream cheese until fluffy. Add sugar gradually (1/3 cup); continue beating until well blended. Add egg yolks one at a time, beating well after each addition. Melt the chocolate bits in a double boiler over hot, not boiling, water. Blend in the coffee, salt and vanilla and then blend all into the cream cheese mixture.

Beat egg whites to soft peaks; add remaining sugar until glossy peaks appear. Fold this gently into chocolate mixture and then pour into prepared crust. Bake 1 hour in 350°F. oven. Do not open the oven door. Turn oven off, but leave cake inside for 1 hour until completely cooled. Remove cake; chill. When ready to serve, whip cream and add sugar. Spread over top of cake.

Bake this cake and gather in your friends for a real treat...

GINGERSNAP CHEESECAKE

Crust:

2 cups finely ground gingersnap
crumbs

1/4 cup sugar
1/4 pound butter, melted

Filling:

1 8-ounce package cream cheese, softened
1 14-ounce can sweetened condensed milk
1/3 cup fresh lime juice
1/3 cup ginger marmalade
1 cup sliced fresh fruit (peaches, pineapple or
nectarines are preferable).

Combine crust ingredients and blend thoroughly. Line the bottom and halfway up the sides of a 9-inch springform pan. Beat cream cheese until light and fluffy. Beat in condensed milk and then the lime juice. Add marmalade and stir until well blended.

Line crust with sliced fruit. Pour cheese mixture over fruit and refrigerate for 2 hours or until cake is set.

This is an excellent summer dessert that requires no baking!

GINGERSNAP CHEESECAKE SUPREME

2 3-ounce packages cream cheese
2 cups chopped pecans
2-1/2 cups gingersnap crumbs
3 tablespoons sugar
2 tablespoons cold water
24 chopped maraschino cherries
1 cup whipping cream
1 tablespoon gelatin

Cream cheese until very soft. Blend in cherries and nuts. Whip cream until it begins to thicken and hold its shape. Beat in the sugar and blend well. Stir in the gelatin which has been softened in cold water and dissolved over hot water. Gradually fold in first mixture.

In a paper-lined pan, arrange alternate layers of gingersnap crumbs and the cheese mixture. Chill about 12 hours before serving.

LEMON CHEESECAKE

A very light and delicious cheesecake; especially good during the summer...no baking necessary!

1 cup sugar
1 8-ounce package cream cheese
1 3-ounce package lemon jello
1 teaspoon lemon flavoring
1 13-ounce can evaporated milk, chilled and whipped
1 cup water

Crust:
1-1/2 cups graham cracker crumbs   4 ounces butter
3 tablespoons sugar

Combine crust ingredients well; press into square baking dish and set aside.

Mix jello with 1 cup boiling water until completely dissolved. Set aside to cool. Mix cream cheese, sugar and flavoring until light and fluffy. Add the cooled jello and milk; pour slowly into crust.

Sprinkle the top evenly with 3/4 cup plain crushed graham cracker crumbs. Refrigerate until well chilled before serving. Cut in squares to serve, if desired.

A star cake...superb!

CHOCOLATE MARBLE CHEESECAKE

Crust:

1 cup graham cracker crumbs
3 tablespoons sugar

3 tablespoons melted butter

Filling:

3 8-ounce packages
  cream cheese
1 cup sugar
3 tablespoons flour
1 teaspoon vanilla

3 eggs
1 1-ounce square
  unsweetened chocolate, melted
6 or 7 tablespoons milk

Combine crumbs, sugar and melted butter; press onto bottom of 9-inch springform pan. Set aside.

Combine softened cream cheese, sugar, flour and vanilla, mixing until well blended. Blend in eggs, mixing well. Blend melted chocolate into 1 CUP BATTER. Spoon plain and chocolate batters alternately over crust; cut through batter with knife several times for marble effect. Bake at 450° F. for 10 minutes. Reduce oven temperature to 250° F.; continue baking 30 minutes. Loosen cake from rim of pan. Spread top of cake with sweetened whipped cream, if desired. Chill before serving.

Always try to bring out the best in your cakes!

WHITE CHOCOLATE CHEESECAKE

1/4 pound butter
2 cups very finely ground
  tea biscuit crumbs

1 ounce white chocolate,
  grated
1/4 cup sugar

Filling:

2 pounds (4 8-ounce packages)
  cream cheese
1-1/4 cups sugar
Pinch of salt

4 large eggs
3 ounces white chocolate,
  shaved or sliced thin

Topping:

2 cups sour cream
1/4 cup sugar

1 teaspoon vanilla
1 ounce white chocolate, shaved

Melt butter and combine with remaining crust ingredients until well blended. Press mixture over sides and bottom of an ungreased 10-inch springform pan.

Combine cream cheese and sugar and beat until soft and fluffy. Add salt and mix well. Add eggs one at a time, keeping mixer on lowest speed, just until egg has been incorporated into batter. Add shaved white chocolate and fold in on lowest speed. Pour into crust and bake 40 minutes in a preheated 350° F. oven Remove cake from oven and be sure to let stand for 10 minutes while you prepare the topping.

Combine sour cream, sugar and vanilla. Spread over top of cake and return to 350° F. oven for 10 minutes. Remove from oven and refrigerate immediately. When completely cooled decorate top of cake with the shaved white chocolate.

Out of a little effort comes an extraordinary cake!

CHOCOLATE SWIRL CHEESECAKE

Crust:
1/4 pound butter
2 cups very finely ground crumbs from Nabisco Famous Wafers (vanilla or chocolate)
1/4 cup sugar

Filling:
2 pounds (4 8-ounce packages) cream cheese
1-1/4 cups sugar
1-1/2 teaspoons vanilla extract
Pinch salt

4 large eggs
1-1/2 ounces German Sweet Chocolate, melted
1/2 teaspoon instant coffee powder

Topping:
2 cups sour cream
3/4 cup sugar

1 teaspoon vanilla

Combine crumbs, melted butter and sugar until well blended. Press mixture over sides and bottom of ungreased 10-inch springform pan. Combine cream cheese and sugar; beat until soft and fluffy. Add vanilla and salt and blend thoroughly. Add eggs, one at a time, keeping mixer at low speed to prevent too much air from destroying the proper consistency of the batter. Mix just until each egg is incorporated into the batter.

Reserve one cup of batter. Pour the remainder into the crust. Add the melted chocolate and instant coffee powder to the reserved cup of batter and blend well. Pour chocolate mixture into center of batter in the pan and cut through with a knife to achieve a swirl effect, but keep most of the chocolate in the center. Bake one hour in a preheated 350° F. oven.

Remove cake from oven and let stand on counter top for 10 minutes while preparing topping. Be sure to do this.

Combine sour cream, sugar and vanilla extract. Spread over top of cake and return to 350° F. oven for 10 minutes. Remove cake from oven and cool. Refrigerate for 8 hours or better, overnight.

One of the best cakes ever!

PRALINE CHEESECAKE

1-1/2 cups graham cracker
  crumbs
1/4 cup sugar

1/4 cup chopped pecans,
  toasted
1/4 cup melted butter

Filling:

3 packages (8-ounce) cream
  cheese, softened
1 cup brown sugar, packed
1 can (5-1/3 ounces) evaporated
  milk
2 tablespoons cake flour
1-1/2 teaspoons vanilla

3 eggs
1 cup pecan halves,
  toasted
1 cup dark corn syrup
1/4 cup cornstarch
2 tablespoons brown sugar
1 teaspoon vanilla

Crust: Combine crumbs, sugar and chopped pecans. Stir in melted butter. Press mixture over bottom and 1-1/2 inches up sides of springform pan. Bake in 350°F. oven for 10 minutes or less, until set.

Filling: Beat cream cheese, 1 cup brown sugar, evaporated milk, flour and 1-1/2 teaspoons vanilla until light and fluffy. Add eggs, beating just until blended. Pour mixture into baked crust and bake in 350°F. oven for 50 to 55 minutes, or until set. Cool in pan for 30 minutes, loosen sides, remove rim from pan. Cool completely. Arrange pecan halves over top.

Before serving, combine syrup, cornstarch and 2 tablespoons brown sugar in small saucepan. Cook and stir until thick and bubbly. Remove from heat, stir in vanilla. Cool slightly. Serve cheesecake with some of the warm sauce over the top.

Expand yourself and begin baking a cake today...

PERFECT CHEESECAKE

Crust:

1/2 cup graham cracker crumbs
1 tablespoon sugar
1/4 teaspoon cinnamon

1/4 teaspoon nutmeg
2 tablespoons melted
  butter

Filling:

1-3/4 cups sugar
3/4 teaspoon salt
3/4 teaspoon grated
  lemon rind
6 eggs
1/4 teaspoon vanilla

3 tablespoons plain flour
3/4 teaspoon grated orange
  rind
5 packages (8-ounce) cream
  cheese, softened
1/2 cup whipping cream

Blend the crust ingredients; press mixture on bottom and

sides of a greased springform pan.

Blend the cream cheese until soft and fluffy. Add the sugar gradually, beating well after each addition. Add eggs, one at a time, continuing to beat well. Add the sifted flour and salt alternately with the whipping cream blending thoroughly. Finally, add the vanilla and grated rinds.

Bake in 325° F. oven for 1 hour or until set. If you would like a topping, add 1 carton sour cream and bake an additional 5 minutes. Cool thoroughly before removing side of springform pan.

The best way to bake a cake is to begin... do this and you are well on your way to success...

SWEET POTATO CHEESECAKE

Crust:

1-2/3 cups graham cracker crumbs   4 tablespoons sugar
1/3 cup butter, melted

Filling:

2 envelopes unflavored gelatin   2 (8-ounce) packages cream
1/2 cup cold water   cheese, softened
3 eggs, separated   1-1/4 cups cooked, mashed
3/4 cup sugar   sweet potatoes
1/2 teaspoon salt   1 cup whipping cream,
1/3 cup milk   whipped
1/2 teaspoon vanilla

Topping:

1 cup whipping cream, whipped and sweetened to taste. Mandarin orange slices (optional).

Combine graham cracker crumbs, butter and sugar and blend well. Press into a 9-inch springform pan and chill.

Soften gelatin in cold water in top of a double boiler; stir in egg yolks, sugar, salt and milk. Place over water and bring water to a boil. Reduce heat, then cook, stirring constantly, until slightly thickened. After cream cheese and sweet potatoes have been combined together until light and fluffy, add the cooked mixture and blend until smooth. Beat egg whites until stiff but not dry. Fold egg whites, whipped cream and vanilla into the mixture. Spoon into prepared pan. Chill until set. Garnish with dollops of whipped cream and orange slices, if desired.

Pleasing, summertime cheesecake!

PUMPKIN CHEESECAKE

Crust:

1-1/2 cups biscuit mix   1/4 cup butter
2 tablespoons sugar

Filling:

1 (8-ounce) package cream   1/4 teaspoon ginger
  cheese, softened   1/4 teaspoon nutmeg
3/4 cup sugar   1 (16-ounce) can pumpkin
3 eggs   1/4 teaspoon vanilla
2 tablespoons flour   6 or 7 tablespoons milk
1 teaspoon cinnamon

Topping:

1-1/2 cups commercial sour cream   1/4 teaspoon vanilla
2 tablespoons sugar

Combine biscuit mix and 2 tablespoons sugar, stirring well; cut in butter with a pastry blender or 2 knives until mixture resembles coarse meal. Press mixture into a 9-inch square baking pan.

Beat cream cheese; gradually add the 3/4 cup sugar, beating until light and fluffy, until sugar dissolves. Add eggs, one at a time, beating well after each addition. Combine flour, cinnamon, ginger and nutmeg; stir well. Add to creamed mixture, beating well. Add pumpkin and 1/4 teaspoon vanilla to creamed mixture, mixing well. Pour batter over crust. Bake at 350° F. for 55 minutes or until set.

Beat sour cream and then add 2 tablespoons sugar and 1/4 teaspoon vanilla; beat until sugar is dissolved and well blended. Spread over cheesecake while hot. Refrigerate for at least 6 hours before serving.

Create a new cake...

Coffeecakes

APPLE COFFEE CAKE

1/4 cup butter
1 egg
2 teaspoons baking
powder
2/3 cup milk
1 cup finely chopped
cooking apples

3/4 cup sugar
1-3/4 cups cake flour
1/2 teaspoon nutmeg
1/4 teaspoon salt
1 teaspoon vanilla
1/3 cup sugar
1 teaspoon cinnamon

Cream butter; gradually add 3/4 cup sugar, beating well. Add the egg, beating well.

Sift together flour, baking powder, nutmeg and salt; add to creamed mixture alternately with the milk, mixing well after each addition. Stir in the vanilla. Pour batter into a greased and floured 9-inch square baking pan.

Combine apples, 1/3 cup sugar and cinnamon; mix well. Sprinkle over batter. Bake at 350°F. for 25 to 30 minutes or until tests done.

APRICOT ORANGE COFFEE CAKE

1 (8-ounce) package dried apricots
1/2 cup chopped pecans
1/4 cup cake flour
2 tablespoons butter
2 teaspoons baking powder
1/2 cup orange juice

1 cup sugar
1 egg
2 cups cake flour
1/4 teaspoon soda
1/4 teaspoon salt
1/4 cup water

Soak apricots in warm water to cover for 30 minutes; drain well and cut into 1/4-inch pieces.

Combine the apricot pieces and pecans; dredge with 1/4 cup flour and set aside.

Combine sugar and butter, beating until light and fluffy. Add egg and beat well. Sift the 2 cups flour, baking powder, soda and salt. Combine orange juice and water. Add flour mixture and orange juice mixture alternately to creamed ingredients, mixing lightly after each addition. Stir in apricots and pecans.

Spoon batter into wax paper-lined and greased 9 x 5 x 3-inch loaf pan. Bake at 350°F. for 1 hour or until tests done.

Bake a cake...it's fascinating!

APRICOT PECAN COFFEE CAKE

1 (16-ounce) can apricot halves
1/3 cup shortening
2 cups cake flour
1/2 teaspoon salt
1/2 cup chopped pecans

1/2 cup sugar
2 eggs
1 teaspoon baking powder
1/2 teaspoon soda

Drain apricots, reserving syrup; press apricots through a sieve or food mill. Add enough reserved syrup to apricots to make 1 cup; set aside.

Cream shortening and sugar until fluffy. Add eggs, one at a time, beating well after each addition.

Sift dry ingredients together and add alternately with apricots to creamed mixture; stir just until all ingredients are moistened. Stir in pecans. Spoon batter into a well-greased 9 x 5 x 3-inch loaf pan. Bake at 350° F. for 50 minutes or until tests done.

BANANA COFFEE CAKE

1/2 cup butter
Pinch of salt
1 cup chopped pecans
3 ripe bananas, mashed

1 teaspoon baking soda
1 cup sugar
2 eggs
2 cups flour

Mix butter, sugar and eggs together. Add dry ingredients, then mashed bananas and nuts. Pour in a greased loaf pan. Bake in 325° F. oven 40 to 50 minutes.

Enrich your life and others...bake one of these coffee cakes!

BANANA DATE NUT COFFEE CAKE

2 cups cake flour
1 teaspoon baking soda
1 teaspoon salt
1/2 cup chopped pecans
1/2 cup chopped dates
1 teaspoon vanilla

1 cup sugar
1/2 cup Crisco
2 whole eggs
2 or 3 small bananas,
  mashed
1/4 cup flour

Sift together flour, soda and salt and set aside. Cream Crisco and sugar until light and fluffy. Add eggs, one at a time, beating well after each addition. Blend in vanilla, then flour mixture alternately with the bananas. Dredge the pecans and dates in 1/4 cup flour and fold in. Pour into a greased and floured loaf pan and bake at 325° F. for around 45 minutes. Delicious plain or with cream cheese.

These coffee cakes turn out beautifully...

BANANA CRANBERRY COFFEE CAKE

2 cups fresh cranberries
1 cup water
2/3 cup sugar
2 cups cake flour
1/2 teaspoon salt
1/4 teaspoon baking soda
1/2 cup chopped pecans

1 cup sugar
1/3 cup Crisco
2 eggs
2 teaspoons baking powder
1 cup mashed bananas

Combine cranberries, 1 cup sugar and water; cook over medium heat about 5 minutes or until cranberries begin to pop. Drain and set aside.

Cream shortening; gradually add 2/3 cup sugar, beating until light and fluffy. Add eggs, one at a time, beating well after each addition. Sift dry ingredients; add to creamed mixture alternately with banana, mixing well after each addition. Fold in cranberries and pecans.

Line a greased 9 x 5 x 3-inch loaf pan with wax paper; grease wax paper. Spoon batter into pan. Bake at 350° F. for 1 hour or until coffee cake tests done. Cool 5 or 10 minutes in pan and then remove.

CHOCOLATE COCONUT COFFEE CAKE

1-1/4 cups milk
2-1/2 cups unsifted flour
1-1/2 teaspoons salt
4 tablespoons butter
1 egg
1 teaspoon vanilla

1 tablespoon lemon juice
1-1/2 teaspoons baking soda
3 ounces cream cheese
1 cup sugar
6 ounces cocoa
1 cup toasted coconut

Combine the milk with the lemon juice and set aside. Combine flour, baking soda and salt and set aside.

Cream the butter and cream cheese and gradually add the sugar, beating well. Beat in the egg and then add the cocoa and vanilla, blending well.

To this mixture, alternately blend in the milk and flour mixtures. Stir in the coconut.

Pour batter into a well greased 9 x 5 x 3-inch loaf pan and bake at 350° F. for 1 hour, or until tests done. Allow to cool for 5 to 10 minutes in pan and then remove to cake plate. Allow to cool completely before slicing.

BANANA SOUR CREAM COFFEE CAKE

1/2 cup chopped pecans
1/4 teaspoon cinnamon
1 cup sugar
1 cup mashed bananas
1/2 cup sour cream
1 teaspoon baking powder
1/4 teaspoon salt

1/4 cup sugar
1/2 cup shortening
2 eggs
1 teaspoon vanilla
2-1/2 cups cake flour
1 teaspoon soda

Combine pecans, 1/4 cup sugar and cinnamon; stir well and set aside.

Cream shortening and 1 cup sugar until light and fluffy. Add eggs, beating well after each addition. Add flour alternately with the sour cream, then stir in the vanilla and bananas just enough to blend.

Sprinkle half of reserved cinnamon mixture into bottom of a well greased Bundt pan; spoon half of batter into pan. Sprinkle remaining cinnamon mixture over batter, then spoon balance of batter into pan. Bake at 350°F. for 40 to 45 minutes or until tests done.

Cool coffee cake 5 minutes in pan on a wire rack. Serve warm or cold.

This cake slices perfectly...rates tops!

CARROT PECAN COFFEE CAKE

1-3/4 cups cake flour
1 teaspoon cinnamon
1 teaspoon soda
1/2 teaspoon salt
3/4 cup salad oil

2 eggs
1 cup sugar
1 cup grated carrots
1 cup chopped pecans

Combine cinnamon, soda, salt and flour and set aside.

Combine oil, sugar and eggs and beat until well blended. Add dry ingredients and mix just until blended. Fold in carrots and pecans and spoon batter into a greased and floured loaf pan; bake at 350°F. for 1 hour and 25 minutes or until coffee cake tests done. Cool in pan for 10 minutes and then remove from pan and cool completely.

This can be a simple family dessert or one for the most discriminating company to enjoy...

CINNAMON BUTTERMILK COFFEE CAKE

2-1/2 cups cake flour
1/2 cup butter
1 egg
1 teaspoon soda
1/2 cup chopped pecans

2 cups brown sugar,
　firmly packed
1/3 cup flour
1 cup buttermilk
1 teaspoon cinnamon

Combine 2-1/2 cups flour and sugar in a large mixing bowl. Cut in butter until mixture resembles coarse meal. Set aside 3/4 cup crumb mixture.

Combine remaining crumb mixture and 1/3 cup flour. Add egg, buttermilk, soda and cinnamon; stir until moistened.

Pour batter into a greased 9-inch square pan. Combine reserved crumb mixture with nuts; sprinkle over batter. Bake at 325° F. for 1 hour or until tests done. Cut into squares.

This coffee cake is tasty and unusual...

CRANBERRY COFFEE CAKE

1/2 cup butter
2 eggs
1 teaspoon baking powder
1 (8-ounce) carton sour
　cream
1/2 cup chopped pecans

1 cup sugar
2-1/2 cups cake flour
1 teaspoon soda
1 teaspoon vanilla
1 (16-ounce) can whole
　berry cranberry sauce

Cream butter and gradually add sugar, beating until light and creamy. Add eggs, one at a time, beating well after each addition. Combine dry ingredients and add alternately with sour cream, beating well. Blend in the vanilla extract.

Spoon 1/3 of mixture into a greased and floured 10-inch tube pan or Bundt pan. Spread 1/3 cranberry sauce over batter. Repeat layers twice more, ending with cranberry sauce. Sprinkle pecans over top.

Bake at 325° F. for 1 hour or until done. Let cool 5 minutes before removing from pan. Drizzle glaze over top.

GLAZE

1 cup confectioners sugar
1/2 teaspoon vanilla extract

2 tablespoons milk

Combine all ingredients; stir well and drizzle over warm cake.

This cake has rich color and pleasing flavor...

CHERRY CHOCOLATE COFFEE CAKE

1 square unsweetened chocolate
2 tablespoons water
1/2 cup shortening
1-1/2 cups cake flour
1 cup sugar
1 teaspoon soda
1/2 teaspoon salt

2/3 cup buttermilk
mixed with 2 tablespoons
cherry juice
1 egg
1/4 cup well-drained
maraschino cherries,
cut in 8ths

Grease an 8 x 8 x 2-inch pan, line bottom with wax paper, grease paper. Set aside. Preheat oven at 350°F.

Put chocolate and water into a custard cup and set in hot water to melt. Stir until smooth and cool.

Cream shortening, then add sugar beating until light and fluffy. Sift flour with soda and salt three times. Add alternately with the buttermilk and cherry juice, beating well after each addition. Add egg and cooled chocolate and beat in well.

Pour batter into the prepared pan. Sprinkle cherries over top of batter. Bake about 35 minutes. Cool in pan on cake rack 5 minutes, then turn out on rack and strip off paper. When cool, spread top with Coffee Butter Frosting.

COFFEE BUTTER FROSTING

3 tablespoons freshly made coffee
1/4 cup softened butter
2 cups sifted confectioners sugar

1/4 teaspoon salt
1 tablespoon light
corn syrup

Cream butter until smooth and shiny; gradually blend in sugar alternately with about 3 tablespoons coffee. Beat in salt and white corn syrup until mixture has good spreading consistency. Very good for Chocolate, White and Yellow cakes.

This delicious cake has rich, appealing flavor!

STRAWBERRY PECAN COFFEE CAKE

3-1/2 cups cake flour
1 teaspoon salt
2 cups sugar
1-1/4 cups vegetable oil
1-1/4 cups chopped pecans

1 teaspoon baking soda
1 tablespoon cinnamon
4 eggs
2 cups thawed sliced
frozen strawberries

Combine dry ingredients. Add eggs, oil, strawberries and pecans; stir just until all ingredients are moistened.

Spoon batter into 2 well greased 9 x 5 x 3-inch loaf pans. Bake at 350°F. for 60 to 70 minutes or until tests done. Cool in pan for 5 minutes; remove to wire rack to cool.

FIG COFFEE CAKE

1/2 cup firmly packed brown sugar
2 tablespoons butter
1/2 teaspoon cinnamon
10 fig-filled bar cookies,
  (Fig-Newtons)
2 eggs
1 teaspoon vanilla extract

3/4 cup sugar
1/3 cup melted butter
2 cups cake flour
1 teaspoon baking
  powder
1/2 teaspoon salt
1/2 cup milk

Combine brown sugar, 2 tablespoons softened butter, cinnamon and crumbled fig cookies; mix well and set aside.

Beat eggs until frothy; add sugar and melted butter and beat well. Sift flour, baking powder and salt and gradually add alternately with the milk, mixing well. Stir in vanilla.

Pour half of batter into a greased and floured 8-inch square pan; top with half of fig mixture. Pour remainder of batter over fig layer. Sprinkle remaining fig mixture on top. Bake at 350° F. for 40 to 45 minutes or until cake tests done.

HONEY COFFEE CAKE

1 cup all-purpose white flour
1 cup whole wheat flour
1 teaspoon salt
1/2 teaspoon ginger
1 cup milk
1/4 cup Wesson oil

1-1/2 teaspoons baking powder
1 teaspoon baking soda
1/2 teaspoon cinnamon
1 large egg
1/2 cup honey
1/2 cup pecans, chopped

Line bottom of 9 x 5 x 3-inch loaf pan with wax paper; grease paper. Combine flours, baking powder, baking soda, salt, cinnamon and ginger and set aside.

Beat egg until foamy; add milk, honey and oil; beat to blend. Add flour mixture and stir until moistened. Stir in pecans. Turn into prepared pan and bake in 350° F. oven until done; 45 to 50 minutes. Cool 5 minutes in pan and then turn on a wire rack. Remove wax paper; turn right side up. Cool completely before slicing.

You can't forget the fine flavor, texture and color of these cakes...

LEMON COFFEE CAKE NO. 1

1/2 cup butter
1 cup sugar
2 eggs
2 cups cake flour
1 teaspoon baking powder

1/2 teaspoon salt
1/2 cup milk
1/2 cup chopped pecans
Grated rind of 1 lemon

Cream the butter and sugar until light and fluffy. Add eggs, one at a time, beating well after each addition. Sift the dry ingredients and add alternately with the milk, mixing well after each addition. Stir in the pecans and lemon rind.

Pour batter into a greased and floured 9 x 5 x 3-inch pan. Bake at 350° F. for 55 minutes or until tests done. Pour glaze over coffee cake. Cool 10 to 15 minutes before removing from pan.

LEMON GLAZE

1/2 cup confectioners sugar   Juice of 1 lemon

Combine ingredients, mixing well. Pour over warm cake.

LEMON COFFEE CAKE NO. 2

3/4 cup butter
3 eggs
1/4 teaspoon salt
1/2 cup buttermilk
3/4 cup chopped pecans
3/4 cup confectioners sugar

1-1/2 cups sugar
2-1/2 cups cake flour
1/4 teaspoon soda
Grated rind of 1 lemon
Juice of 2 lemons

Cream butter and sugar until light and fluffy; add eggs, one at a time, beating well after each addition. Sift together the dry ingredients and add alternately with the buttermilk; stir just until all ingredients are moistened. Stir in lemon rind and pecans. Spoon batter into a greased and floured 9 x 5 x 3-inch loaf pan. Bake at 325° F. for 1 hour and 15 minutes, or until tests done. Cool for 15 minutes and remove from pan.

Combine lemon juice and powdered sugar; stir well. Punch holes in top of warm cake and pour on glaze.

Surprisingly good coffee cakes!

PECAN SUGAR COFFEE CAKE

2/3 cup butter
1 cup sugar
1/2 cup brown sugar,
    firmly packed
1 teaspoon vanilla extract
2-1/2 cups cake flour
1 teaspoon baking powder
2 eggs

1 teaspoon soda
1/2 teaspoon salt
1 teaspoon cinnamon
1 cup chopped pecans
1/2 cup brown sugar,
    firmly packed
1/2 teaspoon cinnamon

Cream butter and 1 cup sugar and 1/2 cup brown sugar until light and fluffy. Add eggs, one at a time, beating well after each addition; stir in vanilla.

Sift together flour, baking powder, salt and 1 teaspoon cinnamon. Add alternately with buttermilk, mixing well after each addition.

Pour batter into a greased and floured 9 x 5 x 3-inch loaf pan. Combine pecans, 1/2 cup brown sugar and 1/2 teaspoon cinnamon; stir well and spinkle over batter.

Bake at 350° F. for 35 minutes or until tests done.

SOUR CREAM COFFEE CAKE

1/2 cup chopped pecans
2 teaspoons cinnamon
1 cup butter
2 eggs
1 teaspoon baking
    powder

2 tablespoons brown sugar,
    firmly packed
1 cup sugar
2-1/2 cups cake flour
1 teaspoon soda
1 cup sour cream

Combine pecans, brown sugar and cinnamon; stir well and set aside.

Cream butter and sugar, beating until fluffy. Add eggs, one at a time and beat well. Sift dry ingredients and add alternately with the sour cream. Spoon half into a greased and floured Bundt pan; sprinkle half of pecan mixture over batter. Repeat layers. Bake at 350° F. for 35 to 40 minutes. Cool 5 minutes and invert onto serving plate. Store overnight in airtight container, after drizzling glaze over top.

Glaze: 1-1/4 cups confectioners sugar, sifted, 1 tablespoon milk, 1/4 teaspoon vanilla extract. Combine all ingredients and stir well.

Don't pass these up...bake one soon!

LEMON LIGHT COFFEE CAKE

3/4 cup evaporated milk
1 teaspoon soda
1 cup sugar
1 teaspoon grated lemon rind
2 teaspoons baking powder
1/2 cup firmly packed brown
   sugar
2 tablespoons lemon juice

2 tablespoons vinegar
1/2 cup butter, softened
2 eggs
1-3/4 cups cake flour
1/2 teaspoon salt
1 tablespoon cinnamon
1 cup sifted
   confectioners sugar

Combine evaporated milk and vinegar; stir in soda and set aside.

Cream butter and sugar until light and fluffy. Add eggs, one at a time, beating well after each addition. Add lemon rind; beat well.

Sift together the dry ingredients; add to creamed mixture alternately with milk, beating well. Spread one half of batter in a greased and floured 10-inch tube pan.

Combine brown sugar and cinnamon; sprinkle half of mixture over batter. Spoon remaining batter into pan; sprinkle with remaining cinnamon-sugar. Bake at 350° F. about 45 minutes or until tests done. Cool in pan 5 minutes and then remove.

Combine confectioners sugar and lemon juice; spoon over warm cake.

This cake can't be beat for flavor...

ORANGE PECAN COFFEE CAKE

1/2 cup butter, softened
2 eggs
2 teaspoons grated orange rind
2-1/2 teaspoons baking powder
3/4 cup orange juice
2-1/2 teaspoons orange juice

3/4 cup sugar
2-1/2 cups cake flour
1 teaspoon salt
1/2 cup chopped pecans
1/2 cup sifted
   confectioners sugar

Cream butter and 3/4 cup sugar until light and fluffy. Add the eggs, one at a time, beating well after each addition. Add grated orange rind, blending well.

Sift flour, baking powder and salt and add alternately with 3/4 cup orange juice. Mix well after each addition. Stir in pecans.

Pour batter into a greased 9 x 5 x 3-inch loaf pan. Bake at 350° F. for 50 to 55 minutes or until tests done. Cool for 10 minutes in pan and then remove and cool completely.

Combine 2-1/2 teaspoons orange juice and powdered sugar; drizzle over loaf. Wrap and store overnight before serving.

A fun cake...fun to make, to give and to get!

SOUR CREAM COFFEE CAKE SUPREME

3 cups cake flour
1-1/2 teaspoons each, baking powder
    and baking soda
1/4 teaspoon salt
3 sticks butter, at room temperature

1-1/2 cups sugar
3 large eggs
1-1/2 cups sour cream
1-1/2 teaspoons vanilla

Filling/Topping:
1 cup firmly packed brown sugar
1 cup walnuts or pecans, chopped
1-1/2 teaspoons cinnamon
2 tablespoons vanilla
2 tablespoons milk
confectioners sugar (garnish)

Butter a 10-inch tube pan. Sift together the flour, baking powder, soda and salt. Combine butter and sugar and beat until soft and fluffy. Add eggs, one at a time, beating well after each addition. Blend in sour cream and vanilla alternately with the sifted dry ingredients, beating well.

Combine the brown sugar, nuts and cinnamon. Put one-third of the batter into the tube pan. Sprinkle half of the brown sugar mixture over it. Repeat with a third of the batter and the remaining brown sugar mixture. Top with remaining third of batter.

Combine the vanilla and milk and spoon over the top. Bake at 325°F. for 60 to 70 minutes. Cool 10 minutes before removing from pan. Dust generously with confectioners sugar.

A memorable coffee cake...

SPECIAL STRAWBERRY JAM COFFEE CAKE

3 cups cake flour
3/4 teaspoon cream of tartar
1 cup butter
1 teaspoon vanilla
4 eggs
1/2 cup buttermilk

1 teaspoon salt
1-1/2 cups sugar
1/2 teaspoon soda
1/4 teaspoon lemon juice
1 cup strawberry jam
1 cup chopped nuts

Combine flour, salt, cream of tartar and soda and set aside.

Combine sugar, butter, vanilla and lemon juice and cream until light and fluffy. Add eggs, one at a time, beating well after each addition. Stir together jam and buttermilk; add to creamed mixture alternately with dry ingredients, mixing just until blended. Stir in nuts.

Spoon batter into 2 greased 9 x 5 x 3-inch loaf pans. Bake at

350°F. for 55 minutes or until cake tests done. Cool 15 minutes; remove from pans onto cooling racks.

Excellent as is and exquisite topped with whipped cream.

SPICY COFFEE CAKE

2-1/2 cups cake flour
1/2 teaspoon salt
1/2 teaspoon nutmeg
1/2 cup chopped pecans
1-3/4 cups sugar

1 teaspoon baking soda
1/2 teaspoon cinnamon
1/2 cup pitted dates, cut fine
3 large eggs
1 cup sour cream

Sift together flour, soda, salt, cinnamon and nutmeg; toss dates with 1/2 cup of mixture and set all aside.

Beat eggs slightly; gradually beat in sugar until thickened; add sour cream and beat to blend. Gradually and gently beat in flour mixture until batter is smooth. Add pecans to date mixture and gently fold into batter.

Pour into a greased 9 x 9 x 1-3/4-inch cake pan. Bake at 350°F. for around 35 to 40 minutes. Center may sink slightly but this will not affect texture. Loosen edges and turn out on a wire rack, then turn right side up and cool completely.

STRAWBERRY COFFEE CAKE

2 cups cake flour
1/4 teaspoon salt
1/2 cup chopped pecans
1/2 cup corn oil
1 teaspoon baking soda

1 cup sugar
2 large eggs
1 10-ounce package frozen
   sweetened strawberries,
   thawed but undrained

Grease and flour a 9 x 5 x 3-inch loaf pan. Sift together the flour, baking soda and salt; stir in sugar and then pecans.

Beat eggs and oil until well blended; add undrained strawberries and beat just until blended. Add flour mixture and beat until mixture is smooth and strawberries are in small pieces. Turn into prepared pan.

Bake at 350°F. for 1 hour or until tests done. Cool before loosening edges and removing from pan. Cool completely. (You may substitute 1 pint fresh strawberries, sweetened to taste when they are in season, if desired).

These coffee cakes are interesting, delicious and nutritious...

SWEET POTATO COFFEE CAKE

1-1/2 cups sugar
2 eggs
2 cups cake flour
1 teaspoon nutmeg
1/2 teaspoon salt
1 cup chopped pecans

1/2 cup Wesson oil
1/3 cup milk
1-1/2 teaspoons cinnamon
1 teaspoon soda
1 cup cooked, mashed
   sweet potatoes

Combine sugar, oil, eggs and milk; beat at medium speed just until combined.

Sift together the dry ingredients and add to egg mixture, mixing just until moistened. Stir in sweet potatoes and pecans.

Spoon batter into 2 greased and floured loaf pans or coffee cans (1-pound size). Bake at 350° F. for 1 hour or until done. Let cool in pans for 10 minutes; remove and complete cooling.

Very simple but incredibly good!

TROPICAL COFFEE CAKE

2 cups cake flour
2 teaspoons baking powder
1 (8-ounce) carton peach-flavored
   yogurt
1/2 cup salad oil
1 cup grated coconut

1 cup sugar
1/2 teaspoon salt
2 eggs
1/3 cup sugar
1 teaspoon cinnamon

Combine oil and 1 cup sugar and beat well. Add eggs, one at a time, beating well after each addition. Add sifted flour, baking powder and salt alternately with the yogurt, blending well. Pour into a greased and floured 9-inch square pan.

Combine coconut, 1/3 cup sugar and cinnamon. Sprinkle over top. Bake at 350° F. for 40 minutes or until cake tests done.

A stimulating change and a delightful blend of ingredients!

Fruitcakes

CHINESE FRUITCAKE

1 pound coconut
1/2 pound candied
cherries, green
1 pound chopped pecans

1/2 pound candied cherries, red
1 pound dates, cut in small
pieces
2 cans sweetened condensed milk

Grease large loaf pan or 2 small loaf pans. Combine all ingredients. blending well. Bake at 300° F. until top is brown (about 1 hour).

JAPANESE FRUIT CAKE

1-1/3 cups butter
4-1/2 cups cake flour
5 eggs
1-1/2 teaspoons vanilla extract

2-2/3 cups sugar
1-1/3 cups milk
2-2/3 teaspoons
baking powder

Use standard cake mixing method and divide batter into two parts. To one part add:

1 teaspoon allspice
1/2 teaspoon cloves

1/4 cup chopped raisins
1/4 cup chopped pecans

Dust raisins and pecans with flour.

Bake four 8-inch layers in two parts at 350° F. for 20 to 25 minutes or until done. Spread with coconut filling and frost with Seven Minute Frosting.

Filling: Juice and finely grated rind of 2 lemons
l large coconut, grated
2 cups sugar
1 cup boiling water
2 tablespoons cornstarch

Put all ingredients, except cornstarch, in saucepan; mix well and place over medium heat. When mixture begins to boil, add cornstarch (dissolved in 1/2 cup cold water). Cook mixture until it turns clear and will drop from a spoon.

Seven Minute Frosting: 2 egg whites, 1-1/2 cups sugar,
1-1/2 teaspoons light corn syrup,
1/3 cup cold water, dash of salt

Mix ingredients in top of double boiler. Water in bottom should be boiling. Have electric mixer ready to beat and cook frosting for seven minutes, beating all the time. Add vanilla and frost entire cake.

A family recipe...at least 50 years old...beautiful color, tantalizing aroma and fine flavor!

FRUIT CAKE (SMALL)

1 cup flour
1/4 teaspoon cloves
1/2 cup each of candied
    orange & lemon peel
1 cup pecans, chopped
3 eggs
1/4 teaspoon allspice
1 cup raisins
1/4 cup maraschino cherry juice

1/4 teaspoon cinnamon
1 cup chopped figs
1/4 cup maraschino
    cherries, chopped
1/2 cup butter
1/2 teaspoon baking powder
1/4 teaspoon mace
1/2 cup brown sugar, packed

Sift together all dry ingredients except sugar. Cream butter and sugar until light and fluffy. Add eggs, one at a time, beating well after each addition. Mix dry ingredients and fruit together, then add cherry juice. Add fruit mixture to creamed mixture. Mix well. Bake in greased pan (8 x 5 x 3-inch) about 2-1/2 hours at 250° F.

SOUTHERN FROZEN FRUIT CAKE

1 cup whipping cream
1/2 cup sugar
1/4 teaspoon salt
1 teaspoon vanilla extract
2 cups vanilla wafer crumbs
1/4 cup candied green cherries
1 cup chopped pecans

2 cups milk
1/4 cup cake flour
2 eggs
1 cup golden raisins
1/2 cup candied red
    cherries

Chill whipping cream and whip; set aside.

Scald milk in top of double boiler. Mix together flour, sugar, salt; add to milk all at once and cook over hot water until smooth and thick. Stir constantly.

Pour mixture over beaten eggs gradually and return to double boiler, cooking about 3 minutes until thickened, still stirring constantly. Add vanilla. Cool. Stir in raisins, crumbs, chopped fruits and nuts. (Reserve a few of the whole green and red fruits and whole pecans for the top). Fold in the whipped cream.

Pour into a 1-1/2 quart loaf pan that you have greased and bottom-lined with wax paper. Arrange the whole fruits and nuts over top. Bake at 300° F. for 1-1/2 hours. Wrap and freeze. This should keep about 2 weeks.

SOUTHERN MOIST FRUIT CAKE

2 cups sugar
3/4 cup milk
1/2 teaspoon salt
6 eggs
1 cup crushed pineapple,
  well drained
1 cup chopped pecans
1/2 box dark seedless raisins
1-1/2 pounds crystallized cherries
  (red and green)

1 cup butter
2 teaspoons soda
3-1/2 cups cake flour
2 cups cooked dried apples
1 teaspoon each; cloves
  nutmeg, and 2 teaspoons
  cinnamon
1/2 box light seedless
  raisins
1 box (8-ounce) dates

Cream butter and sugar until light and fluffy; add eggs, one at a time, beating well after each addition. Sift together flour, soda, salt, cloves, nutmeg and cinnamon. Cut fruits in small pieces. Use 1 cup of flour mixture and dredge fruit well. Add this and remaining flour alternately with the milk to first mixture.

Add pineapple and cooked apples to batter with your hands, mixing thoroughly.

Pour into greased and floured pans. This should make 6 loaf pans (7-1/2 x 3-1/2 x 2-1/2-inches) and two tube pans. Bake loaf pans about 1 hour and tube pans about 1-1/2 hours or until done. Bake at 300° F.

SOUTHERN LEMON FRUIT CAKE

1 pound butter
6 eggs, separated
4 cups cake flour
1/2 pound candied cherries
1 quart pecans

1 pound light brown sugar
3 teaspoons lemon juice
1 teaspoon baking powder
1/2 pound candied pineapple

Cream butter and sugar; add egg yolks, one at a time, beating well after each addition. Add lemon juice and mix well. Sift together 2 cups flour with baking powder and stir in. Cut pineapple, cherries and nuts in small pieces. Stir them into 2 cups flour; stir into the first mixture.

Beat egg whites stiff; fold into cake mixture. Cover and let stand overnight. Next morning, stir well and pour into a tube pan that you have greased and lined with wax paper. Bake at 250° F. for 3 hours or until done.

These are the cakes to send to your friends, in town or out of town...

TEXAS FRUIT CAKES

1 pound pitted dates
1/2 pound candied pineapple
4 cans Angel Flake coconut

1 pound pecans
1/2 pound candied cherries
2 cans Eagle Brand milk

Chop dates, nuts, fruit. Combine all ingredients and mix well. Let stand (covered) overnight in refrigerator.

Place in miniature muffin tins (I use the miniature paper cups). Bake at 325° F. for 28 to 30 minutes or until golden brown. Do not overbake...they tend to harden a bit after cooking.

(Will keep in air-tight tins for weeks).

WHITE FRUIT CAKE SOUTHERN STYLE

1-1/2 cups butter
2 cups sugar
6 eggs
1 teaspoon nutmeg
1 teaspoon vanilla
1/2 cup bourbon

2 teaspoons baking powder
4 cups cake flour
1 pound candied cherries
1 pound candied pineapple,
   cut into large pieces
1 pound chopped pecans

Cream butter and sugar until light and fluffy. Add eggs, one at a time, beating well after each addition. Add nutmeg, vanilla and bourbon. Sift baking powder, 3 cups flour and fold into the batter.

Dredge fruit in 1 cup flour and place fruit in the oven 5 minutes. Add flour-coated fruit to the batter. Pour into tube pan and bake 3 hours at 275° F.

This cake will win compliments...it is moist with good old time flavor...

FRUIT CAKE (UNBAKED)

2 cups raisins
1 cup dates
1 pound graham crackers
1 cup honey
2 teaspoons cinnamon
1/2 teaspoon nutmeg
1 cup each: candied lemon peel,
   candied orange peel

1 cup dried figs
1 cup each
   walnuts and pecans
1 cup butter
2 teaspoons vanilla
1 teaspoon mace
1/2 teaspoon allspice

Cut up fruits and nuts. Roll graham crackers very fine or buy crackers already prepared. Cream butter and honey, add vanilla and let stand 2 hours. Then add spices to cracker crumbs and then combine with fruit-nut mixture.

Pack into loaf pans that have been lined with wax paper. Store in a very cool place. You can half the recipe if you want to.

PERFECT FRUIT CAKE

4 cups chopped pecans
2 cups unchopped crystallized
   cherries
5 slices crystallized pineapple,
   each slice cut into eighths
1 cup flour

1-1/2 teaspoons baking
   powder
1/4 teaspoon salt
4 eggs
1 cup sugar
1 teaspoon vanilla

Grease bottom and sides of a 2 quart tube pan and line bottom with brown paper or parchment paper.

Combine cherries and pineapple in a mixing bowl. Combine the flour, baking powder and salt in a sifter and sift over the fruits.

Combine eggs, sugar and vanilla in another mixing bowl and beat until blended. Pour this over the fruit and stir with a slotted spoon.

Pour batter into the prepared pan and bake 1-1/2 hours at 250°F. At end of that time, set cake pan into a pan of boiling water and continue baking 15 minutes longer.

A moist, delicious cake you will be proud to serve...

Poundcakes

ALMOND POUND CAKE

2/3 cup butter
1 cup sugar
3 eggs
1/2 cup blanched almonds,
    finely ground

1-1/2 cups cake flour
1 teaspoon baking powder
1/4 cup blanched almonds,
    coarsely chopped
1/2 teaspoon almond flavoring

Cream butter, add sugar gradually, then eggs, one at a time, beating well after each addition until soft and fluffy. Add ground almonds and flavoring and mix thoroughly. Add sifted dry ingredients; blend thoroughly. Spoon into greased and floured 9 x 5 x 3-inch loaf pan and sprinkle with the chopped almonds. Bake at 325° F. for 45 to 50 minutes or until tests done.

APRICOT POUND CAKE

1 cup butter
6 eggs
1 teaspoon orange extract
1 teaspoon rum extract
3 cups flour
1/2 cup apricot nectar

2-1/2 cups sugar
1 teaspoon vanilla extract
1/2 teaspoon lemon extract
1/4 teaspoon baking powder
1 cup sour cream
1/4 teaspoon salt

Cream together butter and sugar until soft and fluffy. Add eggs one at a time, blending well after each addition. Stir in the flavorings well. Add the sifted dry ingredients alternately with the sour cream and apricot nectar.

Lightly grease a 3 quart Bundt pan or tube pan and bake at 325° F. for 1 hour and 15 minutes or until done.

Treat each recipe as a special friend...this is the secret...

BUTTERMILK POUND CAKE

3 cups flour
2 sticks butter
5 large eggs
1 teaspoon vanilla

3 cups sugar
3/4 cup buttermilk
1/2 teaspoon baking powder
1/4 teaspoon almond extract

Using 1/2 cup Crisco, grease tube pan well and set aside.

Cream together the butter and sugar until light and fluffy. Add eggs, one at a time, beating well after each addition. Add sifted dry ingredients alternately with the buttermilk and vanilla extract and almond extract. Bake, starting in cold oven, at 350° F. on middle rack for 1 hour and 20 minutes. Cut next day!

You'll need no coaxing to bake this cake...

BEST POUND CAKE

1-1/2 cups butter
1/4 teaspoon baking soda
2-1/4 cups sugar
2 teaspoons vanilla
8 large eggs, separated
3/4 teaspoon cream of tartar

3 cups cake flour
1/2 teaspoon mace
2 tablespoons freshly
squeezed lemon juice
1/4 teaspoon salt
Confectioners sugar

Grease and flour a 3-1/2 quart Bundt pan or a 10" x 4" tube pan and set aside.

Cream butter until light and fluffy. Add the sugar gradually, beating thoroughly. Beat in the egg yolks, one at a time, beating well after each addition. Stir in the vanilla extract and the lemon juice and blend well. Sift the flour, mace and baking soda and salt 3 times, then add one-half cup at a time, beating well after each addition. Beat at least 10 minutes.

Beat the egg whites and cream of tartar until soft peaks form and fold into creamed mixture. Bake at 300° F. for 2 hours or until done. Turn off heat and leave in oven 30 minutes and then let stand in pan on wire rack for 30 minutes. When completely cold, sprinkle with confectioners sugar.

This kind of cake is the real thing...

BANANA POUND CAKE

1 box (1-pound) light brown
sugar
1 cup granulated sugar
1/2 pound real butter
5 eggs
2 large bananas, mashed

3 cups flour
1/2 teaspoon baking powder
1/2 teaspoon salt
1 cup milk
1 teaspoon vanilla
1 cup chopped pecans

Cream sugars with butter until light and fluffy. Add eggs, one at a time, beating well after each addition. Stir in mashed bananas.

Sift flour with baking powder and salt. Add to first mixture alternately with milk and vanilla. Stir in the pecans. Pour into a well greased tube pan and bake at 325° F. for 1-1/2 hours or until done.

Place upside down on a cake rack and when cooled, invert and turn out onto rack.

Really luscious...

CANDY BAR POUND CAKE

1 cup butter

2 cups sugar

4 eggs

8 Hershey bars

1 cup chopped pecans

1 cup buttermilk

1/4 teaspoon baking soda

2-1/2 cups cake flour

2 teaspoons vanilla

Cream butter until light and fluffy, gradually adding the sugar. Add eggs, one at a time, beating well after each addition. Add sifted dry ingredients alternately with the buttermilk. Add melted Hershey bars, vanilla and pecans. (Roll pecans in flour until lightly coated).

Grease and flour tube pan or Bundt pan and bake at 325° F. for 1-1/2 hours or until done.

A great favorite!

CHOCOLATE RIPPLE POUND CAKE

2-1/2 cups sugar

4 cups cake flour

1 tablespoon vanilla extract

1/4 teaspoon almond extract

2 cups butter

10 eggs

2 squares unsweetened
chocolate, melted

Cream butter and sugar until light and fluffy. Add eggs, one at a time, until well blended, after each addition. Add vanilla and almond extracts and blend in thoroughly. Add flour 1/2 cup at a time, beating well after each addition. Cream for 10 minutes.

Grease and flour a 10-inch Bundt pan or 10-inch tube pan. Measure about 7 cups batter into the pan. Into remaining batter, stir chocolate until well mixed. Spoon chocolate mixture over batter in Bundt pan. With rubber spatula cut and twist through batter a few times to obtain "rippled" effect.

Bake 1 hour and 30 minutes at 300° F. or until tests done. Cool cake in pan on rack 10 minutes; remove from pan; cool completely on rack.

Serve plain or with icing of your choice.

There is great value in a well made cake...

BROWN SUGAR POUND CAKE

1 cup butter, softened
1 16-ounce package brown sugar, packed
5 large eggs
3-1/2 cups cake flour
1 cup milk
2 cups chopped pecans

1/2 cup Crisco
1 cup granulated sugar
1/2 teaspoon baking powder
2 tablespoons vanilla

Cream butter and shortening; gradually add sugar, beating until light and fluffy. Add eggs, one at a time, beating well after each addition.

Combine baking powder and flour and sift 3 times; add to creamed mixture alternately with milk, beginning and ending with flour, and beating well after each addition.

Stir in vanilla and pecans.

Pour batter into a greased and floured 10-inch tube pan. Bake at 350°F. for 1 hour and 10 minutes or until tests done. Cool in pan 10 minutes; invert on wire rack and cool completely. Frost with Cream Cheese Frosting.

CREAM CHEESE FROSTING

1/2 cup butter, softened
1 (16-ounce) package confectioners sugar

2 teaspoons vanilla
1 (8-ounce) package cream cheese

Combine all ingredients, mixing until smooth. Frost cake when cooled.

Redouble your efforts and be rewarded when you bake this delicious cake...

CONFECTIONERS SUGAR POUND CAKE

1 box confectioners sugar
6 eggs
1 sugar box sifted cake flour, plus 2 tablespoons

3/4 pound butter
1 teaspoon vanilla
or
1 teaspoon lemon extract

Cream butter and sugar until creamy and fluffy. Add eggs, one at a time, beating well after each addition. Add flavorings. Add flour gradually and beat vigorously for 15 minutes.

Bake at 275°F. for 1 hour or until cake tests done.

This is a very fine textured and delicious pound cake!

CHOCOLATE MOCHA POUND CAKE

1 cup butter
2 cups sugar
3 cups cake flour
1 teaspoon salt
1 teaspoon baking powder
1 teaspoon vanilla
1 cup finely chopped pecans

4 eggs
1 cup buttermilk
3 squares unsweetened
    chocolate
1 tablespoon powdered
    instant coffee

Melt chocolate over hot water, stir in instant coffee and set aside.

Cream together the butter and sugar until light and fluffy. Add eggs, one at a time, beating well after each addition. Add sifted dry ingredients alternately with the buttermilk. Stir in the vanilla and chocolate mixture, blending well. Stir in pecans and bake at 325° F. for 1 hour and 10 minutes or until tests done. When cooled, spread with Chocolate Cream.

CHOCOLATE CREAM

1 tablespoon instant coffee
4 ounces sweet chocolate

1/4 cup heavy cream
2 tablespoons hot water

Whip cream and fold in chocolate mixture after it has been cooled. (Melt chocolate in 2 ounces hot water and stir in instant coffee).

Baking a cake is simple...just be concerned...

CHOCOLATE POUND CAKE

1/2 cup butter
1/2 cup Crisco
3 cups sugar
5 eggs
1 cup milk
1 tablespoon vanilla

3 cups cake flour
1/2 teaspoon baking powder
1/2 teaspoon salt
4 heaping tablespoons cocoa
    (sift these dry ingredients
    together)

Cream butter and Crisco; add sugar gradually, beating well. Add eggs, one at a time. Add flour mixture alternately with milk. Add vanilla. Bake at 325° F. for 1 hour and 40 minutes. When cooled completely, frost.

GERMAN CHOCOLATE FROSTING

1 stick butter
1/2 block German chocolate

1 box confectioners
    sugar

Melt chocolate and butter, stirring. Let cool. Sift in other ingredient and blend well. Use evaporated milk to thin. Frost cooled cake. Add chopped pecans, if desired.

CINNAMON SOUR CREAM POUND CAKE

1 cup butter
2 eggs
1 teaspoon baking powder
1 (8-ounce) carton sour cream
1/2 cup sliced almonds, toasted
2 teaspoons sugar

2 cups sugar
2-1/2 cups cake flour
1/2 teaspoon salt
1 teaspoon vanilla
1/2 teaspoon cinnamon

Cream butter; gradually add 2 cups sugar, beating until light and fluffy. Add eggs, one at a time, beating well after each addition.

Sift flour, baking powder and salt three times. Add 1/3 dry ingredients to creamed mixture alternately with one-half of sour cream, stirring until well blended. Add vanilla, blending well.

Combine almonds, cinnamon and remaining 2 tablespoons sugar; sprinkle a third of mixture in a well-greased and floured 10-inch Bundt pan. Pour in half of batter and sprinkle with another third of almond mixture. Pour remaining batter into pan and top with remaining almond mixture.

Bake at 350°F. for 50 to 60 minutes. Cool 1 hour before removing from pan.

COCONUT POUND CAKE

3 cups sifted cake flour
1/4 teaspoon salt
1 cup butter
2 cups sugar
5 eggs
Juice of 1 lemon

1 teaspoon lemon extract
1/2 teaspoon vanilla
1 cup milk
1 can flaked coconut
(1-1/2 cups)
1 teaspoon baking powder

Cream butter; add sugar gradually, beating until light and fluffy. Add eggs, one at a time, beating well after each addition. Add lemon extract, vanilla and lemon juice. Mix thoroughly.

Add sifted flour, baking powder and salt alternately with milk, then fold in coconut.

Bake at 300°F. 1 hour and 15 minutes or until done. Serve plain or with Buttermilk Icing.

BUTTERMILK ICING

1 cup buttermilk
2 cups sugar

1/2 cup butter

Combine and cook to soft ball stage. Spread on cake.

Practice baking cakes...it is one effective answer to tension...

CRANBERRY PECAN POUND CAKE

2-1/4 cups sifted cake flour
1/2 teaspoon baking powder
1/4 teaspoon salt
1 cup butter
2 cups sugar
1 cup chopped pecans

4 eggs
1 tablespoon vanilla
1/2 cup evaporated milk
1 cup chopped raw
 cranberries

Grease and flour a 10-inch tube or Bundt pan and set aside. Cream together the butter and sugar until light and fluffy. Add eggs, one at a time, beating well after each addition. Blend in vanilla extract. Add the sifted dry ingredients alternately with the milk, then fold in the cranberries and pecans that have been dredged in flour lightly.

Bake at 325° F. for 1 hour and 10 minutes or until done. Dust with confectioners sugar.

These cakes are worth baking!

CREAM CHEESE POUND CAKE

3/4 pound butter
1 package (8-ounces) cream
 cheese, softened
3 cups sugar

6 egg yolks
3 cups cake flour
1 teaspoon vanilla
6 egg whites

Cream butter with cream cheese until soft and fluffy. Add sugar and beat well. Add egg yolks, one at a time, until well blended. Add sifted flour gradually, continuing to blend well. Stir in vanilla. Fold in egg whites that have been stiffly beaten. Spoon into a well buttered and floured tube pan. Bake at 350° F. for 1 hour or until tests done. Delicious as is, or you may prefer a glaze.

A winner!

ELEGANT POUND CAKE

8 eggs, separated
1 pound butter (No Substitute)
1/2 cup whipping cream

2-2/3 cups sugar
3-1/2 cups sifted cake flour
1 teaspoon vanilla

Lightly grease a very large tube pan and set aside. Reserve 1/3 cup of sugar for egg whites.

Cream butter thoroughly and then add sugar gradually; continue to cream, beating for about 10 minutes. Add egg yolks, one at a time, beating well after each addition. Sift flour 3 times; add alternately with the cream and vanilla, beating for another 10 minutes until the mixture is very light. Beat the egg whites until very frothy and then add the 1/3 cup sugar gradually. Fold in by hand to the creamed mixture.

Pour in batter and bake at 300° F. for 1-3/4 hours or until tests done. Let cool in pan for 10 minutes and then turn out and let cool on rack.

Serve plain or with Lemon Glaze. Also good with fresh and sweetened strawberries and whipped cream.

LEMON GLAZE

1/2 cup confectioners sugar,
  sifted and firmly packed
1 teaspoon white corn syrup
2 teaspoons whipping cream

3 teaspoons lemon juice
1 teaspoon soft butter
Dash of salt

Combine all ingredients and beat hard to blend. Drizzle over top of cake. This icing adds flavor and helps to retain moisture.

If you want to bake this delicious and elegant cake...just begin ...you will see amazing results!

FRUIT POUND CAKE

1 cup butter
1-1/2 cups sugar
2-1/2 cups cake flour,
  divided
1 cup chopped mixed
  candied fruit
1/2 cup chopped pecans

1 (8-ounce) package cream cheese
4 eggs
1-1/2 teaspoons baking powder
Grated rind of 1 lemon
1/2 cup golden seedless raisins
1/2 cup dates, chopped
Confectioners sugar

Cream butter and cream cheese; gradually add sugar, beating well until light and fluffy. Add eggs, one at a time, beating well after each addition.

Combine 1-3/4 cups flour and baking powder; gradually add to creamed mixture and beat until well blended. Dredge lemon rind, candied fruit, raisins, dates and pecans with remaining 3/4 cup flour; stir to coat well. Stir mixture into batter.

Spoon into a greased and floured 10-inch tube pan. Bake at 325° F. for about 1 hour and 20 minutes. Cool for 10 minutes; remove from pan. Dust top with confectioners sugar. Garnish with candied cherries and pineapple slices, if desired.

Read these cake-building words and begin, step by step, to build your cake...

ELEGANT SOUR CREAM POUND CAKE

1/2 cup butter, softened
1/2 cup shortening
3 cups sifted cake flour
1/4 teaspoon salt
1 cup sour cream

3 cups sugar
6 eggs, separated
1/4 teaspoon baking powder
1/4 teaspoon baking soda

Cream butter and shortening; gradually add sugar, beating well. Add egg yolks, one at a time, beating well after each addition.

Sift flour, baking powder, soda and salt; add to creamed mixture alternately with sour cream, beginning and ending with the flour mixture. Beat egg whites until stiff; gently fold into batter.

Pour into a greased and floured 10-inch tube pan. Bake at 325° F. for 1-1/2 hours or until tests done.

Cool in pan for 10 minutes; remove from pan and cool completely.

GERMAN CHOCOLATE POUND CAKE

2 cups sugar
1 cup butter
4 eggs
2 teaspoons vanilla
2 teaspoons butter flavoring
1 package German sweet chocolate

1 cup buttermilk
1/2 teaspoon soda
1 teaspoon salt
3 cups flour, sifted

Cream butter and sugar; add eggs, one at a time, beating well. Add flavorings and buttermilk. Sift together flour, soda and salt three times. Melt chocolate in top of double boiler. Add dry ingredients alternately to first mixture with the chocolate. Mix well. Pour into a large well-greased tube pan and bake in a 300° F. oven for 1-1/2 hours. When cake pulls away from sides of pan it is done. Remove from oven and place under a tight fitting cover until it cools. Frost.

CHOCOLATE FROSTING

1/4 cup butter
4 tablespoons cocoa
Some Hot Coffee

1 box Confectioners sugar
1 teaspoon vanilla

Cream butter; add sugar, then cocoa and vanilla. Use enough hot coffee to make spreadable.

A first-class pound cake!

GINGER POUND CAKE

1 cup butter
2 cups light brown sugar, packed
4 eggs, separated
3-1/4 cups cake flour
1 teaspoon baking powder

1 teaspoon nutmeg
1 tablespoon ground ginger
1 teaspoon salt
2 tablespoons minced candied ginger, optional
1/2 cup whipping cream

Grease a tube pan and line with wax paper.

Cream butter and sugar well. Add egg yolks, one at a time, beating well after each addition. Sift together the dry ingredients and add alternately with the cream. Fold in the minced ginger, if used, and then the egg whites that have been beaten stiff, but not dry. Pour batter gently into the tube pan and bake at 325° F. for 1 hour or until done.

Serve plain or with a butter cream glaze, if desired.

Fine flavored, rich cake...

LEMON POUND CAKE

1 stick butter
1/2 cup Crisco
3 cups cake flour
1/4 teaspoon salt
1 tablespoon lemon juice

2 cups sugar
3 eggs
1/2 teaspoon baking soda
1 cup buttermilk
1 tablespoon lemon rind, grated

Cream butter, Crisco and sugar together until light and fluffy. Add eggs, one at a time, beating well after each addition. Add sifted flour, soda and salt alternately with the buttermilk, lemon juice and lemon rind. Pour into a greased and floured tube pan or Bundt pan and bake at 325° F. for around 1 hour or until the cake tests done. Cool 5 minutes in pan and then turn out and cool completely. Cover entire cake with Lemon Icing.

LEMON ICING

1 stick butter
Juice and rind of 2 lemons

1 box confectioners sugar

Cream butter until smooth. Add confectioners sugar and then the juice and rind. Blend thoroughly and then spread on cake immediately.

Hard to beat for flavor...

MOROCCAN POUND CAKE

2/3 cup butter
1/2 cup Crisco
2 cups sugar
4 eggs
3-1/2 cups cake flour
3 teaspoons baking
   powder
1/4 teaspoon salt

1 cup milk
1 teaspoon vanilla
1/2 cup raisins
3/4 cup chopped unsalted
   mixed nuts (any combination)
1 tablespoon cocoa
1 tablespoon cinnamon
Confectioners sugar

Cream the butter, Crisco and sugar until light and fluffy. Add eggs, one at a time, beating well after each addition. Sift together the flour, baking powder and salt, and then add alternately with the milk and vanilla, beating well. Fold in the raisins and nuts. Pour 3/4 of the batter into a greased 10-inch pan lined in bottom with wax paper. Mix remaining batter with the cocoa and cinnamon (sifted). Spoon batter in pan and run a knife through batter to marblelize. Bake at 325° F. for 1 hour and 15 minutes or until done. Let stand 5 minutes and then turn out on cake rack. Peel off paper. Cool and sprinkle with confectioners sugar.

LEMON JELLO POUND CAKE

1 box Lemon Supreme cake mix
1 box lemon jello
4 eggs

3/4 cup Wesson oil
1 cup milk

Mix together the cake mix, jello, eggs and milk. Then add oil and mix well. Bake at 350° F. for 1 hour in a tube pan or until done. Then spread icing over cake.

LEMON ICING

1-1/4 cups confectioners sugar
Juice from 2 lemons

3 tablespoons butter,
   softened

Mix well and pour over cake while it is still hot.

MILLION DOLLAR POUND CAKE

3 cups sugar
1 pound butter
6 eggs

4 cups cake flour
3/4 cup milk
2 teaspoons vanilla flavoring

Cream butter and sugar until light and fluffy. Add eggs, one at a time, creaming well after each addition. Add flour alternately with the milk, beating well. Stir in flavoring. Pour into a well greased and floured 10-inch tube pan. Bake at 325° F. for 1 hour and 15 minutes or longer, if necessary.

MRS. WALKER'S POUND CAKE

6 eggs
2 sticks butter, plus
   1 stick margarine
2 cups sugar

3 cups sifted plain flour
1-1/2 teaspoons vanilla (or 2
   teaspoons lemon flavoring)

Beat sugar and butter until light and fluffy (this is the secret). Add eggs, one at a time, beating after each. Add flour and flavorings alternately. Grease a tube pan and flour it. Bake in 325° F. oven for about 1 hour and 10 minutes, or until it leaves the sides of pan. Let cool slightly in pan, then turn out on rack to finish cooling.

PECAN POUND CAKE

1 cup butter, softened
6 eggs, separated
1/4 teaspoon soda
2 to 4 cups chopped pecans

3 cups sugar
3 cups cake flour
1 cup sour cream

Cream butter and sugar until light and fluffy. Add egg yolks, one at a time, beating well after each addition. Set aside about 1/3 cup flour. Combine remaining sifted flour and soda; add to creamed mixture alternately with sour cream, beating well after each addition. Fold in stiffly beaten egg whites. Dredge pecans in reserved flour and fold into batter.

Spoon batter into a greased and floured 10-inch tube pan and bake at 300° F. for 1-1/2 hours. Cool 15 minutes before removing from pan.

PINEAPPLE POUND CAKE

2 cups Crisco
9 eggs
1 can (small) crushed pineapple

3 cups sugar
3 cups cake flour,
   sifted

Cream shortening well, gradually add the sugar, beating well. Add eggs, one at a time, beating well after each addition. Add sifted flour alternately with the pineapple and juice. Pour batter into a large tube pan. Grease lightly and put wax paper in bottom of pan. Bake at 350° F. for 1-1/2 hours or until tests done. While still warm, drizzle over glaze.

PINEAPPLE GLAZE

1-1/2 cups confectioners sugar
1 can (small) crushed pineapple

1/4 stick melted butter

Mix well and drizzle over warm cake.

OLD FASHIONED POUND CAKE

1 *pound butter*
1 *pound granulated sugar*
1 *pound flour*

9 *eggs, separated*
1 *teaspoon lemon extract*

Cream butter and sugar until light and fluffy. Add egg yolks, one at a time, beating well after each addition. Add lemon extract. Add flour, gradually, beating well after each addition. Fold in stiffly beaten egg whites. Bake in well greased tube pan for 1 hour at 325° F. or until the cake tests done.

A top-notch cake! An old, old recipe and delicious...

ORIGINAL POUND CAKE

1 *pound butter*
1 *pound confectioners sugar*
12 *eggs, separated*
1 *pound flour, (4-1/2 cups, sifted)*

1/2 *teaspoon nutmeg*
1/4 *cup grated lemon peel*
1/2 *cup whipping cream*

Cream butter and sugar; add egg yolks, beating well after each addition. Sift together the flour and nutmeg and add alternately with the cream. Fold in the lemon peel and then the egg whites that have been stiffly beaten. Bake at 325° F. for 1 hour or until cake tests done.

Amazing things begin to happen when you bake a cake...

PEANUT BUTTER POUND CAKE NO. 1

1 *cup butter*
2 *cups granulated sugar*
1 *cup light brown sugar,*
   packed
1/2 *cup creamy peanut butter*
5 *eggs*

1 *tablespoon vanilla*
3 *cups cake flour*
1/2 *teaspoon baking powder*
1/2 *teaspoon salt*
1/4 *teaspoon baking soda*
1 *cup milk*

Cream butter and granulated sugar until light and fluffy. Add brown sugar and peanut butter and continue beating thoroughly. Add eggs, one at a time, beating well after each addition; add vanilla and blend well.

Sift together the dry ingredients and add alternately with the milk. Pour into a very large tube pan. Lightly grease the pan first. Bake at 325° F. for around an hour or until it tests done. Frost, if desired, with the Peanut Butter Frosting; however, it is delicious without the frosting.

PEANUT BUTTER FROSTING

1/2 stick butter
Dash of salt
1 ounce milk or less
(do not use too much)

2 eggs
1/3 cup creamy peanut
butter
1 box confectioners sugar

Combine all ingredients and beat until smooth. Be careful not to use too much milk. Add just enough to make the frosting of spreading consistency.

PEANUT BUTTER POUND CAKE NO. 2

2-1/2 sticks butter
6 eggs
1/2 cup creamy or crunchy
peanut butter
1/4 teaspoon salt
2 cups sugar

1 teaspoon vanilla
2 cups cake flour
1 teaspoon baking powder
1/3 cup finely chopped
peanuts

Cream together butter and sugar until fluffy. Beat in eggs, one at a time, until thoroughly blended. Add vanilla, then slowly beat in peanut butter. Sift together flour, baking powder and salt. Add this, a little at a time, blending well. Lightly grease a 10-inch tube pan and spoon in batter. Bake at 350° F. for 45 minutes; reduce heat to 325° F. and bake an additional 15 to 20 minutes, or until cake tests done. If desired, toward the end of the baking time and while batter is still soft, sprinkle over the chopped peanuts to give the cake a crunchy topping.

Bake and give your own special cake to someone...

SOUR CREAM POUND CAKE

1/2 pound butter, softened
3 cups sugar, sifted 3 times
1 8-ounce carton sour cream
1/4 teaspoon salt

6 large eggs
3 cups flour, sifted
3 times
1/4 teaspoon baking soda

Measure flour and then sift it. Cream butter well. Add sifted sugar gradually, creaming thoroughly. Add eggs, one at a time, beating well after each addition. Add sifted flour, baking soda and salt alternately with the sour cream. Use 1 or 2 teaspoons of any flavoring that you like; vanilla and lemon are especially good. Bake 1-1/2 hours in 325° F. oven. CAUTION: Do not open the oven door until time is up or the cake will fall.

A superb cake for the most festive occasions!

SWEET POTATO POUND CAKE

1/2 cup Crisco	1 teaspoon baking powder
1/2 cup butter, softened	1 cup buttermilk
2 cups sugar	1 cup pureed cooked sweet potato
6 eggs	1/2 teaspoon coconut extract
3-1/2 cups cake flour	1/4 cup slivered almonds, toasted
1/2 teaspoon salt	and finely chopped
1/4 teaspoon baking soda	1/4 cup flaked coconut

Cream shortening and butter; gradually add sugar, beating until light and fluffy. Add eggs, one at a time, beating well after each addition. Sift together the dry ingredients and add alternately with the buttermilk. Stir in sweet potato and flavoring until well blended.

Grease and flour a 12 cup Bundt pan; sprinkle almonds and coconut evenly over bottom. Pour batter into pan; bake at 350° F. for 1 hour or until done. Cool in the pan for 10 minutes; remove and cool completely.

When you give a cake you've baked, you're giving part of yourself away...

Refrigerator Cakes and Desserts

ANGEL FOOD DELIGHT

Angel Food cake or lady fingers
1 3-ounce package orange jello
1 medium can crushed pineapple, drained
1 can sliced peaches, drained and chopped

12 maraschino cherries, chopped
2 heaping cups of miniature marshmallows
1 pint whipping cream, whipped

Line a 9 x 12-inch glass baking dish with sliced angel food cake or lady fingers. Set jello with 1 cup water. Combine fruits and marshmallows. Whip cream; fold into fruit mixture and jello. Pour over cake. Leave in refrigerator overnight.

Expensive but worth the compliments!

ANGEL'S SURPRISE

1 pint milk
4 egg yolks
1 cup sugar
2 tablespoons flour
Pinch salt
1 envelope gelatin
1/2 cup cold water

1/2 pint whipping cream
4 egg whites, beaten stiff
Angel Food cake (large)
1/2 pint whipping cream (for garnish)
1 teaspoon almond extract

Combine egg yolks, sugar, milk, flour and salt and cook until ingredients form a custard or thickens. Then dissolve gelatin in cold water. Add to the custard and cool. Whip 1/2 pint cream and beat egg whites stiff. Add these ingredients to the custard mixture. Add flavoring.

Break the Angel Food cake into large pieces and put in oblong pyrex dish. Pour custard over cake. Refrigerate overnight. Garnish with 1/2 pint of whipped whipping cream and toasted slivered almonds.

A year-round glamour dessert -- rich and refreshing...

BLUEBERRY GLAZE CAKE

1 box vanilla wafers
1 package Dream Whip
1 large package cream cheese

1 can blueberry pie filling
1 cup sugar
1 stick margarine

Crush vanilla wafers. Melt margarine and mix with wafers. Then press in bottom of Pyrex dish, reserving 1/2 cup for topping. Whip Dream Whip as directed. Mix together the cream cheese and sugar, blending well and then add Dream Whip.

Spread one half of this mixture over the crust and cover with pie filling. Then spread the remaining Dream Whip mixture on top. Refrigerate overnight.

This cake is good, but it's good enough to be!

BUTTER CREAM SATIN CAKE

Angel Food cake, lady fingers (30)
or pound cake
1 pint whipping cream, whipped
1/2 cup butter
1 cup confectioners sugar

4 egg yolks
4 egg whites
1 tablespoon vanilla
extract

Line a mold or a large bowl with Angel Food cake pieces, lady fingers or pound cake. Then put the filling and cake in the bowl in layers.

Cream butter; beat in the sugar until fluffy. Beat in the egg yolks, one at a time. Flavor with the vanilla and fold in the egg whites beaten stiff. Chill 12 hours or longer before serving. Serves 6.

Smooth as satin!

CHARLOTTE CAKE

4 egg whites
1 cup sugar
1 quart whipping cream
2 tablespoons plain gelatin

1 cup sherry
1/2 pint whipping cream
Almonds and crystallized
cherries

Whip one quart whipping cream until it is about half as stiff as desired, then add 1 cup sugar and continue to whip. Now beat the egg whites until foamy and add this to whipped cream, folding in carefully. Then dissolve gelatin in 1 cup cold water. Let stand until about the consistency of applesauce; then dissolve it over very low heat (or in top of double boiler). Let stand until it is cool.

Now add gelatin very slowly, stirring carefully, to whipped cream and finally add the sherry slowly. Now line an angel food cake spring mold with lady fingers, then pour the mixture in slowly. Place in the refrigerator for at least two hours.

Unmold on serving platter. To unmold push it very carefully out of mold by pushing the spring bottom. Garnish with 1/2 pint cream, whipped with crystallized cherries and almonds.

A Southern favorite and a very popular cake!

CHOCOLATE COCONUT ICE BOX CAKE

4 squares unsweetened
chocolate
1/2 cup cold water
8 egg yolks
8 egg whites
1 cup sugar, divided
1-1/2 sticks butter, softened
2 cups confectioners sugar

Ladyfingers
1 cup chopped pecans
1 teaspoon vanilla
flavoring
2 dozen coconut
macaroons, crumbled
1/2 pint whipping
cream whipped

Melt chocolate in top of double boiler. Beat egg yolks and add 1/2 cup sugar. Add water and blend with the chocolate. Cook until very thick, stirring constantly. Fold in stiffly beaten egg whites to which you have added the other 1/2 cup sugar. Chill in refrigerator.

Cream butter and gradually add the confectioners sugar, pecans, flavoring and macaroon crumbs. Combine the two mixtures. Line sides of spring form pan and bottom of pan with split ladyfingers. Pour mixture over this. Store in refrigerator overnight. Serve with sweetened whipped cream.

It takes a little time to make this elegant cake, but it is easy once you begin...

CHOCOLATE LOAF CAKE

1 small sponge cake,
bought or homemade
4 ounces chocolate
1/2 cup milk
1/2 cup sugar
4 eggs, separated

1 teaspoon vanilla
1/4 teaspoon salt
1 cup whipping cream,
whipped
1/4 cup confectioners
sugar

Line small loaf pan with wax paper. Cover bottom and sides with thin slices of sponge cake (or ladyfingers). Melt chocolate over hot water. Add milk and continue cooking over hot water until smooth and blended, stirring constantly. Add sugar to slightly beaten yolks and add chocolate mixture slowly, stirring constantly.

Cook until thickened and smooth. Remove from heat and while still hot, fold in stiffly beaten egg whites. Add 1/2 teaspoon vanilla and salt. Pour half of chocolate mixture into cake-lined pan. Cover with a layer of sponge cake, add remaining chocolate mixture and cover with last layer of cake slices.

Chill for 12 hours or overnight. Turn out onto plate. Cover with whipped cream flavored with confectioners sugar and 1/2 teaspoon vanilla.

CHOCOLATE FILLED ANGEL CAKE

1 *large angel food cake*
6 *tablespoons cocoa*
6 *tablespoons sugar*
1/8 *teaspoon salt*

3 *cups whipping cream*
1 *cup sliced, blanched*
   and toasted almonds

Cut a slice about 1-inch thick from top of cake. Remove center from cake, leaving walls and bottom about 1-inch thick. Mix cocoa, sugar and salt with cream and chill thoroughly for 1 hour. Then whip cream mixture stiff and add 1/2 of almonds. Fill cake with 1/3 of cocoa mixture. Place top on cake and frost with remaining cocoa mixture. Sprinkle remaining almonds over cake. Chill 2 to 3 hours before serving. Serves 12.

For a truly regal looking cake...make this one

CARAMEL GINGER-SNAP

1 *can Eagle Brand condensed milk*   *Candied ginger*
   (caramelized*)
2 *dozen ginger snaps*

*To caramelize: Place can of Eagle Brand condensed milk in a kettle of boiling water and keep at boiling point for 3 hours. Caution: Be sure to keep can well covered with water. Cool can before opening.

Beat caramelized milk until smooth and creamy. Spread on ginger snaps. Then stack four ginger snaps on top of each other for each individual portion. Spread top and sides of each portion with caramelized milk. Decorate with candied ginger, cut fine. Chill and refrigerate for 8 hours or longer. Serves 6.

Excellent dessert!

CHANTILLY SPONGE CAKE

1 *large sponge cake*
1 *cup cubed or crushed*
   pineapple, drained
12 *marshmallows, quartered*
1 *cup cut strawberries*

1/2 *teaspoon vanilla*
2 *cups whipping cream,*
   whipped
20 *large whole*
   strawberries

Cut cool sponge cake into halves, crosswise. Fold next four ingredients into whipped cream. Spread the bottom half of cake liberally with the mixed filling. Cover with the top half of cake and spread remaining mixture over top and sides. Chill for 2 to 3 hours before serving. Garnish with whole berries. Serves 12.

Expensive but delightful...

COFFEE ALMOND CAKE

1/2 pound butter, softened
1/2 cup sugar
5 egg yolks
2 teaspoons vanilla extract
1/2 cup strong cold coffee
1-1/2 dozen lady fingers, split

1/3 cup toasted almonds,
 pulverized
Slivers of toasted
 almonds, for garnish
1 pint whipping cream

Cream butter and sugar thoroughly. Add egg yolks, one at a time, beating well. Add pulverized almonds and vanilla and blend. Add coffee gradually and beat until smooth. Line a 2 quart mold with ladyfingers. Spread 1/2 of coffee mixture on top, then a layer of ladyfingers. Spread with other 1/2 of mixture and end with ladyfingers. Refrigerate overnight. Invert and spread sweetened whipped cream evenly over top. Sprinkle with slivered almonds.

A very tasty dessert!

COLONIAL ENGLISH TRIFLE

1 medium can peeled,
 pitted apricots
3 tablespoons strawberry jam
3 eggs
1 tablespoon sugar
Dash vanilla extract
Chopped pecans

1 two-layer sponge cake
1/2 pound macaroons
1 cup sherry
1-1/2 cups milk
1/4 teaspoon salt
1/2 pint heavy cream

Line deep, round glass casserole with drained apricots. Top with layer of sponge cake. Spread on jam. Add other cake layer and broken macaroons. Pour sherry on contents. Make soft custard in double boiler. Scald milk. Beat eggs with sugar and salt. Add to milk and stir until slightly thickened. Cool 15 minutes and add vanilla. Pour custard over cake mixture. Chill until set or overnight. Top with whipped cream and nuts before serving.

A delightful dessert...

DATE AND NUT ROLL

2 cups vanilla wafer crumbs
1 cup chopped dates
1/2 cup chopped pecans

1/2 cup sweetened
 condensed milk
2 teaspoons lemon juice

Combine vanilla wafer crumbs, dates and nuts. Blend together condensed milk and lemon juice. Add to crumb mixture and knead well. Form into a roll 3-inches in diameter and wrap in wax paper. Chill in refrigerator for 12 hours. Cut into slices and serve with whipped cream topping or hard sauce flavored with brandy.

Different and very good...

DELICIOUS BUTTERSCOTCH CAKE

1 tablespoon unflavored gelatin
1/4 cup cold water
2-1/2 tablespoons butter
2/3 cup brown sugar
1-1/2 cups milk
2 eggs, separated

1/4 teaspoon salt
1 cup whipping cream,
  chilled and whipped
1/2 teaspoon vanilla
1 dozen ladyfingers

Soften gelatin in water for 5 minutes. Melt butter, add sugar and cook together until well blended. Add milk, heat and pour over well beaten egg yolks, stirring constantly. Add salt and cook over hot water until mixture coats a spoon, stirring constantly.

Remove from heat and add softened gelatin. Stir until dissolved, then chill until mixture begins to thicken. Fold in stiffly beaten egg whites, whipped cream and vanilla. Pour into a mold lined with separated ladyfingers. Chill until firm.

Attractive...a lovely party cake...

FESTIVE ORANGE DELIGHT

1 cup water
2 envelopes gelatin, plain
8 eggs, separated
1/2 teaspoon salt
2 six-ounce cans frozen
  orange juice

Grated rind of 1 orange
1 cup sugar
1/2 pint whipping cream, whipped
Mandarin oranges, toasted almonds
and whipped cream for garnish

Dissolve gelatin in water in top of a double boiler. Beat the egg yolks and add salt. Add this to the gelatin mixture and beat thoroughly. Place over boiling water and cook, stirring constantly, until mixture begins to thicken. Remove from heat and add the orange juice and rind. Chill until slightly thickened. Whip egg whites until foamy, gradually add sugar and beat until stiff. Whip cream and fold both mixtures into the orange mixture. Pour mixture into a buttered dish and chill. When ready to serve, garnish with almonds, mandarin oranges and sweetened whipped cream, if desired.

Attractive in color and delicious!

ELEGANT LADYFINGER DESSERT

1/2 pound butter, softened
1 cup sifted confectioners sugar
6 eggs

16-ounce can crushed
pineapple, drained
32-34 Ladyfingers

Cream butter until very light, then add sugar gradually, beating well after each addition. Add egg yolks one at a time and mix well. Add pineapple. Beat egg whites until stiff but not dry and fold into above mixture.

Split Ladyfingers and place a layer in a pyrex dish. Cover with half of mixture, then remaining Ladyfingers. Top with mixture again and cover. Refrigerate at least 24 hours before serving. Serve topped with whipped cream.

Dainty and delicious...

FROZEN STRAWBERRY DELIGHT

1 Angel Food cake
1/2 gallon vanilla
   ice cream
1 large carton Cool Whip

2 3-ounce packages strawberry jello
1 large package frozen strawberries,
   slightly thawed or 1 pint fresh
   strawberries, sweetened to taste

Dissolve jello in 2 cups hot water. Add strawberries. Break Angel Food cake into bite-size pieces and place in bottom of greased tube pan. Add a layer of softened ice cream and a layer of Cool Whip. Repeat these layers 3 times. Punch holes in cake and pour over the warm strawberry mixture. Place in freezer. When ready to serve, dip pan in hot water and remove cake to serving plate. Garnish with fresh strawberries.

HEAVENLY FRUIT CAKE

1 pound box graham crackers
1/2 pound cherries, cut up
1/2 pound mixed nuts, chopped
1 pound marshmallows, cut up
1 pound pecans, chopped
1 pound box raisins

1 cup grated coconut
1 can Eagle Brand
   condensed milk
1 pound English walnuts,
   chopped

Mix marshmallows; crush graham crackers, then mix with other ingredients in order given. Blend well. Place in a foil-lined pan and refrigerate for at least 24 hours.

A luxurious cake, expensive but worth the price...

FLOATING ISLAND

Sponge cake or ladyfingers

*1 cup chopped blanched
  almonds
3 cups milk
4 egg yolks
1/2 cup sugar
1-1/2 tablespoons cornstarch*

*Dash salt
1 teaspoon vanilla
1/2 pint whipped cream,
  sweetened
Strawberry jelly, optional
1 tablespoon sherry flavoring*

In top of double boiler, scald milk. Beat egg yolks until thick, then beat in sugar, cornstarch and salt. Gradually beat hot milk into egg mixture. Return milk to double boiler and cook until mixture thickens. Stir in vanilla.

Cover bottom of large bowl with broken cake pieces or ladyfingers. Sprinkle with sherry flavoring, then pour the custard over all. Top generously with sweetened whipped cream, and dab bits of strawberry jelly over it, if desired. Serve from the bowl.

A dramatic, classic dessert!

FROZEN STRAWBERRY CAKE

*1-1/2 cups crushed fresh
  strawberries
2/3 cup sugar
1 tablespoon lemon juice,
  freshly squeezed*

*3 cups graham cracker crumbs
1/2 cup whipping cream
1-1/2 teaspoons vanilla*

Combine ingredients in order listed and blend well. Line a freezing tray with oiled paper. Fill with the mixture and freeze until firm. Cut into squares, top with sweetened whipped cream and some chopped pecans, if desired.

A delicate and flavorful dessert...

MACAROON DELIGHT

*1 dozen almond macaroons
4 egg whites
4 egg yolks*

*1 pint whipping cream, whipped
3/4 cup sugar
1/2 cup sherry*

Leave macaroons out overnight to dry or place in oven for a few minutes. Roll out to make crumb mixture. Beat egg whites until stiff. In a separate bowl, beat egg yolks and gradually add the sugar and then the sherry. Fold in the beaten egg whites.

Line buttered serving dish with 1/2 macaroon crumbs. Pour mixture on top and sprinkle remaining crumbs over top. Freeze until ready to serve.

HOLIDAY CAKE

2 tablespoons unflavored
 gelatin
1 quart milk
2 eggs, separated
3/4 cup sugar
1/4 teaspoon salt

3/4 cup chopped
 maraschino cherries
1/3 cup maraschino juice
1 teaspoon vanilla
1-1/2 cups whipping cream
2 dozen vanilla wafers

Soften gelatin in 1/2 cup milk. In double boiler, scald the remaining milk and pour onto beaten egg yolks. Add sugar, salt and softened gelatin; return to double boiler; cook until mixture coats a spoon. Cool, then add cherries, juice and vanilla. Chill until mixture begins to thicken.

Fold in beaten egg whites and half the cream, whipped. Butter a cake pan and arrange vanilla wafers around it. Pour in filling and cover top with remaining vanilla wafers. Chill overnight. Unmold and frost sides and top of cake with remaining cream, whipped and sweetened.

A snap to make and wonderful eating!

LEMONADE LOAF

1 Angel Loaf Cake
1 6-ounce can frozen pink
 lemonade concentrate

1 quart vanilla ice cream
1 cup heavy cream,
 whipped (optional)

Slice cake lengthwise in three even layers. Stir ice cream to soften. With spoon, zigzag lemonade concentrate through ice cream until marbled; spread between cake layers. Freeze approximately one hour. Before serving, spread top and sides of loaf with whipped cream.

Whipped cream frosting may be omitted, in which case the top layer of the cake should be frosted with part of the ice cream-lemonade mixture.

A sparkling cake!

LEMON BISQUE

1 package (3-ounces) lemon jello
4 tablespoons lemon juice,
 freshly squeezed
Grated rind of one lemon
1-1/4 cups water, hot

1/2 cup sugar
1 13-ounce can evaporated
 milk, chilled
2 cups vanilla wafer crumbs
Pinch salt

Dissolve jello in hot water. Put sugar, lemon juice, rind and salt in pan and heat until thoroughly dissolved. Add softened jello to this hot mixture. Let it cool. Whip chilled evaporated milk until stiff peaks form. Fold gelatin mixture gradually into cream. Do not stir. Butter a square pyrex dish and sprinkle with 2/3 of the crumbs. Press crumbs to set. Pour bisque into dish and sprinkle top with remaining crumbs. Place in refrigerator for at least 6 hours. Best made the day before it is to be served. May be garnished with fresh strawberries.

A delightful lemon colored dessert. After a heavy meal, it's wonderful!

LEMON CHARLOTTE

1 envelope gelatin	*2 teaspoons lemon rind*
1/2 cup water	*1 pint whipping cream, whipped*
4 eggs, separated	*2 dozen ladyfingers, split*
1 cup sugar, divided	*Fresh strawberries and*
Pinch salt	*whipped cream for garnish*
1/2 cup lemon juice, freshly squeezed	

Soften gelatin in cold water and dissolve over hot water. Separate eggs and beat the yolks, adding 1/2 cup sugar gradually and then the salt. Beat until thickened. Slowly add the lemon juice, rind and gelatin. Beat egg whites until foamy and add gradually 1/2 cup sugar, beating until stiff peaks form. Fold into yolk mixture. Fold in whipped cream.

Line a spring form pan with split ladyfingers. Pour in 1/2 of the custard mixture. Place more ladyfingers on top and cover with rest of custard. Refrigerate overnight. Remove from pan and decorate with strawberries and sweetened whipped cream.

A beautiful and delicious dessert!

STRAWBERRY SPLENDOR

1 small sponge cake,	*1/3 cup whipping cream*
homemade or bought	*1/4 teaspoon vanilla*
or 6 ladyfingers	*1 tablespoon chopped*
3 tablespoons sugar	*pecans*
1-1/4 cups fresh, crushed	
strawberries	

Line springform pan with split ladyfingers or sliced sponge cake. Add sugar to strawberries. Whip cream with vanilla. Cover cake with berries. Then add a layer of whipped cream. Repeat in layers until all is used. Save part of cream for top of cake. Sprinkle with the pecans and chill overnight.

LEMON ICE BOX CAKE

12-ounce loaf sponge cake,
bought or homemade
1/2 cup butter
1 teaspoon grated lemon rind
1/4 cup lemon juice,
    freshly squeezed

2 cups confectioners sugar
1/4 cup milk, scalded
1/2 pint whipping cream
1 tablespoon pistachio
    nuts, sliced

Line bottom and sides of an 8-3/4 x 4-1/2 x 2-1/2-inch glass loaf pan with wax paper, extending paper 1/2-inch over sides in order to lift cake out easily.

Cut cake into 12 slices. Cream butter with lemon rind until smooth. Stir in lemon juice and sugar alternately. Add hot milk gradually, beating until fluffy. Arrange 3 cake slices flat on bottom of pan in an even layer. Spread 1/3 of filling evenly over cake. Repeat with cake and filling until all are used, finishing with cake.

Cover tightly with wax paper. Chill 5 to 6 hours. To serve, lift cake to serving plate. Pull paper from sides and cut it off. Spread top and sides with stiffly whipped and sweetened cream, swirling it. Sprinkle with pistachio nuts.

A refreshing party dessert...

MAPLE PECAN CAKE

1 tablespoon unflavored gelatin
1/2 cup cold water
2 eggs, separated
3/4 cup maple syrup
1/4 teaspoon salt

1 cup whipped cream
10 macaroons, rolled
    into crumbs
3/4 cup chopped pecans
2 dozen ladyfingers

Soften gelatin in water for 5 minutes. Beat egg yolks slightly. Add maple syrup and salt and cook over boiling water until slightly thickened. Add gelatin and stir until dissolved.

Cool and add whipped cream, macaroon crumbs and pecans. Fold in stiffly beaten egg whites. Line a mold with separated ladyfingers and fill with maple mixture. Chill.

When firm, unmold and garnish top with whipped and sweetened cream. Add pecan halves for garnish, if desired.

Delectable!

MOCHA CHARLOTTE

2 envelopes unflavored
  gelatin
4 tablespoons cold water
3 egg yolks and whites,
  beaten separately
1 cup sugar

1 cup milk
3/4 cup strong coffee
2 tablespoons kahlua
1 cup whipping cream, whipped
1 dozen ladyfingers, split
Whipped cream, for garnish

Soften gelatin in cold water. Combine egg yolks, sugar, milk in coffee in top of double boiler. Cook, stirring constantly, until mixture coats a spoon. Remove from heat and stir in gelatin. Continue stirring until mixture cools. Mixture will begin to thicken; then fold in beaten egg whites, whipped cream and kahlua. Chill. Line bottom and sides of a spring form pan with split ladyfingers. Pour gelatin mixture into pan. Chill until firm. Unmold on chilled platter when ready to serve. Garnish with sweetened whipped cream.

A delicate and appealing dessert...

OLD-FASHIONED BANANA-WAFER CAKE

1/2 cup sugar
1/4 cup flour
1/4 teaspoon salt
1-1/2 cups milk
2 eggs

2 tablespoons butter
1/2 teaspoon vanilla
24 vanilla wafers
3 large ripe bananas
Whipping cream

Blend sugar, flour and salt in top of double boiler, stir in milk and cook over hot water until thick, about 5 minutes, stirring often. Beat eggs, then stir in 1/2 cup of the hot mixture and return to the double boiler, stir and cook 4 to 5 minutes. Remove from heat and add butter and vanilla. Beat until smooth with rotary beater. Lightly butter an 8-cup round glass casserole. Arrange 9 wafers in bottom, then spoon 1/2-inch thick layer of custard over wafers. Now slice 1 banana over custard and spoon a thin layer of custard over banana. Lay on 10 wafers, then slice the 2 remaining bananas over them. Spread remaining custard over top, completely covering bananas. Crush the remaining 5 wafers fine and sprinkle over custard. Cover and chill from 6 to 8 hours. Serve with sweetened to taste whipped cream.

Hard to beat for flavor...

ORANGE PARTY CAKE

1/2 cup sugar
2 teaspoons flour
2 eggs, separated
1/2 cup scalded milk
1 tablespoon butter
Dash salt

Grated rind of 1/2 orange
Juice of 1 orange
Ladyfingers or spongecake
cut into strips
Whipped cream

Mix sugar and flour with beaten egg yolks. Add scalded milk slowly. Then add butter and salt and cook over hot water until thickened. Add orange rind and juice. Cool slightly and fold in stiffly beaten egg whites.

Split ladyfingers and place a layer in a pan lined with wax paper. Spread with orange mixture. Cover with another layer of ladyfingers and continue until mixture is used. Chill overnight. Serve with sweetened whipped cream.

A perfect party dessert and never served often enough!

PEACH DELIGHT

1 Angel Food cake
1/2 cup lemon juice
1-1/2 envelopes unflavored gelatin

5 eggs
1 cup sugar
1 cup mashed peaches,
crested or fresh

Separate the 5 eggs. Beat the yolks and place in a double boiler. Add lemon juice and 1/2 cup sugar. Cook this until it coats the spoon. Remove from heat and add gelatin which has been dissolved in 1/2 cup water.

Beat the egg whites until stiff. Gradually add sugar and beat until soft peaks form. Fold in the cup of mashed peaches. Add to custard mixture.

Lightly grease a tube pan with butter. Break the Angel Food cake in small pieces and arrange a layer of cake topped with custard. Continue to alternate layers and then refrigerate at least four hours before serving. Remove from pan and slice into serving pieces. Top with whipped cream.

Really luscious!

PEACH DREAM CAKE

1 tablespoon unflavored gelatin
1/4 cup cold water
1/3 cup butter, softened
cup confectioners sugar
2 eggs, separated

1/2 pound marshmallows,
cut into small pieces
4 cups sliced fresh peaches
2 cups vanilla wafer crumbs

Soften gelatin in water for 5 minutes. Cream butter and sugar until light and fluffy. Blend in the egg yolks well. Cook over low heat, stirring constantly until thickened. Remove from heat, add gelatin and stir until dissolved. Cool slightly, then add marshmallows. Blend lightly and chill until mixture begins to thicken. Fold in peaches and beaten egg whites. Arrange alternate layers of cookie crumbs and peach filling in mold, beginning and ending with cookie crumbs. Chill until firm. Unmold and serve with whipped and sweetened cream.

Prepare the night before for a delicious dessert the next day...

PINEAPPLE CRUSH CAKE

1-1/4 cups graham cracker crumbs
1/4 cup sugar
1/4 cup softened butter
2 envelopes unflavored gelatin
1/2 cup cold water
3 egg yolks
1 cup sugar
1/2 cup milk

Dash salt
4 cups cottage cheese
1-1/2 teaspoons grated lemon rind
2 tablespoons lemon juice
3 egg whites, stiffly beaten
1 cup drained canned crushed pineapple
1 cup whipping cream

Combine graham cracker crumbs, sugar and softened butter thoroughly. Pack all but 1/3 cup of this mixture on bottom of a greased 9-inch spring form pan.

Sprinkle gelatin over cold water. Let stand until softened, about 5 minutes.

Beat egg yolks slightly in top of double boiler. Add 1 cup sugar gradually, beating well with rotary beater. Stir in milk and salt. Cook over boiling water, stirring constantly, until slightly thickened and custard coats a spoon. Stir in gelatin until dissolved. Cool slightly.

Press cheese through sieve or beat with electric mixer until smooth. Add lemon rind and juice; mix well. Add slightly cooled custard mixture, beating until thoroughly blended. Let cool until thickened and partially set. Beat with rotary beater (electric or hand) until light and foamy. Fold in egg whites, whipped cream, and pineapple.

Pour into crumb-lined pan. Sprinkle top with remaining crumbs. Chill 2 or 3 hours.

PEPPERMINT STICK CHARLOTTE

2 envelopes unflavored
  gelatin
3/4 cup sugar, divided
1/4 teaspoon salt
4 eggs, separated
2-1/2 cups milk

Red food coloring
2/3 cup finely crushed
  peppermint stick candy
12 Ladyfingers
1 cup heavy cream, whipped

In medium saucepan, mix gelatin, 1/4 cup sugar, and salt. Beat together the egg yolks and milk; stir into gelatin. Place over low heat; stir constantly until gelatin dissolves and mixture thickens slightly, about 5 minutes. Remove from heat and cool slightly. Stir in a few drops of red food coloring and crushed candy. Chill, stirring occasionally, until mixture mounds slightly when dropped from a spoon.

While mixture chills, separate Ladyfingers and stand around sides of a 9" springform pan with rounded sides against pan. Beat egg whites until soft peaks form. Then gradually beat in remaining 1/2 cup sugar and beat until stiff peaks form. Fold into chilled gelatin mixture. Fold in whipped cream and turn into prepared pan. Chill until set.

To serve, remove from pan and garnish with additional whipped cream and crushed candy. Serves 8-10.

You can't forget the fine flavor, texture and color of this cake...

SNOWBALL CAKE

1 large Angel Food cake
2 envelopes unflavored
  gelatin
1 pint whipping cream
  (sweetened & whipped)

1 large can crushed
  pineapple, drained
1 cup pineapple juice
1 large can Angel Flake
  coconut

Mix gelatin with 3 tablespoons cold water. Add 1 cup hot water and the pineapple juice. Add pineapple and chill until firm. Then fold in the sweetened and whipped cream, reserving 1/3 of this mixture for topping.

Break cake into large pieces and alternate layers of cake, topping and coconut in large salad mold, ending with a layer of cake pieces.

Refrigerate for at least 3 hours. Unmold onto a 10-inch plate. Spread the reserved mixture over cake and sprinkle coconut on top.

SPRINGTIME DELIGHT

6 eggs, separated
3/4 cup sugar
3/4 cup lemon juice
2 teaspoons grated lemon
  rind

1 envelope gelatin
1/4 cup cold water
1 Angel Food cake
3/4 cup sugar

Mix egg yolks, 3/4 cup sugar, lemon juice and rind in top of double boiler and cook until thickened. Dissolve gelatin in water and add to above. Make a meringue of the egg whites and 3/4 cup sugar. Then fold custard slowly into meringue.

Line a tube pan with wax paper. Break cake into small pieces and alternate layers of cake and custard in pan. Let stand refrigerated overnight. About 2 hours before serving, ice with whipped cream.

Cookies

ALMOND CRISPIES

1 cup butter
1 cup sugar
1 cup thick sour cream
1/8 teaspoon soda
2 egg yolks
1-1/2 teaspoons grated
  lemon rind

1 teaspoon soda
1/2 teaspoon salt
3 to 3-1/3 cups all-
  purpose flour
3/4 cups almonds
2 tablespoons sugar

Combine butter, 1 cup sugar, cream and 1/8 teaspoon soda in heavy saucepan. Place over heat. Stir until sugar is dissolved. Boil, stirring occasionally, until thick (10 to 15 minutes). Cool to lukewarm. Beat in egg yolks, lemon rind, soda and salt. Add enough flour to make a medium-stiff dough. Roll dough, 1/2 teaspoon at a time, in palm of hands to form small balls. Place 3 inches apart on ungreased cookie sheet. Press flat with bottom of glass dipped in sugar. Sprinkle with mixture of almonds and 2 tablespoons sugar. Bake on ungreased cookie sheets at 325° F. for 10 to 12 minutes, or until edges are browned.

ALMOND DREAM COOKIES

2 sticks butter, softened
3/4 cup sugar
1/2 teaspoon baking powder

1/2 teaspoon vinegar
1-1/2 cups flour
Whole almonds

Cream butter and sugar together until light and fluffy. Add vinegar and flour and blend thoroughly. Drop by teaspoonsful onto lightly greased cookie sheet. Place an almond on top of each cookie before baking. Bake at 300° F. for around 18 to 20 minutes. Cool for several minutes before removing from cookie sheet. Yields around 5 dozen cookies.

ALMOND VANILLA CRESCENTS

1 cup butter
1/2 cup sugar
2 egg yolks
1/8 teaspoon salt
1 teaspoon vanilla

3 cups flour
1 cup blanched, slivered almonds,
  finely ground
Confectioners sugar

Cream butter and sugar together until light and fluffy. Add egg yolks, salt and vanilla. Beat well. Stir in flour and almonds. Chill 1 hour.

Shape into 2 inch crescents. Place on lightly greased cookie sheet. Bake at 325° F. for 20 minutes. Remove immediately from cookie sheets. Coat with confectioners sugar.

APPLE DREAM SQUARES

1/2 cup butter
1-1/2 cups brown sugar,
  divided
1-1/4 cups sifted all-
  purpose flour, divided
2 eggs
1 teaspoon vanilla

1/4 teaspoon salt
1/2 teaspoon baking powder
1 (4 ounce) can flaked
  coconut
2-1/2 cups sliced apples
1 cup chopped nuts

Cream together butter, 1/2 cup brown sugar and 1 cup flour until crumbly. Pat out into greased 9x9x2" baking pan. Bake at 350°F. for 20 minutes. Beat eggs, vanilla and remaining 1 cup brown sugar, 1/4 cup flour, salt and baking powder. Mix well. Add apples, coconut and nuts. Pour over baked crust. Return to oven and bake an additional 20-25 minutes. Cut into squares.

APPLESAUCE COOKIES

1-3/4 cups uncooked
  quick oats
1-1/2 cups flour, unsifted
1 teaspoon salt
1 teaspoon baking powder
1 teaspoon cinnamon
1/2 teaspoon nutmeg
1/2 teaspoon baking soda
1/2 cup butter, softened

1 cup brown sugar, firmly
  packed
1/2 cup granulated sugar
1 egg
3/4 cup applesauce
6-ounce package semi-sweet
  chocolate morsels
1 cup chopped nuts

Heat oven to 375°F. In small bowl combine oats, flour, salt, baking powder, cinnamon, nutmeg and baking soda; set aside. In large bowl cream butter, brown sugar and granulated sugar. Beat in egg. Gradually blend in flour mixture alternately with applesauce. Stir in semi-sweet chocolate morsels and nuts. Drop by level measuring tablespoonsful onto greased cookie sheets. Bake at 375°F. for 14 minutes.

BOURBON BALLS

2 cups vanilla wafer crumbs
2 tablespoons cocoa
1-1/2 cups confectioners
  sugar, divided

1 cup finely chopped pecans
2 tablespoons white corn syrup
1/4 cup bourbon

Mix well the vanilla wafer crumbs, cocoa, 1 cup confectioners sugar and pecans. Add the corn syrup and bourbon and mix well. Shape into 1-inch balls and roll in the remaining confectioners sugar. Store in a tightly covered metal container for at least 12 hours before serving.

APRICOT DATE BARS

1 cup brown sugar	3/4 cup melted butter
1 teaspoon vanilla	Pinch salt
2 cups flour	2 teaspoons baking soda
2 cups quick rolled raw oats	1 cup coconut

Filling

1-1/2 cups mashed, cooked dried apricots	3 tablespoons apricot juice
1 cup dates, cut up	1/2 cup sugar

Cook filling ingredients for 2 or 3 minutes. Combine dry ingredients with butter and vanilla. Press one-half of crumb mixture in pan; spread filling over the top. Then spread remaining crumbs evenly. Bake in 350° F. oven for 30 minutes.

BANANA-OATMEAL COOKIES

1-1/2 cups sifted all-purpose flour	1 egg
1 teaspoon salt	1 cup mashed ripe bananas (approximately 3)
1/2 teaspoon baking soda	1 teaspoon vanilla extract
1/2 teaspoon nutmeg	1-1/2 cups raw quick-cooking oats
3/4 teaspoon cinnamon	
3/4 cup soft butter	1/2 cup coarsely chopped pecans
1 cup sugar	

Sift flour together with salt, soda, nutmeg and cinnamon and set aside. In large bowl of electric mixer (at medium speed) beat butter, sugar and egg until light and fluffy. Beat in bananas and vanilla until smooth. Gradually stir in flour mixture and oats until well combined. Stir in nuts and refrigerate for 30 minutes. Meanwhile, preheat oven to 400° F. and lightly grease cookie sheets. Drop batter by rounded teaspoonsful, two inches apart, onto cookie sheets. Bake for 12 to 15 minutes, or until golden brown. Remove to wire rack and cool.

BUTTER PECAN COOKIES

2-1/2 sticks butter	3 cups flour, sifted
1 cup sugar	1 teaspoon almond extract
2 egg yolks	1 cup chopped pecans

Cream butter and sugar until light and fluffy. Add egg yolks, one at a time, beating well after each addition. Then add sifted flour gradually, blending well. Add flavoring and blend. Then stir in pecans. Drop by teaspoonsful onto ungreased cookie sheet. Bake at 350° F. for around 12 minutes. Yields around 5 dozen cookies.

BLONDE BROWNIES

1 cup flour	2 cups light brown sugar
2 teaspoons baking powder	2 eggs, beaten
1 teaspoon salt	2 teaspoons vanilla extract
1 stick butter, plus	1 cup chopped pecans
2 tablespoons, melted	

Sift flour, baking powder and salt together and set aside. Pour melted butter into mixing bowl. Beat in sugar, eggs and vanilla. Add sifted dry ingredients, mixed with pecans. Spread thinly in well greased and floured pan. Bake at 350° F. 25 to 30 minutes. Cool and then cut into squares.

BROWN SUGAR COOKIES

1 cup butter	2 cups brown sugar
2 eggs	3-1/2 cups flour
1 cup chopped pecans	1 teaspoon baking soda
1 teaspoon vanilla	1/2 teaspoon salt

Sift flour, salt and soda together and set aside. Cream sugar and butter until well mixed. Add eggs, one at a time, beating well after each addition. Add flavoring and blend. Add flour mixture gradually, mixing well. Stir in pecans. Roll in round balls; wrap in wax paper. Refrigerate overnight. Thinly slice cookies and place on an ungreased cookie sheet. Bake at 350° F. for around 10 minutes. Do not burn.

BUTTER COOKIES

1 cup butter	2-1/2 cups flour
1 cup sugar	1 cup nuts, chopped
2 egg yolks	(if desired)
1 teaspoon vanilla	

Cream butter thoroughly; add sugar and continue beating until fluffy. Add egg yolks and vanilla and beat well. Stir in flour and mix well. Divide dough in half if you want half plain and half with nuts. Dip finger tips in cold water and make small cookies by forming balls and pressing flat on ungreased baking sheet. Bake at 400° F. for 10 minutes.

BROWNIE CUP CAKES

3 squares unsweetened chocolate
2 sticks butter
1-1/2 cups broken pecans (optional)
1-3/4 cups sugar

1 cup flour
4 eggs
1 teaspoon vanilla

Melt chocolate and butter over low heat in heavy saucepan. Add nuts and stir to coat. Remove from heat. Combine sugar, flour, eggs and vanilla. Mix only to blend (do not beat). Add chocolate-nut mixture and mix carefully. Put into 20 baking cups. Fill almost to the top as they don't rise much. Bake at 325°F. for 30 to 35 minutes.

BROWNIES SUPREME

1-1/2 squares unsweetened chocolate
1/2 cup crisco
(Melt together and set aside)

1 cup sugar
2 eggs
3/4 cup self-rising flour

1 cup chopped nuts
1 teaspoon vanilla

Add chocolate mixture to sugar and then combine remaining ingredients. Bake 20 minutes at 350°F. Check for doneness.

Icing

1 square unsweetened
chocolate
2 tablespoons butter

1/3 small can evaporated milk
1/2 box confectioners sugar

Combine all ingredients in saucepan and stir over medium heat until it boils around edges. Add capful of vanilla and a dash of salt. Beat until thick enough to spread.

CARAMEL SQUARES

1 stick butter
1 cup light brown sugar,
packed
1 egg
1 cup flour

1 teaspoon baking powder
Dash salt
1 teaspoon vanilla
1 cup chopped pecans
Confectioners sugar

Melt butter with sugar over low heat. Cool. Add egg and beat. Sift the flour, baking powder and salt together. Add to the creamed mixture. Blend in the vanilla and pecans. Spread in a greased baking pan and bake at 350°F. for around 30 minutes. Sift confectioners sugar over top when done. Let cool and cut into squares.

BUTTER STARS

Cream thoroughly:
  1 cup butter

Add:
  1 egg yolk
  6 tablespoons confectioners sugar
  3 cups flour
  1 tablespoon sherry or brandy

Mix thoroughly. Chill. Roll 1/2 inch thick. Cut out with a star cutter.

Beat until stiff:
  1 egg white

Fold in:
  1/2 cup sugar

Put a spoonful on each cookie and sprinkle with chopped almonds.
Bake for 30 minutes at 325°F. Yields 36 cookies.

BUTTERSCOTCH REFRIGERATOR COOKIES

2 cups sifted cake flour
1-1/2 teaspoons baking powder
1/4 teaspoon salt
1 cup shortening
1/2 cup granulated sugar

1/2 cup brown sugar
1 egg, slightly beaten
1 teaspoon vanilla
2/3 cup chopped nuts

Sift flour, baking powder and salt together. Cream shortening with sugars until fluffy. Add egg and vanilla. Mix well and add sifted dry ingredients and nuts. Mix and shape into rolls about 2-1/2-inches in diameter. Wrap in wax paper and chill thoroughly. Cut into 1/8-inch slices and bake on greased cookie sheet in a 400°F. oven for 12 minutes or until browned. (You may use ground raisins or coconut instead of part or all of the nuts.)

CANDY COOKIES

2 cups granulated sugar
1/4 cup cocoa
1 stick margarine
1/3 cup milk

1 teaspoon vanilla
1/3 cup peanut butter
2-1/2 cups walnuts or coconut

Combine the granulated sugar, cocoa, margarine and milk and bring to a rolling boil; boil for one minute. Remove from heat and add vanilla, peanut butter, and walnuts or coconut. Drop from a teaspoon onto wax paper.

CARAMEL COOKIES

1 cup butter
1 cup brown sugar
1 cup granulated sugar
2 beaten eggs
2 teaspoons vanilla

3 cups plain flour
1 teaspoon baking soda
1/2 teaspoon salt
1 cup chopped pecans

Cream the butter and sugars together until light and fluffy. Add beaten eggs and vanilla and blend well. Sift the flour, soda and salt together and add gradually to the creamed mixture. Add the pecans dredged in flour. Make two rolls and chill overnight. Thinly slice cookies and place on ungreased cookie sheet. Bake at 350° F. for 10 minutes.

CHERRY DROPS

1/4 cup butter
1/2 cup sugar
1 egg, unbeaten
1 cup sifted flour
1 teaspoon baking powder

1/4 teaspoon salt
3 tablespoons whipping cream
1/2 teaspoon vanilla
1-1/2 cups drained
    maraschino cherries

Cream butter and sugar together until light and fluffy. Add egg and beat until fluffy. Add sifted flour, baking powder and salt alternately with the cream. Stir in the vanilla. Dip cherries into batter one at a time and form a cherry drop. Place on greased cookie sheet. Bake in 375° F. oven for 10 to 12 minutes. Yields around 50 small cookies.

CHESS SQUARES

2 sticks butter
1 box light brown sugar
1/2 cup granulated sugar
4 eggs
2 cups flour

1 teaspoon baking powder
pinch salt
1 teaspoon vanilla
1 cup chopped pecans

Melt butter and brown sugar together on low heat. Cream granulated sugar into this mixture. Add eggs, one at a time, beating well after each addition. Blend in the vanilla. Add the sifted flour, baking powder and salt gradually. Blend in the pecans. Pour into a greased and floured 9 x 13-inch pan. Bake at 300° F. for 40 to 50 minutes. Cut into bars when slightly cooled and roll in confectioners sugar.

CAROB GOODIES

1 cup sugar
1 stick butter
5 tablespoons carob powder
1/2 cup milk

1 cup pecans, chopped
1 teaspoon vanilla
3 cups rolled oats
1 cup peanut butter

Combine the sugar, butter, powder and milk in a large saucepan and cook for 15 minutes. Then add pecans, vanilla, oats and peanut butter and mix together thoroughly. Cool slightly and drop by teaspoonsful on wax paper. Let cool before serving.

CHOCOLATE BALLS

1-1/2 cups butter, softened
3/4 cup sugar
2 cups flour
1/8 teaspoon salt

1/2 cup cocoa
2 cups chopped pecans
1 teaspoon vanilla
Confectioners sugar

Cream butter and sugar until light and fluffy. Sift together the flour, salt and cocoa. Gradually add to creamed mixture, then blend in the pecans and vanilla. Refrigerate for around 2-1/2 hours. Shape into 1-inch balls and place on an ungreased cookie sheet. Bake at 350°F. for around 20 minutes. When slightly cooled, roll in confectioners sugar. Yields around 6 dozen balls.

CHOCOLATE CAKE SQUARES

2 cups plain unsifted flour
2 cups sugar
1 cup water
2 sticks butter
5 tablespoons cocoa

1/2 cup buttermilk
1/2 teaspoon baking soda
2 eggs
1 tablespoon vanilla

Preheat oven to 400°F. Mix sugar and flour together. Bring water, butter and cocoa to a boil. Pour into flour-sugar mixture. Add buttermilk, soda and vanilla. Stir into this mixture the slightly beaten eggs. Pour into a lightly greased baking pan. Spread with Icing when you remove from oven and let cool before cutting into squares.

Icing

1 stick butter
6 tablespoons milk
4 tablespoons cocoa

1 box confectioners sugar
1/2 cup chopped pecans
1 tablespoon vanilla

Melt butter and add milk and cocoa. Remove from heat and stir in sugar, pecans and vanilla. Spread on cake immediately.

CHOCOLATE PEANUT DREAMS

6 ounce package semi-sweet
  chocolate pieces
16 large marshmallows
1/3 cup crunchy peanut butter
2 tablespoons butter

2 tablespoons milk
1 cup coconut
1/3 cup salted peanuts
1 cup Quick Quaker Oats

Melt chocolate pieces, marshmallows, peanut butter and butter in top of double boiler over hot, not boiling water. Stir until smooth. Remove from heat. Stir in milk, coconut, peanuts and oats. Mix thoroughly. Drop by teaspoonsful onto wax paper. Chill thoroughly. Store in refrigerator.

CHOCOLATE CRINKLES

1/2 cup Wesson oil
4 squares unsweetened
  chocolate (4-oz. melted)
2 teaspoons vanilla
2 teaspoons baking powder

1 cup confectioners sugar
4 eggs
2 cups sugar
2 cups flour
1/2 teaspoon salt

Mix oil, chocolate and granulated sugar. Blend in one egg at a time until well blended. Add vanilla. Stir sifted flour mixture into oil mixture. Chill several hours. Shape into balls and roll in confectioners sugar. Bake at 350°F. for 10 to 12 minutes. Do not overbake.

CHOCOLATE CRISPS

3 squares unsweetened
  chocolate, melted
1 cup butter
2 cups sugar

4 eggs, unbeaten
1 cup flour, sifted
1 teaspoon vanilla
1 cup pecans, finely chopped

Melt chocolate in 1/4 cup butter. Cool slightly. Cream sugar with the rest of butter; add eggs and then melted chocolate, mixing all well. Stir in flour and vanilla. Spread evenly on ungreased cookie sheet. Sprinkle chopped nuts evenly on top of batter. Bake at 375°F. for 15 to 17 minutes. Cut in small squares and take out of pan while warm or they will stick. Keep in tin or other tight container.

CHOCOLATE MINT BROWNIES

1/2 cup butter
1 cup sugar
2 eggs
1 teaspoon vanilla
2 squares chocolate, melted
1/2 cup flour
1/2 cup nuts

1 cup confectioners sugar
2 tablespoons butter
1 tablespoon whipping cream
1/4 to 1/2 teaspoon peppermint extract
Melted chocolate

Cream butter and sugar. Beat in eggs and vanilla. Blend in chocolate. Stir in flour and nuts. Bake in 8 x 8-inch greased pan for 25 minutes in 325°F. oven. Cool. Combine remaining ingredients and spread on top of cooled brownies. Drizzle with desired amount of melted chocolate.

CHOCOLATE-PEANUT BUTTER COOKIES

2 cups all-purpose flour
1 cup butter, softened

1/2 cup sugar
2 teaspoons vanilla

In large mixer bowl, combine all ingredients and mix well. Drop by level teaspoons onto greased cookie sheets. Flatten to 1/4-inch with a glass, greased on the bottom then dipped in sugar. Bake at 325°F. for 15-18 minutes. Spread warm cookies with peanut butter topping. Drizzle with chocolate glaze. Let stand until glaze is set. Makes 54-60 cookies.

Peanut Butter Topping

1/4 cup butter
1/3 cup peanut butter

1/3 cup firmly packed brown sugar

Cream all ingredients together until light and fluffy.

Chocolate Glaze

1/2 cup semi-sweet chocolate pieces
2 tablespoons milk

1/3 cup sifted powdered sugar

Melt chocolate pieces with milk in a saucepan over low heat, stirring constantly. Remove from heat. Add powdered sugar; stir until smooth.

CHOCOLATE-CHIP COOKIES

1 cup plus 2 tablespoons
   sifted flour
1/2 teaspoon baking soda
1/2 teaspoon salt
1/2 cup granulated sugar
1/4 cup light brown sugar,
   firmly packed

1 egg
1 teaspoon vanilla
1/2 cup soft butter
1/2 cup chopped pecans
1 package (6-oz.) semi-sweet
   chocolate morsels

Sift flour, soda and salt together into large mixing bowl. Add sugars, egg, vanilla and butter. With wooden spoon, or portable electric mixer at medium speed, beat until smooth and well combined -- approximately 1 minute. Stir in nuts and chocolate morsels. Drop by teaspoonsful, 2-inches apart, onto ungreased cookie sheets. Bake at 375° F. for 10-12 minutes, or until golden brown. Remove to wire rack and cool.

CHOCOLATE PINWHEELS

1-1/2 cups sifted flour
1/2 teaspoon baking powder
1/8 teaspoon salt
1/2 cup shortening
1/2 cup sugar

1 egg yolk, well beaten
1 teaspoon vanilla
3 tablespoons milk
1 ounce (square)
   chocolate, melted

Sift flour, baking powder and salt together. Cream shortening with sugar until fluffy. Add egg yolk and vanilla and beat well. Add flour alternately with milk, mixing well after each addition. Divide dough into two parts. To one part, add chocolate and blend. Chill until firm enough to roll. Roll each half into rectangular sheet, 1/8-inch thick and as nearly the same size and shape as possible. Place plain sheet over chocolate sheet and roll as for jelly roll. Chill overnight or until firm enough to slice. Cut into 1/8-inch slices. Bake on ungreased baking sheet in 400° F. oven for 5 minutes.

CHURCH WINDOWS

1 12-ounce package
chocolate morsels
1 10-1/2 ounce package multi-
colored miniature marshmallows

1/2 cup butter
1 cup finely chopped pecans
Flaked coconut

Melt chocolate and butter over low heat; cool. Add marsh-mallows and nuts to chocolate mixture. Shape into two rolls 1-1/2 to 2 inches in diameter; roll each in coconut. Refrigerate. When rolls are thoroughly chilled, slice into 1/2-inch slices.

COTTAGE WALNUT COOKIES

1 cup brown sugar
1/2 cup butter
1 egg
1/2 teaspoon salt
1 cup small curd cottage cheese

1 cup chopped pecans
1-1/2 teaspoons vanilla
1-1/2 cups sifted flour
1 teaspoon nutmeg
1/2 teaspoon soda

Cream sugar and butter until fluffy; beat in egg, cottage cheese and vanilla. Add flour which has been sifted with nutmeg, salt and soda, mixing well. Stir in pecans and drop by teaspoonsful onto a lightly greased cookie sheet. Flatten to 1/4-inch thickness with the bottom of a glass which has been lightly buttered and dipped into a dish of white sugar. Bake at 375°F. for 15 minutes or until lightly brown.

CREAM CHEESE COOKIES

1 stick real butter
1 3-ounce package cream cheese
1 cup sugar

1 cup plain flour
1/2 teaspoon vanilla
1/2 cup chopped pecans

Cream butter and cheese. Add sugar and mix well. Add flour, vanilla and nuts. Drop by teaspoonsful on ungreased cookie sheet. Bake at 375°F. until brown. (Do not let these burn.) Makes approximately 3 dozen.

CHOCOLATE REFRIGERATOR COOKIES

4 cups sifted cake flour
4 teaspoons baking powder
1/2 teaspoon salt
1-1/4 cups softened shortening
1-1/2 cups sugar

2 eggs, unbeaten
4 ounces (squares)
   chocolate, melted
1 teaspoon vanilla
2 cups broken walnuts

Sift flour, baking powder and salt together. Cream shortening and sugar until fluffy. Add eggs, chocolate and vanilla, beating until blended; then add nut meats. Add sifted dry ingredients gradually, mixing well. Shape into two rolls, 1-1/2-inches in diameter, and wrap in waxed paper and chill thoroughly. Cut into 1/8-inch slices and bake on ungreased baking sheet in 350°F. oven for 10 minutes.

CHRISTMAS COOKIES

1 cup butter
1-1/2 cups sugar
3 eggs
1 teaspoon vanilla

3-1/2 cups sifted flour
2 teaspoons cream of tartar
1 teaspoon baking soda
1/2 teaspoon salt

Cream butter and sugar until light and fluffy. Add eggs, one at a time, beating well after each addition. Stir in vanilla. Sift flour, cream of tartar, baking soda and salt together and gradually add to the creamed mixture. Chill in refrigerator for 3 to 4 hours. Then roll out and cut in desired shapes. Place on ungreased cookie sheets and bake at 375°F. for 6 to 8 minutes. Decorate with Ornamental Frosting.

Ornamental Frosting

1 egg white
1/8 teaspoon cream of tartar
1/8 teaspoon vanilla

1-1/4 cups sifted
   confectioners sugar
Food coloring

Mix and beat first 3 ingredients. Gradually add sugar until mixture stands up. Tint and decorate cookies.

CINNAMON SQUARES

1 cup butter
1 cup sugar
1 egg, separated
2 cups sifted all-purpose flour

1-1/2 tablespoons cinnamon
1 teaspoon salt
1-1/2 cups chopped nuts

Grease and flour a 15-1/2 x 10-1/2 x 1" pan. Cream the butter and sugar. Add the egg yolk and sifted dry ingredients. Press batter into the prepared pan. Beat the egg white until foamy and spread sparingly over the batter. Press on the nuts. Bake at 325° F. for 30 minutes. Cool and then cut into squares.

COCOA PECAN COOKIES

2 sticks butter
1/2 cup sugar
1-3/4 cups flour
1/4 cup cocoa

2 teaspoons vanilla
2 teaspoons instant coffee
1/8 teaspoon salt
2 cups chopped pecans

Cream butter and sugar until light and fluffy. Add sifted flour, cocoa, coffee and salt. Blend in the vanilla. Mix thoroughly and then fold in the pecans. Shape dough into 3/4 inch balls and place on a greased cookie sheet one inch apart. Bake at 325° F. for about 15 minutes. Cool. Then roll in confectioners sugar. Yields around 6 dozen cookies.

COCONUT BALLS

1 cup margarine
1/2 cup sugar
2 teaspoons vanilla
2 cups sifted flour

1/4 teaspoon salt
1/2 pound pecan halves
Shredded coconut

Cream together margarine, sugar and vanilla until light and fluffy. Sift together flour and salt. Add to creamed mixture and blend thoroughly. Shape dough around pecan halves to form one inch balls. Roll in shredded coconut and place on an ungreased baking sheet. Bake at 325° F. for around 20 minutes. Remove to wire rack and cool.

COCONUT-CARROT COOKIES

1 cup shortening
3/4 cup sugar
2 eggs
1 cup mashed cooked carrots
2 cups flour

2 teaspoons baking powder
1/2 teaspoon salt
3/4 cup shredded coconut
Orange Butter Icing

Heat oven to 400°F. Mix shortening, sugar, eggs and carrots. Blend in flour, baking powder and salt. Stir in coconut. Drop dough by teaspoonsful about 2 inches apart onto lightly greased baking sheet. Bake 8 to 10 minutes or until no imprint remains when touched lightly. Immediately remove from baking sheet. Cool. Frost with Orange Butter Icing.

Orange Butter Icing

3 tablespoons soft butter
1-1/2 cups confectioners sugar

2 teaspoons grated orange peel
1 tablespoon orange juice

Blend butter and sugar. Stir in orange peel and juice. Beat until frosting is smooth and of spreading consistency. Frost cookies. Yields around 4 dozen cookies.

COCONUT-DATE BALLS

1 egg, beaten
1 cup sugar
1 8-ounce box chopped dates
1 cup coconut

1 teaspoon vanilla
2-1/4 cups rice crispies
1 cup chopped pecans

Combine egg, sugar, dates and cook until dates are melted. Remove and add vanilla, pecans, coconut and rice crispies. Roll in confectioners sugar.

CREAM CHEESE COOKIES SUPREME

1 cup butter
2 3-ounce packages cream
  cheese
1 cup sugar
1/4 teaspoon salt

1 teaspoon vanilla
1 egg
1 tablespoon milk
2 cups flour
1/2 cup toasted flaked coconut

Cream butter and cream cheese until fluffy. Add sugar, vanilla and salt and blend well. Add egg and beat well. Stir in the milk. Add flour gradually and then add the coconut. Mix well and then drop from a teaspoon onto a greased cookie sheet. Top with pecan halves, if desired. Bake at 325°F. for about 20 minutes.

COCONUT PRALINES

2 cups granulated sugar
1 cup firmly packed
brown sugar
3 tablespoons light corn
syrup

1 cup light cream
2-2/3 cups flaked coconut
1 teaspoon vanilla
1/4 cup butter

Combine sugars, corn syrup, and cream in a heavy saucepan. Bring to a boil over low heat, stirring constantly. Continue to boil gently, without stirring, until a small amount of mixture forms a soft ball in cold water (or to a temperature of 236° F.). Remove from heat. Add coconut, vanilla, and butter. Stir to blend. Cool to lukewarm (110° F.) without stirring.

Then beat vigorously just until mixture begins to thicken, about 1 to 2 minutes. Drop by spoonsful onto wax paper. Allow to stand until firm, about 3 hours. To store, wrap each praline in wax paper. Makes about 2 dozen pralines.

CORN FLAKE MACAROONS

2 egg whites
1 cup sugar
2 cups corn flakes

1/2 cup chopped nuts
1 cup dry coconut
1 teaspoon vanilla extract

Beat egg whites until stiff, but not dry. Fold in sugar a small amount at a time. Fold in corn flakes, nuts, coconut and vanilla. Drop by teaspoonsful on a well greased cookie sheet. Bake at 350° F. about 15 - 20 minutes until light brown.

Place cookie sheet on a damp towel to remove cookies.

Very, very good!

DROP SUGAR COOKIES

2-1/2 cups sifted all-purpose
flour
1/2 teaspoon soda
1/2 cup solid shortening
1 teaspoon vanilla or
lemon extract

2 tablespoons milk
3/4 teaspoon salt
1/2 cup margarine
1 cup sugar
1 egg

Sift flour, salt and soda. Cream butter and shortening together with electric mixer. Gradually add sugar, vanilla and egg until light and fluffy. Add flour mixture and milk and beat until smooth. Drop by teaspoonsful onto greased baking sheet. Flatten with bottom of glass dipped in sugar. Bake at 400° F. for 12 minutes, or until brown around edges. Makes about 5 dozen.

DATE NUT FINGERS

Dissolve over low heat:

1 *stick margarine*
1 *cup sugar*
1 *8-ounce package pitted dates*

Stir and mash. Remove from heat and add:

1 *cup rice crispies*
1 *cup chopped nuts*
1 *teaspoon vanilla extract*

Roll into finger shapes or balls and then roll in sifted powdered sugar.

Delicious!

DATE SWIRLS

1/2 *pound pitted dates,*
  finely cut
1/4 *cup sugar*

1/3 *cup water*
1/2 *cup chopped nuts*
Pinch salt

Cook dates, sugar and water together for five minutes. Remove from heat and add nuts and salt. Let mixture cool while mixing cookie dough.

Cookie Dough

1/2 *cup shortening*
1/2 *teaspoon salt*
1/2 *teaspoon soda*
1/2 *teaspoon lemon extract*

1/2 *cup brown sugar*
1/2 *cup granulated sugar*
1 *egg*
2-1/4 *cups flour*

Cream shortening, salt, soda and lemon extract. Add sugar and blend thoroughly. Blend in egg and add flour. Mix well, then roll dough out on wax paper. Roll out thin; spread date mixture over top. Roll and chill for several hours. Slice thinly and bake at 375° F. for about 12 minutes.

DREAM BALLS

2 *pounds confectioners sugar*
1 *can Eagle Brand condensed milk*

1 *stick margarine*
2 *cups chopped nuts*

Mix together; make into balls using butter to grease hands. Chill thoroughly. Meanwhile melt 4 squares unsweetened chocolate with one half pound parafin in double boiler. Add chocolate to parafin. Using toothpicks to hold candy balls, dip each ball into hot chocolate mix. Put on wax paper to cool.

DOUBLE CHOCOLATE DROPS

1 package (6-oz.) semi-sweet chocolate morsels
1 cup sifted all-purpose flour
1/2 teaspoon baking soda

1/2 teaspoon salt
1/2 cup soft butter
1/2 cup sugar
1 egg
1/2 cup chopped pecans

In top of double boiler, over hot not boiling water, melt 1/2 cup chocolate morsels. Let cool. Sift together flour, soda and salt and set aside. In large bowl of electric mixer (medium speed) beat butter, sugar and egg until light and fluffy. At low speed, beat in melted chocolate and 1/4 cup warm water. Then beat in flour mixture, just until combined. With spoon, stir in remaining chocolate morsels and nuts. Refrigerate for 30 minutes. Meanwhile, preheat oven to 375° F. Lightly grease cookie sheets. Drop batter by teaspoonsful, 3-inches apart, onto cookie sheets. Bake for 10-12 minutes and remove to wire rack to cool.

EASY MACAROONS

2 8-ounce packages shredded coconut
1 15-ounce can Eagle Brand condensed milk

2 teaspoons vanilla

Mix ingredients; drop from teaspoon onto well greased cookie sheet. Bake at 350° F. for 10-12 minutes. Cool slightly and remove to rack to finish cooling.

FESTIVE COOKIES

1/2 cup butter, softened
1 cup sugar
1 egg, beaten
1 teaspoon vanilla
1 tablespoon whipping cream

2 cups sifted all-purpose flour
1-1/2 teaspoons baking powder
1/2 teaspoon salt
Colored sugar

Preheat the oven to 375° F. for 10 minutes before the cookies are ready to go in. Grease a cookie sheet. Cream the butter and sugar. Add the egg, vanilla, cream and sifted dry ingredients. Chill in the refrigerator several hours. Roll out, cut, and sprinkle with colored sugar. Place at least 3-inches apart on the prepared cookie sheet (they spread quite a bit). Bake at 375° F. for 15 minutes. Store in a covered container to retain crispness.

FIG COOKIES

2-1/4 cups sifted flour
1/2 teaspoon cinnamon
1 teaspoon baking soda
1/2 cup shortening

1 cup brown sugar
2 eggs, beaten
2 tablespoons sour cream
1 cup chopped figs

Sift flour, cinnamon and soda together. Cream shortening with sugar until fluffy; add eggs, cream and figs. Add sifted dry ingredients. (Add more flour if necessary.) Chill thoroughly. Roll out on lightly floured board to 1/8-inch thickness. Cut with cookie cutter and bake on greased cookie sheet in 350°F. oven for 10 to 12 minutes, or until browned.

FORGOTTEN COOKIES

Turn oven to 350°F. while mixing.

2 egg whites
2/3 cup sugar
1 teaspoon vanilla extract

1 cup chopped pecans
1 small package chocolate chips

Beat egg whites until stiff; add sugar gradually, beating well. Add vanilla extract. Fold in pecans and chocolate chips. Line cookie sheet with aluminum foil. Drop by teaspoonsful 1-1/2 inches apart. Put in oven and turn off heat. Leave in oven overnight. Yields around 30 cookies.

FROSTED APRICOT BARS

4 eggs
2 cups sugar
2 teaspoons soda
1 teaspoon salt

2 teaspoons cinnamon
1-1/3 cups cooking oil
2 cups flour
3 small jars apricot baby food

Beat eggs well. Add sugar, soda, salt, cinnamon, oil and flour; mix well. Add apricots and fold into mixture. Pour on a well greased 11 x 15" cookie sheet and bake at 350°F. for 40 minutes, or until brown. Cool and frost. Cut into bars.

Frosting

4 tablespoons margarine
6 ounces cream cheese

1/2 teaspoon vanilla
1/2 to 1 box 10-X powdered sugar

Blend margarine and cream cheese well; add vanilla and powdered sugar to thin spreading consistency.

FRUIT ROCKS

1/2 pound butter	2 quarts chopped pecans
1 pound candied cherries, chopped	1/2 teaspoon salt
	1/2 teaspoon allspice
1 pound candied pineapple, chopped	1/2 teaspoon cinnamon
	1/2 teaspoon nutmeg
2-1/2 cups flour	5 eggs
1-1/4 cups sugar	2 tablespoons sherry

Mix chopped fruit with 1 cup flour and set aside. Cream butter and sugar until light and fluffy. Add eggs, one at a time, beating well after each addition. Add flour, spices, fruit, nuts and sherry and mix well. Drop by teaspoonsful on ungreased cookie sheet. Bake at 375° F. for about 15 minutes.

GLAZED CHOCOLATE COOKIES

1-1/4 cups sifted all-purpose flour	1 egg
	1 teaspoon vanilla
1/4 teaspoon salt	2 squares unsweetened chocolate, melted
1/4 teaspoon baking soda	
1/2 cup soft butter	1/2 cup buttermilk
1 cup light brown sugar, firmly packed	1 cup coarsely chopped pecans

Sift together flour, salt and soda and set aside. In large bowl of electric mixer (medium speed) beat butter, sugar, egg and vanilla until light and fluffy. Add chocolate and mix well. At low speed, beat in flour mixture alternately with buttermilk until well combined. Stir in nuts. Mixture will be soft. Drop by rounded teaspoonsful, 2-inches apart, onto ungreased cookie sheet. Bake at 375° F. for 8 to 10 minutes. Remove to wire rack and partially cool.

Glaze

3 cups sifted confectioners sugar	1 teaspoon vanilla extract
	1 square unsweetened chocolate, melted
1/4 cup light cream	

In medium bowl, combine sugar, cream and vanilla. With spoon, beat until smooth. Add melted chocolate; mix well. (If glaze is too stiff to spread easily, add a little more cream). Glaze top of cookies while slightly warm.

GERMAN CHOCOLATE COOKIES

2 4-ounce packages German
  chocolate
1 tablespoon butter
2 eggs
3/4 cup sugar
1/4 cup unsifted flour

1/4 teaspoon baking powder
1/8 teaspoon cinnamon
1/8 teaspoon salt
1/2 teaspoon vanilla
1 cup chopped pecans

Melt chocolate and butter over hot water. Stir and cool. Beat eggs, then add sugar gradually until thickened and well blended. Stir in chocolate. Add flour, baking powder, cinnamon and salt. Blend well, then stir in the vanilla and pecans. Drop by teaspoonsful onto a greased baking sheet. Bake in 350° F. oven until cookies are set, around 10 minutes. Yields around 3 dozen cookies.

GIANT CHOCOLATE CHIP COOKIES

1/2 cup butter
1/2 cup shortening
1 cup light brown sugar,
  firmly packed
1/2 cup sugar
2 eggs
2 teaspoons vanilla

2-1/2 cups flour
1 teaspoon baking soda
1/2 teaspoon salt
1 12-ounce package semi-
  sweet chocolate
  morsels
1 cup chopped pecans

Cream butter and sugar until light and fluffy. Add eggs, one at a time, beating well after each addition. Blend in the vanilla. Combine flour, soda, and salt; add to creamed mixture, beating well. Stir in chocolate morsels and pecans.

Drop dough by 1/4 cupsful onto ungreased cookie sheets. Bake at 375° F. for 10 to 12 minutes. Cool slightly and then remove to wire racks to complete cooling.

HEDGEHOGS

2 cups pecans
2 cups coconut
2 eggs

7 ounce package dates
1 cup brown sugar

Grind dates, pecans and coconut with coarse blade. Beat eggs, add sugar and blend. Add ground mixture and stir together. With dampened hands, shape into oblong pieces about one inch long. Place on greased cookie sheet. Bake at 350° F. for 12 minutes. May be rolled in confectioners sugar or left plain.

HOLIDAY SNOWBALLS

1/2 cup butter
2 tablespoons sugar
1-1/4 cups sifted all-
purpose flour

1 cup ground pecans
Confectioners sugar
1 teaspoon vanilla

Cream butter and sugar together until light and fluffy. Blend in vanilla, flour and pecans. Chill for several hours. Shape into 1-inch balls; place on cookie sheet and bake at 350°F. for 15 to 20 minutes. While still hot roll in confectioners sugar. Cool on wire rack; roll again in confectioners sugar.

HONEY COOKIES

1/2 cup shortening
1/2 cup sugar
1/2 cup honey
1 egg
1/2 cup chopped nuts

2-1/2 cups sifted flour
1 teaspoon baking powder
1/4 teaspoon soda
1/4 teaspoon salt

Cream together shortening, sugar and honey until light and fluffy. Stir in egg. Add nuts and mix well. Sift together flour, baking powder, soda and salt. Add to honey mixture and blend well. Divide dough in half. Shape each half into a long roll. Wrap in wax paper and chill in refrigerator about 2 hours. Cut into slices about 1/8 inch thick. Place slices on ungreased baking sheet. Bake at 400°F. for 8 to 10 minutes.

LEMON BARS DELUXE

2 sticks butter
1/2 cup confectioners sugar
2 cups flour
4 eggs, beaten well
1/2 teaspoon salt
2 cups sugar

8 tablespoons lemon juice
1/2 tablespoon grated
lemon rind
4 tablespoons flour
1 teaspoon baking powder

Cream first three ingredients together. Spread evenly on ungreased cookie sheet. Cook at 350°F. for 15 minutes or until brown. Beat eggs and mix with remaining ingredients. Add on top of cooked pastry. Bake at 325°F. for 30 minutes. Sprinkle with confectioners sugar. Cool for 15 minutes, then cut in oblong "finger" shapes. Makes about 32. Store in refrigerator. Can be made several days ahead.

JANIE'S COOKIES

1 stick margarine,
room temperature
1 package Bix Mix (buttermilk)
1 package Spud Flakes
(Martha White)

1 cup sugar
1 egg
1 tablespoon coconut
flavoring

Mix in order given and make in small marble size balls. Place these on an ungreased cookie sheet, not too close together, as they will spread when hot.

Bake at 350° F. 10 to 12 minutes. Slide off with a spatula while warm onto wax paper.

JELLO COOKIES

4 cups flour
1 teaspoon baking powder
1 cup margarine
1/2 cup Crisco

1 cup sugar
1 egg
1 teaspoon vanilla
1/4 cup strawberry Jello

Sift flour and baking powder. Cream margarine. Add sugar, jello, eggs, and vanilla and beat well. Gradually add flour and mix well. Put through cookie press onto ungreased cookie sheet. Bake at 350° F. for about 10 minutes.

LEMON FILLED SQUARES

1 stick butter, softened
1 cup sifted flour

1/4 cup confectioners sugar

Cream butter well. Add flour and confectioners sugar and blend. Press mixture into an 8-inch square baking dish. Bake in 350° F. oven until light brown, around 15 minutes. Cool.

Filling

2 eggs
1 cup sugar
2 tablespoons flour
1/2 teaspoon baking powder

3 tablespoons lemon juice
Grated rind of 1 lemon
Confectioners sugar

Beat eggs until frothy. Add next 5 ingredients and blend well. Pour into the cooled crust. Bake at 350° F. for around 25 minutes or until set. Cool at least 2 hours and then cut into squares. Dust with confectioners sugar.

LEMON CREAM BARS

1 17-ounce package
lemon cake mix
1/2 cup melted butter
1 slightly beaten egg

1 package (13-ounce lemon
frosting mix)
1 8-ounce package cream cheese
2 eggs

Combine cake mix, butter and 1 egg. Mix with fork until moist. Pat into a 13 x 9-inch greased pan. Blend frosting mix into softened cream cheese. Reserve 1/2 of this mixture. Add 2 eggs to remaining half. Beat about 5 minutes. Spread over cake mixture. Bake at 350° F. for 30 to 40 minutes. Cool. Spread with remaining 1/2 of frosting. Cut into bars.

LUCKY DATE CAKES

2 packages active dry yeast
1/2 cup warm water (not hot water)
6 tablespoons sugar
1/4 teaspoon salt
3/4 cup softened margarine
3 eggs

2-3/4 cups unsifted flour
1 cup chopped pecans
1 package chopped and
pitted dates
cinnamon to taste

Butter Cream Icing

Dissolve yeast in warm water in a large warm bowl. Stir in sugar, salt, margarine, lightly beaten eggs and 1 cup flour. Beat until thoroughly blended. Stir in an additional 1-3/4 cups unsifted flour. Mix well. Cover tightly. Refrigerate for 2 hours.

MAY NOW BE USED FOR ROLLS OR SWEET ROLLS OR LUCKY DATE CAKES.

Divide in half - on floured board, roll two 12 x 10 inch rectangles. Sprinkle with granulated sugar, 1 cup chopped pecans, 1 package chopped and pitted dates, and cinnamon. Roll up, jelly roll fashion. Seal edges and ends tightly. Place on a greased baking sheet curving to form narrow U-shapes. Cover and leave in a warm place for 1-1/4 hours to rise, until light to the touch. Now bake in 350° F. oven 18-20 minutes. Spread with Butter Cream Icing while still warm.

BUTTER CREAM ICING

4 tablespoons soft butter
2 cups confectioners sugar

3 tablespoons milk
1 teaspoon vanilla

Cream butter well, then add sugar and milk alternately, a little at a time, stirring until smooth after each addition. Stir in vanilla. When smooth, pour over cakes and let stand until set before cutting.

MARDI GRAS COOKIES

2 cups sifted flour
1/2 teaspoon baking soda
1/2 teaspoon salt
1/2 cup shortening
1 cup brown sugar
1 egg

1/2 teaspoon vanilla
1/4 cup sour cream
1 cup chopped pecans
1 cup chopped gum drops
(omit black gum drops)

Sift together flour, baking soda and salt. Cream shortening and brown sugar. Add egg and vanilla. Beat. Add half of the sifted dry ingredients to the creamed mixture and blend thoroughly. Add sour cream, pecans and gum drops. Add remaining dry ingredients. Mix well. Drop by teaspoonsful, about 2-inches apart, on a greased cookie sheet. Bake in a hot oven (400° F.) for 10-12 minutes. Yield: 5 dozen cookies.

MARTHA'S COOKIES

1 stick butter
2 eggs
2 cups light brown sugar
1 teaspoon vanilla

1 cup all-purpose flour
1 teaspoon baking powder
1 cup chopped nuts

Combine and put into greased square pan. Bake 25 minutes at 350° F. Cut and roll in confectioners sugar while warm.

MELT IN YOUR MOUTH BARS

1 stick butter
1-1/2 cups graham cracker crumbs
1 package chocolate morsels
1 package butterscotch morsels

1 can coconut
1 cup chopped pecans
1 can Eagle Brand
condensed milk

Melt butter in bottom of a 13x9x2-inch pan. Sprinkle crumbs over butter. Add layers of chocolate morsels, butterscotch morsels, pecans and coconut. Pour the condensed milk over top and bake at 350° F. for 25 minutes. Cool in pan for around 10 to 15 minutes, then cut into bars.

MERINGUE PUFFS

4 egg whites
1 cup sugar

1 teaspoon vanilla
Dash salt

Beat egg whites until stiff. Add other ingredients. Drop by teaspoonsful onto cookie sheet (greased). Bake at 250° F. for 1-1/2 hours.

MOLASSES BALLS

1 cup sugar
3/4 cup shortening
1 egg
2 tablespoons molasses
2 cups flour

1 teaspoon ginger
1 teaspoon cinnamon
1/2 teaspoon cloves
1-1/2 teaspoons baking soda
Granulated sugar

Mix together the sugar, shortening, egg and molasses. Sift the dry ingredients together and then combine both mixtures. Shape into balls. Roll in sugar. Bake at 350° F. for 12 to 15 minutes on an ungreased cookie sheet. Yields around 4 dozen balls.

NO BAKE COOKIES

2 cups sugar
1 cup milk
1 stick margarine

3 cups miniature marshmallows
4 cups graham cracker crumbs
1 cup chopped pecans

Cook sugar, milk and margarine over medium heat until a small amount forms soft ball when dropped into cold water. Add the miniature marshmallows and beat until melted. Add the graham cracker crumbs and chopped pecans; mix. Drop by teaspoonsful onto wax paper.

NUT KISSES

1/2 teaspoon vanilla
3/4 cup light brown sugar

1 egg white
2 cups pecan halves

Beat egg white until stiff. Add sugar a little at a time, continuing to beat until all is added. Add vanilla. Stir in the pecan halves and drop onto buttered cookie sheet one at a time. Bake at 200° F. for 1-1/2 hours. Cut off oven and let cool in oven.

OATMEAL COOKIES

1 cup shortening
1 cup brown sugar
1/2 cup white sugar
2 eggs
1 teaspoon cinnamon
1 teaspoon vanilla

2 cups oatmeal
1 cup chopped nuts
2 cups flour
1/2 teaspoon soda
1/2 teaspoon baking powder

Blend all ingredients well. Drop on greased cookie sheet from teaspoon two inches apart. Bake at 375° F. for 10 minutes or until slightly browned.

OATMEAL DATE-FILLED COOKIES

Filling:

1 cup sugar	1 pound dates
1 cup water	1/2 cup pecans, chopped

Mix and cook until thickened. Set aside.

Pastry:

1 cup brown sugar	2-1/2 cups flour
1 cup butter	2-1/2 cups quick cooking
1/2 cup cold water	oatmeal, raw
1 teaspoon baking soda	

Combine all ingredients and mix well. Roll into thin layers on well floured board. Cut with cookie cutter or glass top. Place on greased cookie sheet. Drop filling in center and put another cut pastry on top. Seal edges. Bake at 350° F. about 15 minutes or until lightly browned.

OLD FASHIONED SUGAR COOKIES

1 cup butter, softened	1 teaspoon vanilla
1 cup granulated sugar	4 cups, plus 4 tablespoons flour
1 cup powdered sugar	(sifted and then measured)
2 eggs, beaten	1 teaspoon baking soda
1 teaspoon salt	1 teaspoon cream of tartar
1 cup oil	

Cream butter and sugars. Add eggs and salt. Beat well. Add oil and vanilla. Sift dry ingredients together and add. Beat well. Makes a very soft dough. Drop by teaspoonsful on ungreased cookie sheet. Flatten with the bottom of a glass which has been lightly buttered and dipped into a dish of white sugar. Bake at 350° F. for 8 to 10 minutes.

OLD FASHIONED TEA CAKES

2 cups sugar	1 cup butter
1/2 cup milk	2 eggs
1 teaspoon vanilla flavoring	Flour
Dash of salt	

Cream butter and sugar together; beat in eggs. Add salt and flavoring. Stir in enough sifted flour to make a medium stiff dough. Roll out on floured board and cut with cookie cutter. Bake in 350° F. oven until lightly browned. Makes about 4 dozen tea cakes.

PARTY BUTTER COOKIES

2 cups sifted flour
3/4 cup butter
1/2 cup sugar

1 egg yolk
1/2 teaspoon vanilla

Cream butter and sugar well. Add egg yolks and beat well. Then add sifted flour in small amounts, mixing after each addition. Add vanilla and blend. Shape dough into rolls 1-1/2 inches thick and roll in wax paper. Chill until firm enough to slice. Cut in 1/8 inch slices. Bake on ungreased baking sheet in hot oven at 400° F. for 8 to 10 minutes or until the edges are lightly browned. Yields around 6 dozen.

PEANUT BLOSSOMS

1 cup granulated sugar
1 cup packed brown sugar
1 cup butter
1 cup creamy peanut butter
2 eggs
1/4 cup milk
2 teaspoons vanilla

3-1/2 cups sifted all-
   purpose flour
2 teaspoons baking soda
1 teaspoon salt
2 10-ounce packages milk
   chocolate candies

Cream sugars, butter and peanut butter. Beat in eggs, milk and vanilla. Sift together flour, soda and salt; stir into egg mixture. Shape into balls; roll in additional granulated sugar. Place on ungreased cookie sheet and bake in 375° F oven for 10-12 minutes. Remove from oven and immediately press a chocolate candy into each.

PEANUT BUTTER BROWNIES

1/3 cup butter
1/2 cup peanut butter
1 cup sugar
1/4 cup firmly packed
   brown sugar
2 eggs

1 cup flour
1 teaspoon baking powder
1/4 teaspoon salt
1 package (6-ounce)
   semi-sweet chocolate bits
1/2 teaspoon vanilla

Cream butter and peanut butter well. Add sugar and blend thoroughly. Cream with the sugar until light and fluffy. Add eggs, one at a time, beating well after each addition. Add sifted flour, baking powder and salt. Then blend in the chocolate bits and vanilla.

Pour into a greased pan and bake at 350° F for 25 to 30 minutes. When cooled, cut into squares.

PEANUT BUTTER COOKIES

1/2 cup shortening
1/2 cup peanut butter
1/2 cup sugar
1/2 cup brown sugar (packed)
1 egg

1/4 teaspoon salt
1-1/4 cups flour
1/2 teaspoon baking powder
3/4 teaspoon soda

Mix shortening, peanut butter, sugars and egg thoroughly. Blend all dry sifted ingredients and stir into shortening mixture. Chill dough. Roll into 1-1/4 inch balls. Place 3-inches apart on lightly greased baking sheet. Flatten criss-cross style with fork dipped in flour. Bake at 375° F. 10 to 12 minutes.

PEANUT BUTTER-MARSHMALLOW COOKIES

1/2 cup shortening
1/2 cup sugar
1/2 cup firmly packed
    brown sugar
1/2 cup peanut butter
1 cup miniature marshmallows

1-1/4 cups all-purpose flour
3/4 teaspoon baking soda
1/4 teaspoon salt
1/4 teaspoon baking
    powder
1 egg, beaten

Cream shortening, sugars, peanut butter, and beaten egg. Combine dry ingredients. Add to creamed mixture. Fold in marshmallows. Form into balls about 1-inch in diameter. Bake on greased cookie sheets at 350° F. for 8 to 10 minutes.

PECAN BARS

1-1/3 cups flour
1/2 teaspoon baking powder
1/3 cup butter
1/2 cup light brown sugar
1/4 cup chopped nuts
2 eggs

3/4 cup dark corn syrup
1/4 cup brown sugar
3 tablespoons flour
1/2 teaspoon salt
1 teaspoon vanilla
3/4 cup nuts, chopped

Sift flour and baking powder together and set aside. Cream butter and 1/2 cup brown sugar well. Add the sifted flour mixture. Mix until blended. Add 1/4 cup nuts. Pat firmly into a 9 x 13-inch pan. Bake for 10 minutes at 350° F. Beat eggs until foamy. Add remaining ingredients. Pour over crust. Bake 25 to 30 minutes longer at 350° F. Let cool in pan. Cut into bars.

PECAN DROPS

1/2 cup flour, sifted
1/4 teaspoon salt
1/4 teaspoon baking powder
1/4 cup butter, softened
1/2 cup sugar

1 egg
1-1/2 teaspoons vanilla
1-1/2 squares unsweetened
   chocolate, melted
2 cups chopped pecans

Sift together the flour, baking powder and salt. Cream the butter and sugar until light and fluffy. Add the egg and mix well. Blend in the vanilla. Stir in the chocolate and flour mixture, blending well. Fold in the pecans. Drop by teaspoonsful onto greased cookie sheet about 1 inch apart. Bake at 350°F. for 10 minutes and watch carefully. Yields 2-1/2 dozen.

PECAN TOPPED BARS

3/4 cup butter
3/4 cup sugar
2 eggs

3 cups sifted all-purpose flour
1/2 teaspoon baking powder
Rind of 1 lemon, grated

Preheat the oven to 375°F. for 10 minutes before the dough is ready to go in. Grease and flour two 9 x 9 x 2-inch baking pans. Cream the butter and sugar; add the eggs and lemon rind and beat well. Sift the flour and baking powder together; add to the creamed mixture and beat well. Chill the dough until it is firm enough to handle. Press the dough onto the bottom of the prepared pans. The dough will be approximately 1/8-inch thick. Prick all over with a fork. Bake 12 to 15 minutes at 375°F. or until the dough looks half done. Remove from the oven and spread with Pecan Topping.

Pecan Topping

1 cup butter
1 cup light brown sugar,
   packed

1 cup honey
1/4 cup whipping cream
3 cups chopped pecans

Put the butter, sugar and honey in a deep, heavy saucepan; boil, stirring constantly, for 5 minutes. Remove from the heat. Cool slightly and add the cream and chopped pecans; mix well. Spread the topping evenly over the surface of the partially baked sugar dough using a buttered flexible spatula. Bake at 350°F. for 30 to 35 minutes. Cool and cut into 1 x 2-inch bars.

PECAN TARTS

1/4 cup firmly packed
   light brown sugar
1 tablespoon butter, melted
1 egg, slightly beaten
1 teaspoon vanilla extract

2/3 cup chopped pecans
Cream cheese shells
Sweetened whipped cream,
   optional

Combine first 5 ingredients, mixing well. Spoon 1 teaspoon filling into each pastry shell. Bake the tarts at 350°F. for 17 minutes. Garnish with whipped cream if desired. Yield: 2 dozen.

CREAM CHEESE SHELLS

1 3-ounce package cream cheese,
   softened

1/2 cup butter, softened
1 cup all-purpose flour

Combine cream cheese and butter; cream until smooth. Add flour, mixing well. Refrigerate dough for 1 hour. Then shape into 24 balls. Put each ball in a greased miniature muffin tin, shaping into a shell. Bake at 350° F. for 15 minutes before filling. Yield: 2 dozen.

PECAN PASTRIES

1/2 pound softened butter
6 tablespoons confectioners
   sugar
2 teaspoons vanilla

2 cups plain flour
   (measure before sifting)
2 cups chopped pecans

Mix butter and sugar until well combined; add flour, vanilla and nuts. Make crescent shapes using 1 teaspoonful at a time. Put on an ungreased cookie sheet. Bake at 325°F. until light brown. Remove from oven and gently slide onto wax paper, using a spatula. When almost cool, sift powdered sugar over cookies and on all sides.

These will melt in your mouth!

PECAN PUFFS

1 egg white
1/4 teaspoon salt
1/4 teaspoon soda

1 cup light brown sugar
3 cups chopped pecans

Beat egg whites until stiff. Add salt, soda and sugar. Mix well. Coat pecans with mixture. Spoon one puff at a time on a lightly greased cookie sheet. Bake at 300°F. for 30 to 40 minutes until brown. Let stand and cool before removing from cookie sheet.

PECAN TWISTS

1-1/2 cups flour
3 tablespoons sugar
1 tablespoon baking powder
1/4 teaspoon salt

1/3 cup shortening
1/2 cup, plus
1 tablespoon milk
1 cup chopped pecans

Combine flour, sugar, baking powder and salt; cut in shortening until mixture resembles coarse meal. Stir in milk with a fork until all ingredients are moistened. Stir in the pecans.

Roll dough to 1/2-inch thickness on a lightly floured surface. Cut into 4 x 1/2-inch strips. Twist strips into S shapes; place on lightly greased baking sheets. Bake at 400°F. for 6 to 8 minutes or until lightly browned.

PINEAPPLE DATE BARS

1 cup flour
1 teaspoon butter flavoring
1 cup sugar
1 cup chopped pecans
1/2 cup chopped or
    crushed pineapple

1/4 teaspoon baking powder
1/4 cup melted butter
2 eggs, beaten
1/2 cup chopped dates
8 maraschino cherries,
    halved

Combine the flour and baking powder then mix in the other ingredients in the order given. Line a 13 x 9-inch shallow pan with wax paper and spread batter evenly. Bake at 350°F. for 25 to 30 minutes. Let stand until slightly cooled; then cut into bars. Turn out on rack and peel off paper. Sprinkle with confectioners sugar.

PINEAPPLE NUT COOKIES

1/2 cup margarine
1/2 cup brown sugar
1/2 cup white sugar
1/2 cup crushed pineapple,
    well drained

1/2 cup chopped nuts
1 egg
2 cups flour
1/4 teaspoon salt
1/2 teaspoon soda

Mix all ingredients together and drop by teaspoonsful onto greased cookie sheet. Bake at 375°F. for 10-12 minutes.

PRALINE SQUARES

1 cup butter
1 cup light brown sugar

1 cup chopped pecans
30 graham crackers

Put graham crackers on cookie sheet with sides. Melt butter and mix in sugar, stirring well, until dissolved. Stir in nuts. Spread on crackers. Bake for 10 minutes at 350°F. and then cool for 10 minutes. Cut into small pieces for serving. Do not overcook.

POTATO CHIP COOKIES

1/2 pound butter
1 cup granulated sugar
1 cup dark brown sugar
2 eggs
1 teaspoon vanilla

2 cups crushed potato chips
1 6-ounce package chocolate
or butterscotch bits
2-1/2 cups plain flour
1 teaspoon baking soda

Cream butter and sugar; add eggs, vanilla, crushed potato chips, chocolate or butterscotch bits, flour and baking soda and mix well. Make large balls and then flatten slightly as you place on a greased cookie sheet. Place a pecan half in center of each cookie if desired. Bake at 350°F. for 10 to 12 minutes.

POUND CAKE COOKIES

1 pound butter
2 cups sugar
4 egg yolks

5 cups plain flour
2 teaspoons vanilla

Cream together butter and sugar, mixing lightly and only until well mixed. Add egg yolks, beating constantly. Stir in vanilla and then flour. Mix well. This will make a firm batter. Pinch off dough about the size of a walnut and roll into a ball. Then flatten with the palm of your hand. Place on cookie sheet and bake in 350°F. oven only until lightly browned around the edges.

RAISIN-SPICE DROPS

3 cups all-purpose
flour
1 teaspoon baking soda
1 teaspoon salt
1 teaspoon cinnamon
1 cup shortening

1-1/2 cups light brown sugar,
firmly packed
3 eggs
1 teaspoon vanilla
2 cups seedless raisins
1 cup coarsely chopped pecans

Sift flour with soda, salt, cinnamon and set aside. In large bowl of electric mixer (medium speed) beat shortening, sugar, eggs and vanilla until light and fluffy. At low speed, beat in flour mixture until well combined. Stir in raisins and pecans. Refrigerate for 30 minutes. Drop batter by rounded teaspoonsful onto a lightly greased cookie sheet and bake at 375°F. for 10-12 minutes. Remove from oven and partially cool on wire rack. May be glazed, if desired.

Glaze

3 cups sifted confectioners sugar   1 teaspoon vanilla
1/4 cup milk

In medium bowl, combine sugar with milk and vanilla; stir until smooth. Use to glaze tops of slightly warm cookies. You may decorate the cookies with raisins or nuts if desired.

SCOTCH LACE COOKIES

1 package instant butterscotch   3/4 cup butter
pudding mix (3-1/2-ounce size)   1/2 cup sugar
2 cups quick cooking oats, raw   1 teaspoon vanilla
1/2 cup chopped pecans

Mix all ingredients together with your hands. Shape into balls. Place on ungreased cookie sheets, about 3 inches apart. Flatten with spoon slightly. Bake at 350° F. for 10 to 12 minutes.

SCOTCH SHORTBREADS

Cream thoroughly:
1 cup butter

Add gradually, while beating
1/2 cup confectioners or light brown sugar

Sift together:
2 cups flour
1/4 teaspoon salt
1/4 teaspoon baking powder

Add to the mixture. Mix well and roll out 1/4 inch thick. Cut in squares or rounds. Prick with a fork. Bake at 350° F. until delicately brown. (Approximately 20 to 25 minutes).

SHAMROCKS

1 cup sugar   1/2 teaspoon nutmeg
2/3 cup butter   1 teaspoon soda, dissolved
2 eggs   in small amount of water
1-1/2 cups flour   1 pound seedless raisins
1 teaspoon cinnamon   1 cup chopped pecans
1 teaspoon cloves

Mix in order given and drop on greased cookie sheet. Bake at 350° F. until edges begin to brown.

SHORTBREAD COOKIES

1 cup butter
1/2 cup confectioners sugar
2-1/2 cups sifted flour

1/4 teaspoon baking powder
1/8 teaspoon salt
3 tablespoons milk

Cream butter and sugar together thoroughly until well blended. Sift flour, baking powder and salt together. Add to butter mixture alternately with the milk. Mix just enough to moisten. Roll out on floured board to about 1/4-inch thickness and then cut into 2-inch squares. Place on cookie sheet. Bake at 350°F. for 20 to 25 minutes or until lightly browned. Yields about 50 squares.

SOUR CREAM WAFERS

1/3 cup butter
1/3 cup shortening
2 cups brown sugar,
   firmly packed
1 tablespoon vanilla
1 egg
1/2 cup sour cream

3-1/2 cups sifted flour
1 teaspoon baking soda
1/2 teaspoon salt
1/2 teaspoon nutmeg
1 cup semi-sweet chocolate
   morsels, finely chopped

Cream together butter, shortening and sugar until light and fluffy. Add vanilla and egg. Beat well. Stir in sour cream. Sift together flour, soda, salt and nutmeg. Add to creamed mixture and blend well. Stir in chocolate. Line a 10 x 15 x 3" loaf pan with wax paper. Pack dough firmly into pan. Chill overnight. Slice loaf lengthwise into thirds; then cut each third into slices 1/8 inch thick. Place on ungreased baking sheet. Bake at 400°F. for 8 minutes.

STRAWBERRY BARS

3/4 cup butter
1 cup firmly packed
   brown sugar
1-1/2 cups flour
1 teaspoon salt

1/2 teaspoon baking soda
1-1/2 cups quick cooking
   oats, uncooked
1 10-ounce jar strawberry jam

Cream butter and sugar until light and fluffy. Sift flour, salt and soda and combine with oats; add to creamed mixture.

Press half of crumb mixture into a greased 13 x 9 x 2-inch pan. Spread jam over crumb mixture. Sprinkle remaining half of crumb mixture over the jam. Bake at 400°F. for 20 minutes. Cool and cut into bars. You may substitute other fruit jams or preserves, if desired.

SNICKERDOODLES

1 cup butter (no substitute)
1-1/4 cups sugar
2 eggs
1/2 teaspoon vanilla
1/2 teaspoon almond extract
1 teaspoon freshly squeezed
  lemon juice

2-3/4 cups all-purpose flour,
  measured before sifting
2 teaspoons cream of tartar
1 teaspoon soda
1/2 teaspoon salt
1 teaspoon grated orange rind

Beat butter and sugar thoroughly in large bowl of electric mixer. Add eggs one at a time, beating after each addition. Then add flavorings and lemon juice. Sift dry ingredients together and add to mixture. Stir in orange rind by hand. Refrigerate for one hour. Drop by teaspoonsful into bowl of granulated sugar, turning each to coat with sugar. Then place about 1-1/2-inches apart on greased baking sheet. Bake at 350° F. for about 14 minutes, or until lightly browned. Remove from pan immediately. The nature of Snickerdoodles is to rise spectacularly during baking and then collapse as they brown. For a crisp cookie, allow them to bake until this falling occurs. If you prefer a chewy cookie, you may underbake them.

SUGAR JUMBLES

3/4 cup butter
1-1/2 cups sugar
3 eggs
1 teaspoon baking powder

1/4 teaspoon salt
About 2 cups
all-purpose flour
3 tablespoons milk

Cream butter and sugar until light and fluffy. Add eggs, and beat well. Sift baking powder, salt and flour together and add to creamed mixture. Add the milk. This dough should be stiff enough to roll. Roll and sprinkle with sugar. Cut and bake on a greased cookie sheet at 350° F. for 8 to 10 minutes.

TOFFEE BARS

1 cup butter
1 cup light brown sugar
1 teaspoon vanilla
2 cups flour

1 6-ounce package semi-sweet
  chocolate bits
1 cup chopped pecans

Cream butter and sugar until light and fluffy. Add flour and vanilla and mix well. Fold in remaining ingredients. Press into a 15-1/2 x 10-1/2 inch pan. Bake at 350° F. for 20 to 25 minutes. Yields around 5 dozen bars.

SOUR CREAM COOKIES

1 cup all purpose flour
1 cup cake flour
2 teaspoons baking powder
1/2 teaspoon baking soda
1/2 teaspoon salt
1/2 teaspoon nutmeg

1 cup light brown
    sugar, packed
1/2 cup butter
1 egg
1/2 cup sour cream
1 cup chopped pecans

Sift flours, baking powder, soda and salt and set aside. Put brown sugar through coarse sieve. Cream butter and sugar until light and fluffy. Beat in egg, continuing to beat well. Add the dry ingredients alternately with the sour cream, beating well. Stir in the pecans. Drop heaping teaspoonsful 2 inches apart onto a greased cookie sheet. Bake 8 to 10 minutes at 400° F. or until no imprint is left when pressed lightly. Remove at once to cake rack to cool. Yields around 3 dozen.

VIENNESE NUT BALLS

1-1/2 cups finely ground
    pecans
2 tablespoons cognac

1/2 cup confectioners sugar
2 tablespoons light corn syrup

Mix pecans and sugar. Add cognac and syrup. Mix well. Shape into bite sized balls and let dry out on a cookie sheet for a few hours. Store in an airtight container in a cool place. These will keep well. Yield: Approximately 40 small balls.

WHITE COOKIES

1 cup powdered sugar
1 cup white sugar
1 cup margarine
1 teaspoon vanilla
1 teaspoon cream of tartar

1 cup Crisco oil
2 eggs
5 cups flour
Dash of salt
1 teaspoon soda

Mix the sugars, margarine and Crisco oil. Add eggs and vanilla, beating well. Add the flour, salt, soda and cream of tartar. Shape dough into small balls and press down with fork which has been dipped in sugar. Bake at 350° F. until done. Approximately 10-12 minutes.

VANILLA CRISPIES

1-1/3 cups all-purpose flour
1 teaspoon baking powder
1/4 teaspoon salt
1 cup sugar

1/2 cup butter
2 teaspoons vanilla
2 eggs

Sprinkle an ungreased cookie sheet with flour, then lightly tap to leave only a thin film of flour. Preheat oven to 400°F. Sift flour, baking powder and salt together. Cream butter and sugar together until light and fluffy. Beat in eggs, one at a time, beating well after each addition. Stir in the vanilla. Blend in the flour mixture, mixing until smooth. Drop by teaspoonsful 1-1/2 inches apart onto the prepared cookie sheet. Bake about 8 minutes or until delicately browned. Remove from baking sheet immediately to cake rack to cool. Yields about 5 dozen cookies.

VIENNA BARS

1 cup (2 sticks butter)
1-1/2 cups sugar (divided)
2 egg yolks
2-1/2 cups flour

1/4 teaspoon salt
1 jar (10-ounces) strawberry jelly
4 egg whites
2 cups finely chopped nuts

In mixing bowl, cream butter and 1/2 cup of the sugar. Beat in egg yolks. Add flour and salt; knead with fingers. Pat batter out on greased 9 x 9 inch pan. Bake at 350°F. for 15-20 minutes, or until lightly browned. Remove from oven, spread with jelly. Beat egg whites until stiff. Fold in remaining 1 cup sugar and nuts. Gently spread on top of jelly. Return pan to oven. Bake 25 minutes longer. Cut into squares while still warm. Makes about 2 dozen bars.

MEASUREMENTS AND EQUIVALENTS

Pinch . . . . , ... Less than 1/4 teaspoon
3 level teaspoons . . . . 1 Tablespoon or (1/2 Ounce)
4 Tablespoons . . . . 1/4 cup
8 Tablespoons . . . . 1/2 cup
16 Tablespoons . . . . 1 cup
1 cup . . . . 8 ounces (1/2 pint)
2 cups . . . . 1 pint (1 pound)
2 pints . . . . 1 quart
1 pint milk . . . . 1 pound

1 pound - 2 cups
1/2 pound - 1 cup
1/4 pound - 1/2 cup

Sugar:

1 pound granulated - 2 cups
1 pound confectioners - 3-1/2 cups
1 pound brown - 2 cups

Flour:

1 pound all purpose - 4 cups sifted
1 pound cake - 4-1/2 cups sifted

Whipping Cream: ### Chocolate:

1 cup - 2 cups whipped   1 square - 3 Tablespoons cocoa
                                       plus 1 Tablespoon butter

Nut Meats (coarsely chopped):

1 pound - 3-1/2 cups

Eggs:

2 large - 3 small

Handy Substitutions:

1 cup sifted cake flour or 1 cup all-purpose flour minus
2 Tablespoons

Equivalents: Cocoa, 1 pound - 4 cups
              Evaporated milk, 6 ounce can - 3/4 cup
                               14-1/2 ounce can - 1-2/3 cups

HELPFUL HINTS

TO MEASURE FLOUR -- Always sift flour once before measuring. Heap flour lightly into cup with a scoop or spoon, level off top with straight edge of a knife. Never dip into flour, as it packs down. Be careful not to jar or rap filled cup on the table. This causes flour to settle and results in too much flour being used.

TO MEASURE SUGAR -- Fill cup with granulated or white sugar and level off with straight edge of a knife. Brown sugar is measured differently from other dry ingredients. It is packed so firmly that when turned out it will hold its shape.

TO MEASURE BAKING POWDER, SODA, SALT, SPICES, ETC. -- Use standard measuring spoon. Fill spoon heaping full, level off with straight edge of a knife.

TO MEASURE LIQUIDS -- Place cup on a level surface to fill. Pour liquids into cup or measuring container. Do not dip spoon or utensil into container.

BUTTER OR SHORTENING -- Makes the cake tender. Use a shortening or butter with a mild, sweet flavor and one which will cream easily.

SUGAR -- Fine granulated sugar is used in all recipes unless otherwise indicated. Coarse sugar makes a coarse-textured cake. Brown sugar and maple sugar add flavor in addition to sweetening cake.

EGGS -- Remove eggs from refrigerator several hours before using so that they will beat up to their greatest volume. In separating it is important that none of the yolk gets into the white. Make sure the bowl is dry and also be certain the beaters are dry. Moisture prevents whites from whipping to a stiff foam.

FLOUR -- Two types of flour are used in cake making. Cake flour is made from soft winter wheats and all-purpose flour made from spring or winter wheats. Cake flour produces a lighter, more tender cake. If all-purpose flour is used instead of cake flour, reduce the amount of flour by 2 Tablespoons per cup and avoid over-beating the batter.

LIQUID -- Milk, sweet or sour, is most commonly used in baking cakes; however, cream, buttermilk, water, fruit juices and coffee may be used.

DRIED FRUITS -- In recipes calling for dried fruits to be cut up, use kitchen scissors and dip them occasionally in warm water. (Dates, raisins, prunes, apricots, etc.)

(Helpful Hints continued)

CHOCOLATE HINTS -- Melt chocolate in any of these ways: (1) Place in heavy saucepan over very low heat, stirring until smooth. (2) Place in heat-safe custard cup and set in pan of hot water until melted. (3) Place in top of double boiler and melt over hot water. Do not boil the water as this will curdle the chocolate.

Mix a little unsweetened cocoa in the flour when you are greasing and flouring cake pans for baking chocolate cakes. This will avoid a streaky look.

Handy cocoa substitution: If recipe calls for unsweetened chocolate use 3 Tablespoons cocoa plus 1 Tablespoon shortening or salad oil (NOT butter or margarine) for each 1 ounce of chocolate called for.

TO MAKE A PERFECT CAKE, one that you can be proud to serve, be sure to use only the freshest and best ingredients, measure accurately and follow instructions carefully. When you "put together" a cake, you are creating a miracle. No two cakes are ever exactly alike. How exciting! And what a wonderful adventure in cooking and baking.

COUNTRY CAKES RE-ORDER BLANKS

Blair of Columbus, Inc., P. O. Box 7852, Columbus, Georgia 31908

Please send me _____ copies of COUNTRY CAKES at $10.95 plus $1.50 postage and handling. GA. residents add 44¢ for state sales tax.

Enclosed is my check or money order for $ _____. Make check payable to COUNTRY CAKES.

Please charge my ( ) VISA/BankAmericard ( ) Master Charge/ Inter Bank No. ( ).

_____ Card No. (_____)
Signature of Cardholder

Card
Expiration Date _____

Name _____

Street _____

City _____ State _____ Zip _____

COUNTRY CAKES RE-ORDER BLANKS

Blair of Columbus, Inc., P. O. Box 7852, Columbus, Georgia 31908

Please send me _____ copies of COUNTRY CAKES at $10.95 plus $1.50 postage and handling. GA. residents add 44¢ for state sales tax.

Enclosed is my check or money order for $ _____. Make check payable to COUNTRY CAKES.

Please charge my ( ) VISA/BankAmericard ( ) Master Charge/ Inter Bank No. ( ).

_____ Card No. (_____)
Signature of Cardholder

Card
Expiration Date _____

Name _____

Street _____

City _____ State _____ Zip _____